AF322730

THE EU THROUGH THE EYES OF ASIA

VOLUME II

NEW CASES, NEW FINDINGS

This publication is a partnership between:

With the support of the European Commission:

THE EU THROUGH THE EYES OF ASIA

VOLUME II

NEW CASES, NEW FINDINGS

Editors

Natalia Chaban
National Centre for Research on Europe

Martin Holland
National Centre for Research on Europe

Peter Ryan
Asia-Europe Foundation

Partner research institutes include:
Ateneo de Manila University, Universitas Indonesia, Vietnam National University

With the support of the European Commission:

World Scientific

NEW JERSEY · LONDON · SINGAPORE · BEIJING · SHANGHAI · HONG KONG · TAIPEI · CHENNAI

Published by

World Scientific Publishing Co. Pte. Ltd.

5 Toh Tuck Link, Singapore 596224

USA office: 27 Warren Street, Suite 401-402, Hackensack, NJ 07601

UK office: 57 Shelton Street, Covent Garden, London WC2H 9HE

British Library Cataloguing-in-Publication Data
A catalogue record for this book is available from the British Library.

THE EU THROUGH THE EYES OF ASIA, VOLUME II
New Cases, New Findings

ISBN-13 978-981-4289-81-8
ISBN-10 981-4289-81-7

Typeset by Stallion Press
Email: enquiries@stallionpress.com

Printed by FuIsland Offset Printing (S) Pte Ltd, Singapore.

Message from the Asia-Europe Foundation

On behalf of the partners of the European Studies in Asia (ESiA) network, namely, the Asia-Europe Foundation and the National Centre for Research on Europe, I have the honour of presenting the new publication entitled *The EU through the Eyes of Asia Volume II: New Cases, New Findings.*

This second volume of *The EU through the Eyes of Asia* series presents the findings of an eighteen month international research project carried out across three different ASEM member countries through the partnership and dedication of Ateneo de Manila University, Universitas Indonesia and Vietnam National University. The data collected throughout the research project provides scientifically valid feedback of the perceptions of the EU in Vietnam, Indonesia and The Philippines, along with that of the previous six locations, Mainland China, Hong Kong SAR, Japan, South Korea, Singapore and Thailand. The information supplied by the research project is essential reading for EU stakeholders and opinion leaders both locally and internationally, as it provides key data to encourage better mutual understanding between the regions.

The publication of the findings of this significant study comes at a very timely period for the Asia-Europe Foundation, as we seek to expand the ongoing research in the area of Euro-Asian perceptions. At a recent meeting in Kuala Lumpur, Malaysia, ASEF announced the expansion of the research project to include three further research locations of India, Macau and Malaysia. This expansion sees Jawaharlal Nehru University, University of Macau and the Asia-Europe Institute (University of Malaya) added to our long list of prestigious partners for this project. In addition to the expansion of "The EU through the Eyes of Asia", we have recently announced, during the International Convention of Asia Scholars 6 held in Daejeon, Korea, the implementation of a further ASEF initiative examining the perceptions of Asia amongst Europeans.

Perhaps the most important aspect of extensive Asia-Europe research projects such as these, is the platform they provide to help forge partnerships, to encourage active participation across many sectors and to strengthen networks in the two regions. These projects are of paramount importance for the ESiA network, given its main objective of deepening the understanding between the two regions through knowledge transfer and assisting the development of European Studies in Asia.

Since its establishment in 1997 ASEF has brought together over 15000 participants from Asia and Europe through a variety of fora and from a multitude of sectors, all of these activities have fallen under one of the guiding principles of ASEF, to promote better "mutual understanding". It is my personal view that to promote this mutual understanding between the two regions of Asia and Europe, it is necessary for us to first gauge our existing understanding of one another. The insights identified by "The EU through the Eyes of Asia" research project provide a unique opportunity to examine multi-level perceptions of the EU in Asia, assisting in identifying areas where misunderstandings and misperceptions prevail, thus allowing them to be addressed and mitigated.

September 2009

Ambassador Dominique Girard
Executive Director
Asia-Europe Foundation

Foreword

Ambassador Rosario G. Manalo

ASEF Board Governor for the Philippines

As the Philippine representative on the ASEF Board of Governors and the Director of the European Studies Programme at Ateneo de Manila University, it gives me great pleasure to provide the foreword for this new publication, which is the result of an 18 month collaboration between the European Studies in Asia coordinators, the Asia-Europe Foundation (ASEF) and the National Centre for Research on Europe (NCRE), University of Canterbury, and, three partner institutions in Vietnam National University, Universitas Indonesia and Ateneo De Manila.

The roots of the European Studies in Asia (ESiA) Network stem back to 2005, when ASEF entered into a partnership with the NCRE to contribute towards the stimulation of European Studies in Asia. The interest among Asians in European studies at the time was noticeably low in comparison to the thirst for knowledge on Asia in Europe, with many of the funding grants going to traditional European studies centres in East Asia and very little investment in burgeoning centres in the ASEAN region. The concept of ESiA was to build upon the existing infrastructure, while avoiding any kind of replication. As the network progressed and through the progress of its flagship research project "The EU through the Eyes of Asia", ESiA has been able to provide greater leverage to newly established centres focusing on European Studies. This leverage has allowed traditional and non traditional institutes the opportunity to link with European institutes and has spurred stronger partnerships, providing for shared practices and collaborative projects. It is through providing opportunities to meet one another that the ESiA network can help build capacity for European Studies throughout Asia.

The ESiA network has now grown into a fully functioning academic network providing a platform for students through its newly established Young Academics Workshop, for high level academics and programme coordinators through its work on Curriculum Development and of course the flagship research project that feeds directly into policy makers and stakeholders with scientifically based feedback. The ESiA Network has developed immensely since its inception and now occupies a unique space in the Asian context whereby it reaches out to students, academics and policy makers alike.

As well as being an essential tool for policy makers, 'The EU through the Eyes of Asia' research project operates as a space for leading universities in Asia to collaborate and share mutual research interests. The project has thus far allowed nine separate institutes in the different research locations to come together to build strong partnerships and build long lasting relationships. It is a project that has been very well received in both Asia and Europe, with stakeholders in Brussels paying great interest in its findings.

Contents

Asia's Visions of the European Union: Introducing the Volume

Martin Holland, Natalia Chaban and Peter Ryan

European Commissioner Margot Wallström in her 2005 "Plan D" initiative identified the major obstacle between the European Union (EU) and Europe's citizens to be the lack of any "common narrative" about the nature of European integration: as the Commissioner noted, "the real problem in Europe is that there is no agreement or understanding about what Europe is for and where it is going".[1] This absence of an EU consensus on the end goal of European integration has also created a confused and perplexing image for those outside the borders of the EU27. As a result, the EU's international role often appears ambiguous both within and outside the Union. The recent priority given to understanding how the EU is viewed externally has led to the creation of the European Studies in Asia (ESiA) consortium. From its launch in 2005, the ESiA network has embraced the Commission's imperative and sought to better communicate the EU to Asian audiences. One mechanism utilised by ESiA to achieve this

---

[1] Wallström, Margot, 'Communicating Europe in Stormy Waters: Plan D', <http://europa.eu/rapid/pressReleasesAction.do?reference=SPEECH/05/396&format=HTML&aged=1&language=EN&guiLanguage=en>, accessed 31 April 2007.

goal has been the development and successful execution of the "EU in the Eyes of Asia" research project, the results from Phase III of which form the substance of this publication on how the EU is perceived in Asia. This inaugural project has become emblematic of ESiA's relevance to the Asia Europe Meeting (ASEM) process and has contributed to the profile of EU Studies in Asia more generally.

The choice of EU perceptions as a research theme reflects both practical and conceptual motivations. At a policy analysis level, the surprising reality is that little reliable prior knowledge exists on this important topic, and what information did exist tended to be impressionistic, haphazard, ill-informed and lacking scientific empirical evidence on how Asian citizens and the media saw the European Union. This deficit appears remarkable when the EU's international involvement with Asia is considered, both through region-to-region agreements (such as ASEM and EU-ASEAN relations) as well as on a country-to-country basis. For all of the localities examined in this publication, the EU is among the most significant economic partners and a major development aid donor (in terms of direct assistance, project support and preferential trade agreements). Moreover, the EU is increasingly seen as a partner for political dialogue. Conceptually, a focus on perceptions helps to inform us about the global importance of the EU and how this is being interpreted outside of Europe. As noted in an influential 2002 report for the Commission, "Europe does not exist without non-Europe" and "Europe can only be realized in the mirror of Others".[2] To understand the European Union itself we need to have an external reflection in order to interpret its meaning.

STUDIES OF THE EU EXTERNAL PERCEPTIONS WITHIN THE ESiA FRAMEWORK

This publication is the latest in a series of research projects undertaken by ESiA partners. This interest in EU perceptions began modestly in

---

[2] Stråth, Bo, 'Introductory Report', *Intercultural Dialogue,* Office for Official Publications of the EU, 2002.

2002 with a study of New Zealand conducted by the National Centre for Research on Europe (NCRE), University of Canterbury, New Zealand.[3] It then developed in 2004–5 into a trans-national comparative project covering Thailand, South Korea and Australia, in addition to New Zealand. The project was supported by an EU Commission grant and was again led by the NCRE.[4] The major findings of this multidisciplinary comparative research project have been presented in a number of publications,[5] including the volume "The European Union and the Asia–Pacific: Media, Public and Elite Perceptions of the EU" published in 2008.[6] Since 2006, with support from ASEF, the project has expanded to include Japan, China, Hong Kong SAR, South Korea, Singapore and Thailand (Phase II) and Vietnam, Indonesia and the Philippines (Phase III) with Phase IV commencing in July 2009 to include India, Malaysia and Macau.[7] Early results from this 'EU External Perceptions' research were presented in a volume "The EU through the Eyes of Asia" published in 2007.[8] Perceptions of the EU in Vietnam, the Philippines and Indonesia are the main focus of this book. Looking ahead somewhat ambitiously, it is envisaged that eventually the research will cover all Asian ASEM partners.

The complexity of such cross-national studies, let alone securing the funding base, remains a constant challenge, both methodologically and in geographical scope. The academic contributors to this

---

[3] See "EU External Perceptions" website <http://www.euperceptions.canterbury.ac.nz/NZperceps/index.shtml>.

[4] See "EU External Perceptions" website <http://www.euperceptions.canterbury.ac.nz/comparitive/index.shtml>.

[5] See "EU External Perceptions" website <http://www.euperceptions.canterbury.ac.nz/pubs.shtml>.

[6] Chaban, Natalia, and Martin Holland (eds.) *The European Union and the Asia–Pacific: Media, Public and Elite Perceptions of the EU*, Routledge: London, 2008.

[7] See ESiA website <http://esia.asef.org/>.

[8] Holland, Martin, Peter Ryan, Alojzy Nowak, and Natalia Chaban (eds.), *The EU through the Eyes of Asia: Media, Public and Elite Perceptions in China, Japan, Korea, Singapore and Thailand*, Singapore-Warsaw: University of Warsaw, 2007.

volume (together with those from previous volumes) collectively constitute the most significant and established EU scholars in Asia involved in the research of international perceptions of the EU. Importantly, within the framework of this project, these experienced academics established local teams of early career academics. Benefiting greatly from this mentoring, the new researchers have advanced their research training and acquired new knowledge about the EU, thus helping to ensure the sustainability of EU studies in the region. In keeping with ESiA's inclusive philosophy, participation in future phases of this research is open to all eligible and interested parties.

The approach taken in this research project is innovative and original. While some other studies have considered the EU's periphery, such as Turkey and Ukraine, in terms of European perceptions, as well as within the EU itself through the *Eurobarometre*, studies so distant from the EU are rare.[9] The methodology of this particular study is

---

[9] Although, in recent years such research has become more fashionable: Global-scale surveys include *World Powers in the 21st Century*, Bertelsmann Stiftung, Berlin, 2006, (<www.cap.lmu.de/download/2006/2006_GPC_Survey_Results.pdf>); 2007 'Voice of the People' annual survey carried out by Gallup International in collaboration with the European Council on Foreign Relations. It was conducted in 52 countries with 57,000 respondents (reported in *EUObserver*, <http://euobserver.com/9/25036/?rk=1>); GARNET (2007) 'The External Image of the European Union', Working Paper No. 17/07, <http://www.garnet-eu.org/index.php?id=27>. In Asia specifically several studies have touched on perceptions: Final Report 'Survey Analysis of EU Perceptions in South East Asia', January 2003. Framework Contract AMS/451-Lot 7. A.R.S. Progetti S.r.l. Ambiente, Risorse e Sviluppo; 'Perceptions of the EU's role in South East Asia', Framework Contract Commission 2007, EuropeAid/123314/C/SER/multi, Lot n°4; Lisbonne-de Vergeron, Karine, *Contemporary Indian Views of Europe*, London: Chatham House, 2006; Lisbonne-de Vergeron, Karine *Contemporary Chinese Views of Europe*, London: Chatham House, 2007; Shambaugh, David, Sandschneider, Eberhard and Zhou Hong (eds.), *China-Europe Relations: Perceptions, Policies and Prospects*. London: Routledge, 2007; Tsuruoka, Michito, *How External Perspectives of the European Union are Shaped: Endogenous and Exogenous Sources*, paper prepared for the 20th World Congress of the International Political Science Association (IPSA), Fukuoka, Japan, 9–13 July 2006; Tsuruoka, Michito, *EU — Asia Relations and Security Matters (RCO3 on European Unification)*, <web. uvic.cakeurope/ipsa-rc3/IPSMTsuruoka.pdf>. Yet importantly, all these studies remain sporadic, not linked to each other and conducted in *ad-hoc* manner not prioritising a systematic, empirical approach.

multi-disciplinary in focus involving social science and humanities disciplines and has been successfully tested in the previous studies cited above. The research of EU perceptions in Indonesia, Vietnam and the Philippines discussed in this book ran for eighteen months (January 2008–June 2009), and involved analysis of EU imagery in reputable news media as well as in public and 'elite' opinion. Most importantly, the analysis embraced the local language in each country and was not restricted to an English-language medium. The local research teams used materials in their original languages which were subsequently transposed, for comparative purposes, into an English-language dataset. In this way we believe we have successfully accessed what is locally perceived and communicated not only across the three research countries (which are explored in a greater detail in the first part of this volume), but across all nine Asian locations which have been involved in the project since 2006 (a comparative analysis of the EU imagery across those nine localities is a subject of the second part of this book).

The national findings reported in the first three chapters allow the reader to see the subtleties in the values and scope of meanings assigned to the concept 'the EU' in each individual location. This collection of ideographic cases, addressing a set of common topics, allows this comparative volume exercise an approach to cross-national comparisons known as "nation as object of study".[10] In contrast, the following three chapters employ a different approach to cross-national communication research, namely "nation as a unit of analysis",[11] by selecting nine Asian ASEM countries as members of a common framework and developing thematic comparisons to interpret the imagery of the EU in the Asian region. According to Livingston, in this approach, "given the prior identification of a number of measurable dimensions along which nations vary (...),

---

[10] Kohn, Melvin, 'Introduction', In Kohn, Melvin (ed.), *Cross-national Research in Sociology*, Newbury Park: Sage, 1989, as cited in Livingstone, Sonia, 'On the Challenges of Cross-National Comparative Media Research' (on line), London: LSE: Research Online, <http://eprints.lse.ac.uk/archive/00000403>, pp. 12–16.

[11] *Ibid.*

systematic relations are sought among these dimensions".[12] The comparative theory underlying this model "seeks to understand the diversity of different national contexts, achieving it by representing the specificity of each country using a common conceptual language".[13] The combination of these two approaches adds to the methodological strength of this volume.

Respectively, Chapters 1–3, co-authored by the research teams from three locations, detail comprehensive empirical insights into the EU's present-day perceptions and images in each society: Chapter 1 by Alma Maria Salvador, Leslie Advincula-Lopez and Manuel Enverga examines the EU imagery in the Philippines; Chapter 2 by Pham Quang Minh, Bui Hai Dang and Trần Bách Hiếu explicates EU perceptions in Vietnam; and Chapter 3 by Cornelis Pieter Frederik Luhulima, Edward Panjaitan and Anika Widiana discusses EU imagery in Indonesia. The three following chapters present comparative case-studies bringing together data from nine Asian locations, including Vietnam, Indonesia and the Philippines. Chapter 4 by Martin Holland explores the EU's perceived profile as an economic and political actor in four North-East Asian locations of Japan, China, Hong Kong SAR, South Korea, and five South-East Asian nations of Singapore, Thailand, Indonesia, Vietnam and the Philippines. Chapter 5 by Natalia Chaban investigates the visibility and content of the EU's imagery in these Asian societies in the fields of social affairs, environment and development. Chapter 6 by Lai Suet-yi and Natalia Chaban compares the visions of the ASEM process in media, public and stakeholders' discourses in the same nine locations. Chapter 7 by Peter Ryan offers a summary of the major findings of this next phase of the ESiA project and presents how studies of EU external perceptions could be instrumental in facilitating an informed policy formulation when developing the EU-Asia dialogue.

---

[12] Livingstone, Sonia, 'On the Challenges of Cross-National Comparative Media Research' (on line), London: LSE: Research Online, <http://eprints.lse.ac.uk/archive/00000403>, pp. 12–16.

[13] *Ibid.*

The research design underpinning this project incorporated three elements. The first explored EU images in the news media; the second involved a survey about the general public's perceptions of the EU; while the third involved a series of interviews with selected political, economic, civil society and media decision- and policy-makers. It is assumed that reputable newspapers and television are still major sources, indeed *the* major sources, for forming political ideas and information in the regions we have examined. This assumption was confirmed by the public opinion survey respondents who clearly preferred these two traditional media for accessing international news. It can be debated whether the internet will supersede traditional print and television, and hence requiring a modified methodology in future, but in the cases examined in 2006 and in 2008, newspapers and television, and not the internet, remained the dominant information mediums for Asian societies. Rather than repeat the common methodology across each of the studies reported in Chapters 1–6, this introduction provides a comprehensive description of the methods used, criteria and concepts that construct the datasets. In order to follow the arguments within each of the country-reporting and thematic chapters, readers are urged to first inform themselves with this short and jargon-free methodological section.

METHODOLOGICAL INSIGHTS

This section delves into the basic methodological techniques and guidelines that informed this multidisciplinary and multi-methodological cross-national research. The difficulties associated with such ambitious multilingual research are not inconsiderable: however, the multiple methodologies employed here and the experience of conducting several earlier "EU External Perceptions" studies elsewhere in the Asia-Pacific region provides a high level of confidence that can be placed on the empirical findings. Inevitably, all methodologies involve compromises largely derived from limited resources and this study is no different. The budget, while generous from ASEF and participating ESiA institutions, was not inexhaustible: the resulting compromises in methodology are, we believe, comparatively minor and do not detract from the scientific value of this pioneering empirical analysis of EU perceptions with Asia.

The three methodological elements — media analysis, public opinion surveys and 'elite' interviews — are described below. The research teams who were responsible for gathering the data were formally trained during four regional training workshops (held in Manila, Singapore, Hanoi and Christchurch). A key methodological strength of the project was the inter-coder reliability, as well as the enhanced comparability and consistency that were established during the week-long training sessions.

The element of news media analysis was included into the "EU External Perceptions" study since "the regularity, ubiquity and perseverance of news media will in any case make them first-rate competitors for the number-one position as international image-former".[14] The media data for this three-country study came from the daily monitoring of three prime-time television newscasts and nine reputable newspapers over the six months of 2008. To identify the 'EU' element in a news story, the following procedure was adhered to: the news story had to reference the 'EU' (or 'European Union') or its institutions ('European Central Bank'/'ECB', 'European Commission'/'EC', 'European Parliament'/'EP', and 'European Court of Justice'/'ECJ') or 'Asia-Europe Meeting'/'ASEM' at least once, even if only briefly, in order to be included in the media database. The research was explicitly EU focused; consequently, items that were about individual Member States without any EU reference were not included in the database.

In each location, the teams monitored four media outlets: a primetime news bulletin on a television channel with the highest rating and a nation-wide outreach; a reputable national daily newspaper with the highest national circulation; a business daily targeting specialised audiences possibly involved in business dealings with the EU; and an English-language newspaper read by educated locals who wish to profess their skills in English, foreigners wishing to learn about the locations and expatriates residing in the country. The respective

---

[14] Galtung, Johan and Mari Holmboe Ruge (1965) 'The Structure of Foreign News', *Journal of Peace Research*, Vol. 2, No. 1, pp. 64–91, p. 64.

media outlets analysed were: *Kompas, Bisnis Indonesia, Jakarta Post* and *TVRI* in Indonesia; *Philippines Daily Inquirer, Business World, Manila Bulletin* and *GMA 7–24 Oras* in the Philippines; and *Tien Phong, The Vietnam Economic Times, Vietnam News* and *VTV1* in Vietnam. All outlets are described in a greater detail in Chapters 1–3.

The methods and techniques of the media study in this volume were grounded in the tenets of content and discourse analysis theories, as well as cross-national comparative media research. The media methodology for this project followed that of the groundbreaking 1985 UNESCO comparative media study,[15] as well as a series of pioneering investigations of EU visibility in the EU media,[16] and of

---

[15] Sreberny-Mohammadi, Annabelle with Kaarle Nordentreng, Robert Stevenson and Frank Ugboajah (eds), *Foreign News in Media: International Reporting in 29 Countries*, Paris: UNESCO, 1985.

[16] Research by Amsterdam School of Communication (among its many studies there are de Vreese, Claes, Susan Banducci, Holli A. Semetko and Hajo Boomgaarden, 'The News Coverage of the 2004 European Parliamentary Election Campaign in 25 Countries', *European Union* Politics, Vol. 7, No. 4, 2006, pp. 477–504; de Vreese, Claes. *Framing Europe: Television News and European Integration*, Amsterdam: Askant, 2004; Peter Jochen, Holli A. Semetko and Claes de Vreese, 'EU Politics on Television News', *European Union Politics*, Vol. 4, No. 3, 2003, pp. 305–327; Semetko, Holli A. and Patti M. Valkenburg, 'Framing European Politics: A Content Analysis of Press and Television News', *Journal of Communication*, Vol. 50, No. 2, 2000, pp. 93–109. Other researchers that have contributed to the field are: Van de Steeg, Marianne 'Rethinking the Conditions for a Public Sphere in the European Union', *European Journal of Social Theory*, Vol. 5, No. 4, 2002, pp. 499–519; Meyer, Christoph, 'The Europeanization of Media Discourse: A Study of Quality Press Coverage of Economic Policy Co-ordination since Amsterdam', *Journal of Common Market Studies*, Vol. 43, No. 1, 2005, pp. 121–48; Trenz, Hans-Joerg, 'Media Coverage of European Governance: Exploring the European Public Sphere in National Quality Newspapers', *European Journal of Communication*, Vol. 19, No. 3, 2004, pp. 291–319; Kevin, Deirdre, *Europe in the Media*, Lawrence Erlbaum Associates: London, 2003; Gavin, Neil T., 'Imagining Europe: Political Identity and British Television Coverage of the European Economy", *British Journal of Politics and International Relations*, Vol. 2, No. 3, 2000, pp. 352–373; Norris. Pippa, 'Blaming the Messenger? Political Communications and Turnout in EU Elections', in *Citizen Participation in European Politics, Demokratiutredningens skrift*, Stockholm: Statens Offentliga Utredningar, 2000a; Norris, Pippa, *A Virtuous Circle: Political Communications in Postindustrial Societies*, Cambridge: Cambridge University Press, 2000b.

the EU's imagery in the Asia-Pacific public discourses.[17] This current study's methodology involved quantitative and qualitative measures, and it is the combination of these two that provided a particular sophistication in the analysis. Quantitative tools included the volume of coverage of the EU, its institutions and officials in the media; the monthly distribution; type of media outlet; and news sources.[18] Two other categories used in this analysis — the *degree of centrality*[19] and *focus of domesticity*[20] — were instrumental in a more nuanced study of the EU's media visibility. The former one, evaluating if the EU was presented from a major, secondary or minor perspective, helped to identify the importance and intensity with which the EU was presented to the news audiences in each location. The latter one helped to assess the context and relevance of the EU. This category included four instances in analysis, namely whether the reportage of the EU's actions was grounded locally, regionally, in the European/EU context, or in the context of the third party (neither the EU nor the locality in question). Both the degree of centrality and focus of domesticity categories used qualitative assessment which was later classified creating a quantitative reality.

---

[17] List of publications resulting from this project (2002–2009) has included more than 50 various publications (for more details see "EU External Perceptions" website <http://www.euperceptions.canterbury.ac.nz/pubs.shtml>.

[18] Such quantitative categories as the *placement* and *length* of articles were also used in the study of EU media imagery in this proejct, however they were not in focus of analysis in this particular volume.

[19] The notion of *degree of centrality* of news used in this volume is similar to the definition used by Kevin, Deirdre, *Europe in the Media*, London: Lawrence Erlbaum Associates, 2003, p. 54.

[20] The notion of *focus of domesticity* of news used in this volume is also similar to the "concept of domesticity of EU stories" used by Peter, Jochen, Holli A. Semetko, and Claes de Vreese, 'EU Politics on Television News', *European Union Politics*, Vol. 4, No. 3, 2003, pp. 305–327, p. 310, p. 313, p. 318 and the "domestic or European" focus used by Claes de Vreese, *Framing Europe: Television News and European Integration*. Amsterdam: Aksant, 2003, p. 81, pp. 85–86, p. 92, pp. 103–105. See also Shulz, Winfried, *Foreign News in Leading Newspapers of Western and Post-Communist Countries*, paper at the 51st Annual Conference of the International Communication Association, Washington D.C.: USA, May 24–28, 2001.

Two qualitative measures, namely, the notion of *frames* and the concept of *evaluation*, have also been employed in the analysis.[21] The notion of a *frame* — defined here as the "selection of some aspects of perceived reality to make them more salient in a communication text, in such a way as to promote a particular problem definition, caused interpretation, moral evaluation and/or treatment recommendations"[22] — was used to categorise whether the EU was being presented (traditionally) as an economic actor, a political actor (something that is possibly emerging), a social actor (setting social norms, values, legislation, etc.) or whether the EU was now being understood internationally more as an environmental actor (advocating environment protection inside the European continent as well as globally), or as a leading developmental actor (providing assistance world-wide in general and in the region/country in particular)? All the data generated by the project used these five frames to describe the media framing of the EU and thereby facilitated the comparative analysis of how the various media in different countries interpret the EU.

Media representations of the EU as an actor were further analysed using the second qualitative measure — *evaluation*. This notion, while contentious and despite its ambiguity, is widely used in related communication studies.[23] The case-studies presented in this volume involved the assessment and coding of the explicit judgment and/or tone of an article towards the EU by native speaking coders. Depending on an articles' approach towards the EU and its style,

---

[21] Such qualitative categories as *conceptual metaphors, journalistic attitudes* and *character of news* were also used in the analysis of EU media images in this project, yet they were not in focus of analysis in this particular volume.

[22] Entman, Robert, 'Framing: Toward Clarification of a Fractured Paradigm', *Journal of Communication*, Vol. 43, No. 4, 1993, pp. 51–58, p. 52.

[23] Peter, Jochen, Holli A. Semetko and Claes de Vreese 'EU Politics on Television News: A Cross-National Comparative Study', *European Union Politics*, Vol. 4, No. 3, 2003, pp. 305–28 and de Vreese, Claes, Susan Banducci, Holli A. Semetko and Hajo Boomgaarden, 'The News Coverage of the 2004 European Parliamentary Election Campaign in 25 Countries', *European Union Politics*, Vol. 7, No. 4, 2006, pp. 477–504.

three categories were identified in this analysis: neutral, negative and positive. Rigorous training and cross-coding assessments were undertaken to ensure the coding reliability of this variable. Evaluation was considered to be a tool to triggering emotional responses from the readers and thus a key for "interpreting discursive representations".[24] The inclusion of evaluation as an important affective component in discourse analysis rests on the assumption formulated by Ross who addressed the notions of emotions and affects in the international relations: "[W]hereas feelings are subjective ideas, affects cut across individual subjects and forge collective associations from socially induced habits and memories. Moreover, they are experienced by decision-makers and publics alike."[25]

This comprehensive and internationally benchmarked methodology creates a high degree of confidence and reliability in the media analysis. Other methodological qualifications notwithstanding, the validity of this methodology is broadly acceptable and has been rigorously executed.

The second element in the project design was an analysis of the general public opinion on the EU. The rational to include this particular information was formulated by Stephen Twigg who claimed that "for the Union to prosper it must project a positive image of itself to opinion formers and to the 'man in the street' both within and beyond its borders."[26] While the survey's conception, design and analysis were undertaken by the NCRE and ESiA research group, the administration of the surveys was sub-contracted to a professional social research company — an established Asia-Pacific survey company, TNS-Global.com. This partnership ensured a very high level of methodological precision in collecting the data thus warranting a higher reliability of the findings. The surveys in the

---

[24] Ross, Andrew, 'Coming in from the Cold: Constructivism and Emotions', *European Journal of International Relations*, Vol. 12, No. 2, 2006, pp. 197–222, abstract.

[25] *Ibid.*, p. 199.

[26] Twigg, Stephen, 'Preface' in de Gouveia, Philip Fiske de and Hester Plumridge, *European Infopolitik: Developing EU Pubic Strategy*, London: The Foreign Policy Centre, 2005, p. VI.

Philippines and Vietnam were administered via telephone. The survey in Indonesia was conducted in a face-to-face format, taking into account the low level of telephone technology penetration.

The public opinion fieldwork was conducted in November–December 2008 (including a pilot phase prior to administering the survey in early November). The sample size — 400 respondents in each location — was dictated by budgetary constraints and gave a ±4.9% degree of accuracy. While a total of 1,200 respondents were approached in this stage of the ESiA project, the nine-country sample (explored in the three comparative chapters in this volume) resulted in an impressive sample of 3,600 members of the general public in the region. Each sample was stratified by age (18–64) and gender for each local population. The identical questionnaires administered in local languages used in this study comprised 20 questions (including two open-ended questions, nine structured questions and nine demographics questions). Transcribed verbatims in local languages were subsequently translated into English for comparative purposes. The quantitative data was analysed using SPSS, while the extensive verbatim answers in the open-ended questions were assessed qualitatively.

Turning to the methodology used in the study of the national stakeholders' opinion on the EU, the sampling strategy, data collection methodology, and data analysis techniques were chosen to guarantee the "output of the rigorous and reliable data which could be used in providing evidence-based policy recommendations"[27] and thereby ensure a reliable measure of the EU–Asia dialogue. Indeed, as Michael Brecher argued, "decision makers act in accordance with their perception of reality, not in response to reality itself".[28] These surveys of 'elite' opinion of the EU were conceived as a series of 'snap-shots' of perceptions across time as well as across diverse groups of local decision- and policy-makers. This approach corresponded to

---

[27] Enticott, Gareth, 'Multiple Voices of Modernization: Some Methodological Implications', *Public Administration*, Vol. 82, No. 3, 2004, pp. 743–756.

[28] Brecher, Michael, *India and World Politics: Krishna Menon's View of the World*. New York and Washington: Frederick A. Praeger Publishers, 1968, p. 298.

the goals of the project — to identify the comprehensive range of perceptions of and attitudes towards the EU that exist in Asian public discourses.

A target of thirty-two interviews in each location was set (eight for each sector — business, political, media and civil society). The random selection of respondents in each of the three locations resulted in a 96-person sample.[29] The overall sample from the nine countries examined in the three comparative chapters of this volume was 265 respondents. Information was collected through individual semi-structured, in-depth, face-to-face interviews that lasted for up to one hour in duration.[30] This technique has proven to be particularly effective for approaching 'key informants' — it is more personal, flexible, respects privacy and status, and can generate greater openness and trust between interviewer and interviewee.[31] Interviewees were given the option of their comments either being anonymous or associated with them directly.

Predictably, this methodology leant towards qualitatively rich discursive comments and a wider utilisation of open-ended responses in contrast to the more structured online public opinion surveys — the pre-tested 18-question questionnaire featured only two structured questions. The study used two versions of the questionnaire — one for business, political and civil society respondents, and another slightly modified for media practitioners. The question order rotated depending on the flow of conversation.

---

[29] In Vietnam, 33 respondents were interviewed, in Indonesia 32, and in the Philippines 31.

[30] This particular method of information gathering was preferred to focus group discussions (a method used by A.A.R.S. Progetti S.r.l. in a 2003 study of elite perceptions on the EU in South East Asia). Schedule flexibility in arranging face-to-face interviews, undivided attention to the interviewee by the researcher during the conversation, and more open atmosphere during the individual interviews decided for that particular method against the focus group option.

[31] Walker, Richard and Gareth Enticott, 'Using Multiple Informants in Public Administration: Revisiting the Managerial Values and Actions Debate', *Journal of Public Administration, Research and Theory*, Vol. 14, No. 3, 2004. pp. 417–34.

The sampling strategy for the 'elite' interviews involved the selection of key informants in each location and across the four designated sectors. This approach allowed for a better categorisation and integration of the results and provided an insight into the nature of current links that domestic decision- and policy-makers had with the EU, as well as their personal knowledge, perceptions and attitudes towards the Union. The selected political stakeholders were identified from members of national parliaments, or equivalents, representing different political views. Media 'elites' were identified as the editors/news directors and lead reporters of the reputable media outlets. Civil society members were representatives of various national and international non-governmental organisations. Business respondents were identified from members of national business round-tables and other official business networks, as well as leading international traders. The interviews took place in relevant political and economic centres — Manila, Jakarta, Hanoi and Ho Chi Minh City, during March–September 2008.

The study's analysis utilised qualitative interpretative methodology capitalising on its strong insight and interpretation. To improve the reliability of this particular attitudinal research, the collected data was analysed using content analysis methodology incorporating cognitive semantics tools. The employed methodology revealed the categories which 'mapped' the concept 'EU' via re-constructing mental 'schemata' of that concept.

Significantly, the three elements of this research in each location — media content analysis, the general public survey and the interviews with the national stakeholders — were ultimately designed and positioned within a framework of a large-scale cross-national comparative study — a type of research which is described as "exciting but difficult, creative but problematic".[32] According to Blumler *et al.*,

---

[32] Livingstone, 'On the Challenges of Cross-National Comparative Media Research', 2003, p. 3.

[33] Blumler, Jay, Jack McLeod, and Karl Erik Rosengren, 'An Introduction to Comparative Communication Research', in Blumler, Jay, Jack McLeod, and Karl Erik Rosengren (eds.), *Comparatively Speaking: Communication and Culture across Space and Time*, Newbury Park: Sage, 1992, pp. 3–18, p. 8.

comparative research has "a more creative and innovative role — opening up new avenues",[33] yet it features numerous theoretical, methodological, empirical and practical challenges. The consistent standards of research methods and techniques exercised in this volume, the extensive contextualisation and a two-tier approach to the comparison (i.e., 'nation as a object of study' and 'nation as unit of analysis') are argued to be instrumental in overcoming the above listed challenges. Most importantly, using the words of Livingston, this comparative work "reli[ed] not only on time, funding and mutual interest, but also on good will, on trust, and on what Hochschild (1983) terms 'emotional labour'...".[34] It is hoped that our readers will feel and share excitement and passion our multinational team experienced when working together and writing this volume.

CONCLUDING REMARKS

The audience for this publication straddles academics, students, politicians, officials and the media, and the goals and expected results intentionally combine academic concerns with those of policy. First, the findings reported here will help to develop a wider knowledge about the international perceptions of the EU: the external image of the EU constitutes a fundamental component of the ongoing process of EU identity construction, linking the perceptions of 'Others' and self-perceptions. Second, the analysis provides scientifically valid feedback that can assist better informed policy and suggests recommendations to the EU, third countries and the media and contribute to more effective public diplomacy. Misperceptions or ill-informed views of the EU's global role puts the EU at risk of being overlooked or undervalued by third countries for whom the EU is a significant partner. Similarly, low awareness of the EU exposes third countries to the risk of slipping off the EU's 'radar'. Third, this publication is just one mechanism that will be used to disseminate the results of the research among academic communities and EU policy-makers. The

---

[34] Livingstone, 'On the Challenges of Cross-National Comparative Media Research', 2003, p. 10.

dataset that has been collected will be available from ESiA for secondary analysis by academics and graduates alike throughout ASEM. Furthermore, complementary scholarly publications, media publications, seminars, conferences and workshops targeting young scholars, academics, political practitioners and media professionals will be organised in order to increase awareness and access to ESiA's on-going research on EU perceptions in our region.

The content of this publication is empirically rich and the research has produced a series of fundamental questions relating to the EU's international identity and global role. Are there cognitive and communication gaps between the EU and the external world? What are the implications for the EU's negotiation effectiveness and perception? And, what conclusions for the media and public diplomacy emerge? Hopefully, the recommendations from this study will go some way to addressing these key questions and demonstrate how the EU is understood and seen from third countries and help to identify and define Europe for itself and better inform EU public diplomacy.

Chapter 1

Orientalism Reversed: Images and Perceptions of the EU in the Philippines

Alma Maria O. Salvador, Leslie V. Advincula-Lopez and Manuel Enverga

ORIENT AND OCCIDENT: EU–PHILIPPINE RELATIONS

The first recorded interaction between Europe and the Philippines is said to have occurred during the Spanish exploratory expedition of Ferdinand Magellan, which made landfall in the territory of present-day Philippines on March 17, 1521. This initial contact was not a congenial one, and Magellan "was defeated and killed in battle"[1] just one month after arriving in the archipelago. Only a fraction of the original 235 men in the expedition were able to return to Europe. After three more expeditions from the Spanish colony Mexico, a colonial government under the rule of a Governor-General was established, with the seat of power located in Manila. The Spanish Colonial period in the Philippine islands lasted around three centuries, with

---

[1] Agoncillo, Teodoro, *History of the Filipino People*, 8th edn, Garotech Publishing: Manila, 1990, p. 72.

significant institutional reforms being implemented throughout much of the country.

Historically, the Philippines has experienced two differing Western colonial influences — European and North American. The Philippines were ceded to the USA in 1898, in the Treaty of Paris. Intriguingly, the USA (the Philippines' more recent colonial power) was to become more influential to the independent Philippines than Spain, and by connection, Europe had been to the colony. Even after the USA removed its military bases from the Philippines in 1991, the present-day relationship between the two is on-going and strong. It is clamed to be directed towards "economic development...and continued cooperation in maintaining security in the region".[2]

This is not to say, however, that relations between Europe and the Philippines were non-existent after the end of Spanish Colonial rule. During the American Colonial Period, the Philippines maintained relations with certain European countries, particularly the United Kingdom (UK) in commerce and trade. Simultaneously, Spanish clergy in the Philippines ensured that a link was maintained between the Philippines and its former colonial rulers. Despite these European–Philippines interactions during that period, the link was weak, and US relations took increasing precedence over those with Europe.

When the Philippines gained independence from the United States, relations with Europe remained relatively weak. On the one hand, Europeans were reluctant to form strong ties with the Philippines due to "a perception shared by the United Kingdom, France, and by the [former] Soviet Union of limited political and economic independence from the United States".[3] The Philippines, on the other hand, "also dealt with Europe in a remote and less urgent manner".[4] The first

---

[2] Jose, Ricardo T., 'One Hundred Years of Philippine–United States Relations: An Outline History', *Philippine External Relations, A Centennial Vista*, Foreign Service Institute: Manila, 1998, pp. 433–434.

[3] Salvador, Alma O., 'Philippine–European Relations: Beyond 100 Years', *Philippine External Relations a Centennial Vista*, Foreign Service Institute: Manila, 1998, p. 481.

[4] *Ibid.*, p. 488.

attempts to forge diplomatic links between the Philippines and Europe happened in the 1940s with Treaties of Friendship being made between the Philippines and individual European states such as France, Italy and Spain. An Air Transport Agreement was signed with Greece in 1949.[5] From the 1940s onwards, relations between the Philippines and individual European states gradually began to strengthen.

The creation of the European Community (EC) presented a new European intergovernmental entity for the Philippines to engage with, and relations between the two only developed slowly. Nevertheless, by the 1970s, the EC had become a significant aid donor to the Philippines with the latter receiving "twenty-six percent of total EC assistance for the [Southeast-Asian] region".[6] The relationship was further strengthened when, in 1972, informal relations were established between the EC and ASEAN.[7] Relations between the two regions was formalised in 1980 with the EC-ASEAN cooperation agreement,[8] with the Philippines a part of this process. However, a permanent and stable dialogue between the two was not established until after the fall of the Marcos dictatorial regime in the Philippines.

In 1986, "with the return of democracy to the Philippines, a long-term relationship between the EU and the Philippines ensued…[and] the Delegation [of the European Commission in the Philippines] was officially opened in May 1991".[9] At present, the Philippines cooperates with the EU in a number of policy areas, particularly trade and development aid. The EU27 is the third largest market for Philippine exports after China and ASEAN.[10] The

---

[5] *Ibid.*

[6] *Ibid.*

[7] Forster, Anthony, 'The European Union in Southeast–Asia: Continuity and Change in Turbulent Times', *International Affairs*, Vol. 75, No. 4, (1999), pp. 743–758, p. 744.

[8] *European Commission Delegation in the Philippines*, 'EU-Philippines Relations', <http://www.euphil.org/index.cfm?pagename=eu-phil>, accessed on 15 February 2009.

[9] *Ibid.*

[10] *Ibid.*, 'Trade', <http://www.euphil.org/index.cfm?pagename=stats>, accessed on 15 February 2009.

significance of the EU as a development aid donor in the Philippines has been substantial, with the European Investment Bank and EU Member States collectively accounting for "US$1.9 billion in Overseas Development Assistance (ODA) for the Philippines"[11] between 1992 and 2004. This makes the EU the 4th largest donor of development assistance to the Philippines.

Despite the fact that the EU–Philippines relationship has steadily become more institutionalised and formalized, the colonial experience with and present-day influence of the US on the Philippines has meant that the Philippines has preferred to 'turn to' America rather than to Europe. Undoubtedly, this explicit 'pro-USA' orientation of the Philippines, as well as the geographical and cultural distance between Europe and the Philippines, have impacted on how the Philippines perceives the EU. The combination of these factors indicates at the very least that European actors must exert more effort in order to be more visible in the Philippines' setting. It is on the issues of visibility and perception of the EU that this chapter focuses, looking specifically at news media representations of the Union and its images among the general public and national decision- and policy-makers.

VIEW FROM THE SIDES: EU IMAGERY IN THE NEWS MEDIA IN THE PHILIPPINES

The Philippines has been described as a country that takes pride in its free press. Throughout much of its history, even when it was colonised or under a political dictatorial regime, Philippines' journalists were seen as "remarkably outspoken, and the society in general [is] notably receptive to debate and open disputes. Filipinos strongly adhere to press freedom as a basic human right, [and] as an inalienable right inherent in the exercise of democracy".[12] The Philippines'

---

[11] *European Commission Delegation in the Philippines,* 'EU–Philippines Relations', <http://www.euphil.org/index.cfm?pagename=eu-phil>, accessed on 15 February 2009.

[12] Valdez, Violet, 'Philippines', *The ASIA Media Directory*, Konrad Adenauer Foundation: Singapore, 2004, p. 145.

reputation as a 'haven' for free press in Asia was shaken though, in 2009 when the International Federation of Journalists reported the country as the "second most deadly place for journalists after war-torn Iraq".[13] Despite this, the media, whether through newspapers or television, continues to exist and shape Philippine public opinion.

The first Philippine newspaper *Del Superior Govierno* came into circulation in 1811.[14] Under the American Colonial Regime, (during which "journalism was anglicized"),[15] the Philippines press was said to have flourished. The trend towards the use of English broadsheet newspapers has continued to the present and past attempts made to create broadsheets in the Filipino language have generally been short-lived.[16]

Local television broadcasts began in 1953:[17] since then, the television media has evolved with most channels being a "part of five major TV networks — ABS–CBN Broadcasting Corporation, Associated Broadcasting Corporation, GMA Network Inc., Intercontinental Broadcasting Corporation (IBC), Radip Philippines Network (RPN), and People's Television Network, Inc".[18] ABS–CBN and GMA Network are the two largest. The former was founded in 1956 while the latter traces its roots to 1961.

Selected Media

The newspapers selected for this research were the *Philippine Daily Inquirer*, the *Manila Bulletin* and *Business World*, and the television station was *GMA Network Channel 7* with its prime-time news show "*24 Oras*". *The Philippine Daily Inquirer* was established in 1985,

---

[13] *UCLA Asia Institute,* 'Philippines: Journalism Turns Deadly in the Philippines', <http://www.asiamedia.ucla.edu/article-southeastasia.asp?parentid=23871>, accessed on 24 February 2009.

[14] Violet Valdez, 'Philippines', *The ASIA Media Directory*, p. 145.

[15] *Ibid.*

[16] *Ibid.*, p. 146.

[17] *Ibid.*, p. 147.

[18] *Ibid.*

when it began as one of the newspapers of "the 'mosquito'[19] press during the last days of the Marcos regime and gained credibility through its hard-hitting stories exposing the regime's abuses".[20] After the fall of the Marcos dictatorship, the *Inquirer* has grown to become one of the country's mainstream newspapers, while at the same time maintaining its characteristic criticism of the government. As such, it may be seen as the main opposition newspaper in the Philippines. In 2009, the *Inquirer*'s circulation was 257,416 on weekdays and 268,575 on Sundays.[21]

The Manila Bulletin was established in 1900 making it one of the oldest newspapers in the Philippines. It is printed in English, and has a circulation of 280,000 on weekdays and 300,000 on Sundays,[22] making it the most popular and widely read newspaper in the Philippines.

The final newspaper examined was the nation-wide *Business World* marketed towards the business sector. This newspaper is a 'reincarnation' of the *Business Day*, "the country's first business daily",[23] which closed after a labour dispute and re-opened as the *Business World* in 1967.

Finally, the television *GMA Network Channel 7* was founded in 1961, and, through constant innovation, has become one of the two top television networks in the Philippines. The television show "*24 Oras*" is well recognised as the most viewed prime-time news bulletin in the Philippines.

EU Media Visibility

Throughout the six-month observation period, the EU appeared in just 256 news items in the three monitored newspapers. The *Manila*

---

[19] The 'mosquito' press refers to the opposition press which existed during the Marcos regime in the Philippines. Not sponsored by the state, it specialized in presenting stories that exposed the regime's abuses.

[20] Valdez, Violet, 'Philippines', *The ASIA Media Directory*, p. 154.

[21] *Ibid.*

[22] *Ibid.*

[23] *Ibid.*, p. 149.

Bulletin accounted for nearly half of these (127 items) with the *Business World* next (72) followed by the *Philippine Daily Inquirer* (57). The "*24 Oras*" registered only one (!) news item which referenced the EU in the monitored period.

The majority of the EU news sources came from foreign sources, particularly international wires. Of the 256 news items published, only 51 (a fifth) were sourced locally. Among the foreign sources of EU news, the major international wire used was *Agence France-Presse (AFP)* (71 entries from the three newspapers); *Reuters* was second with 60 entries; the *Associated Press (AP)* was third with 25, followed by the *New York Times, Financial Times, DPA, Dow Jones* and *Guardian*. The choices of sources have obvious implications on how the EU is represented in the newspapers, and this is discussed later in this chapter. However, it appears that foreign sources have become a primary source of EU news since the Philippines newspapers do not have the budgets to maintain correspondents abroad (and in Europe in particular).

With regard to the degree of centrality — the importance of the EU in the news story — 121 articles portrayed the EU the major focus, 58 indicated it was the secondary focus and in 77 the EU played a minor role (Table 1). Comparing the three newspapers in terms of distribution of the degree of centrality, both the *Business World* and the *Philippine Daily Inquirer* portrayed the EU as typically a major actor, while in the *Manila Bulletin's* reports, the EU was

Table 1:   Distribution of the degree of centrality across three newspapers (January–June 2008)

Degree of Centrality	*Philippine Daily Inquirer*		*Business World*		*Manila Bulletin*	
	Number	% of Total	Number	% of Total	Number	% of Total
Major	26	10.2	57	22.2	38	14.8
Secondary	9	3.5	3	1.2	46	18.0
Minor	22	8.6	12	4.7	43	17.0

mainly profiled as a secondary actor. It is possible that due to the *Manila Bulletin*'s status of a 'popular' newspaper (i.e., a paper that targets a general readership rather than specialised audiences), its portrayal of the EU was not very focused.

With regard to the focus of domesticity, 119 of the articles reported the EU in the European context, 86 focused on the EU's activities in third countries, eight focused on the EU acting in the region and 43 looked at the EU actions grounded locally in the Philippines (Table 2). This specific dominant framing of the EU (i.e. 'acting elsewhere in the world but not locally') may have been influenced by the fact that many of the media outlets sourced their news from foreign sources, which are more likely to focus on the EU acting either in Europe or around the world, rather than domestically or regionally.

Continuing with the theme of visibility, a number of institutions and people were prominent in the Philippines news media. Among the institutions, the European Commission was the most represented, appearing in 90 of the monitored news items. The European Council was a distant second, appearing just 11 times, followed by the European Central Bank (10), the European Parliament (8) and in last place the European Court of Justice referenced only once. By far, the most widely cited EU official was the Head of the Commission Delegation to the Philippines, Ambassador MacDonald, who

Table 2:   Distribution of the foci of domesticity in three newspapers (January–June 2008)

	Philippine Daily Inquirer		*Business World*		*Manila Bulletin*	
Degree of Centrality	Number	% of Total	Number	% of Total	Number	% of Total
EU	27	10.5	41	17.6	51	19.9
3rd	20	7.8	23	10.9	43	17.0
Local	10	3.9	8	3.1	25	9.8
Regional	0	0	0	0	8	3.1

appeared in 20 articles outstripping EU Trade Commissioner Peter Mandelson (11 times), President José Manuel Barroso (10 times), and Javier Solana, who appeared in only 6 news stories.

EU Framing in Media Sources

In the monitored news media, the EU was most dominantly presented as an economic actor, with 139 news items on EU economic actions. This was followed by political reports of the EU, with 69 items. EU environment themes were featured 22 times, and finally EU actions in the areas of development and social, cultural and intellectual affairs were only sporadically mentioned (Table 3).

The economic representation of the EU was the most visible not only in the local 'business' daily (which was predictable) but also in the *Manila Bulletin*, a 'popular' newspaper. Interestingly, the *Manila Bulletin* represented the EU across a greater variety of topics fitting all five possible frames identified in this analysis (although this could be attributed to a higher volume of EU news production by this specific outlet). Articles reporting EU business- and finance-related news items were more visible accounting for 30 items. For politics, the news focused mainly on EU political activities on the international

Table 3: Distribution of the leading frames in EU reportage in three newspapers (January–June 2008)

Framing	*Philippine Daily Inquirer*		*Business World*		*Manila Bulletin*	
	Number	% of Total	Number	% of Total	Number	% of Total
Economic	22	8.6	54	21.1	63	24.6
Political	23	9.0	11	4.3	35	13.7
Social, Cultural and Intellectual Affairs	8	3.1	1	0.4	9	3.5
Environment	1	0.3	6	2.3	15	5.9
Development	3	1.2	0	0	5	2.0

stage rather than the EU's actions within the Union. This was the same for the reporting of EU environment actions where issues of climate change advocacy were prevalent. Finally, with regard to the reportage of EU social, cultural and intellectual affairs, the main topic here was immigration to Europe (specifically, of Philippine citizens to the EU). This was not surprising given that the Philippines relies heavily on local migrants' labour overseas to sustain its own economy.

In contrast, the *Philippine Daily Inquirer* gave balanced political-economic news in its reportage of the EU. This newspaper highlighted EU economic issues in the areas of business and industry. Similarly to the *Bulletin*, when representing the EU as a political actor, the *Inquirer* focused on the EU acting in the context of third parties rather than on the EU's internal politics. Development-themed news focused on the EU's development aid given to the Philippines and the one item on environment focused on the EU's internal environment policy. Finally, as in the case of the *Manila Bulletin*, social, cultural and intellectual affairs news were mainly about immigration.

Although not as varied in its coverage, the *Business World* reportage provided more than just economic news even if the overwhelming majority (54 out of 72 news items) were related to the economy. There were 11 news articles on EU politics, six on environment and one on social and intellectual affairs. The emphasis on news pertaining to economy was expected, considering that *Business World*, as the name implies, is a 'business' newspaper. Aside from businessmen, the target clientele of the paper also includes expatriates and members of the diplomatic corps. The reported economic news items (27) about the EU in the context of trade were followed by articles about EU agricultural activities (11). Only a sprinkling of economic news dealt with EU business and finance actions (7) as well as banking and state of its economy (4). Lastly, six of the eleven news articles on politics reported the Union's internal policies and actions, and this was followed by EU representations in the areas of external politics (2) and local governance (2). The six articles on the environment talked about the EU acting both externally and internally. Only two publications reported the EU in the context of climate change.

Evaluation of the EU in Media Sources

In terms of the evaluation of the EU in the Philippine media, 206 news items referenced the EU in neutral tone. Whenever there was an evaluation expressed, a positive assessment of the EU actions was more prevalent than a negative one (38 and 12 respectively) (Table 4).

The EU reportage in the *Manila Bulletin* was predominantly neutral across all frames, with the only difference being found in the development frame where the EU was seen in a majority of articles from a positive angle. In this frame, the *Manila Bulletin* reported the EU-sponsored development projects taking place in the Philippines where the EU was seen as contributing positively to the local community. In all other frames, however, a neutral evaluation dominated. Indeed, most of the items in this paper were simply a report of facts about current events which were perceived to have little direct effect on the Philippines. Furthermore, the use of international wires as main data sources seemed to contribute to the neutral evaluation pattern since international wires typically report facts in a largely objective and neutral manner.

The *Philippine Daily Inquirer* echoed evaluation patterns discovered in the *Manila Bulletin*. The evaluations of the EU were mainly

Table 4: Distribution of evaluations in EU reportage in three newspapers (January–June 2008)

Evaluation	Philippine Daily Inquirer		Business World		Manila Bulletin	
	Number	% of Total	Number	% of Total	Number	% of Total
Positive	17	6.6	3	1.2	18	7.0
Neutral	37	14.5	64	25.0	105	41.0
Negative	3	1.2	5	2.0	4	1.6

neutral followed by positive assessments. There were only three entries where the EU was evaluated negatively.

Out of the 72 items in the *Business World*, 64 covered the EU from a neutral perspective. The neutral valence assigned to the EU by this newspaper was not surprising — it is a business newspaper with a reputation of providing neutral and objective news coverage. Furthermore, similarly to *Manila Bulletin*, most of the EU news in this outlet came from international wires known for their impartiality. However, in contrast to the other two papers in this study, the second most visible evaluation in the *Business World* was negative. Negatively-coloured articles were found in a variety of economic sub-frames, including agriculture, trade, business, as well as banking and finance. The ECB, for example, was mentioned due to its inability to curb inflation in the region and its inability to de-couple from the then downward spiral of the US economy. Though limited in number, there were also three news items portraying the EU positively. The EU, for instance, was reported to be providing a substantial development assistance package to uplift the economic, social and political well-being of the battle-scarred Mindanao region.

EU Perceptions among the Newsmakers in the Philippines

Attempting to identify the reasons behind newsmakers' choices in reporting the EU, this study approached Philippines' media professionals inquiring into their processes of news production. Media practitioners in this study (working at the *ANC*, *Japan News Agency*, the *Philippine Daily Inquirer* and the *German News Agency*) admitted they do not treat EU news in a focused manner. An interviewee from *ANC*, a television news channel owned by *ABS–CBN*, said that he indeed "covered news involving Europeans", but only in light of their participation in sports. However, foreign news practitioners from the *Japan News Agency* in the Philippines reported that the *Agency* has regional desks which responded to regional assignments. These desks, for example, would cover a story on the relations between the Philippines and the EU with regard to human rights issues.

The respondents noted that the official policy on reporting foreign news in general (and EU news in particular) was to write about news that sells. According to a *Philippine Daily Inquirer* interviewee, national, local and foreign news in *the Inquirer* is basically in a "competition for space". Another interviewee noted that the news writer "can write about the EU in (their) locality", meaning that pure foreign news is seen only as an important one only if it demonstrates its local relevance. While a journalist's writing skills were considered to be essential ("if the copy is well written then it would have won half the battle"), the decision about what actually gets published is shaped by a combined criteria of marketing and creativity. Generally, news selection is shaped by a set of requirements, such as "oddity", "intrigue", "news value" and "consequence". In addition, the news should also meet demands for "accuracy", "fairness" and "speed" in writing and reporting.

Philippines' television news reporting was said to be influenced by considerations of ratings (according to a respondent working at *ANC*). According to the source, the demand for "infotainment" and competition for the ratings has "eased out any European or foreign affairs reporting". Nevertheless, *ANC* has a policy aiming to globalise its news and viewership. When it comes to Europe, the respondent claimed that most of the news is oriented at the role of Europe as a destination for Filipino migrant workers (or "Overseas Filipino Workers") and seldom moves beyond that.

When asked about the balance of news reporting respondents in both media noted that it is "overwhelmingly in favour of local news". Such a preference for local news means that EU news which is grounded in European and international contexts is less likely to be reported. In general, only one or two pages in a Philippines press outlet are dedicated to foreign news. In addition, according to some interviewed newsmakers, there was a shared sentiment that "Filipinos are not interested in foreign news". This assumption, coupled with the need to pursue higher ratings and sales, adds to the newsmakers' 'list of rationales' of why not to emphasise EU news.

This analysis of EU representations in the Philippine media leads to a number of conclusions. The visibility of the EU remains low, especially on television. However, despite the low numbers, most of the news in the national press portrayed the EU either as a major or secondary actor, thus partially raising the Union's media profile. Yet, a dominant neutral evaluation of the EU suggests a lack of any special attachment to what is happening in or with the Union. Moreover, a minimal local positioning of the EU's actions suggested a certain distance between the EU and the local audiences. Interviews with local newsmakers provided several useful insights into the dominant patterns in EU news representations. The EU's low media profile was explained by a lack of marketability and sales-value of EU news. These peculiarities in media framing of the EU in the Philippines are likely to have an effect on and manifestations in the opinions on the EU among the members of the general public and national stakeholders, as discussed in a greater detail in the following sections of this chapter.

VIEW FROM THE TOP: STAKEHOLDERS' PERCEPTIONS OF THE EU

The Importance of Different Regions to the Philippines (in the Present and in the Future)

Following the format used in each of the countries examined in this volume, selected key stakeholders were asked a series of questions. The generalised findings from their interviews are presented below.

Representatives of the political, business, civil society and media 'elite' cohorts, were asked to identify the perceived importance of the EU in comparison with other international partners of the Philippines. Typically, the USA was seen as the most important partner at the present, reflecting arguably the fact that the USA was the Philippines' ally and coloniser for 45 years.

For political 'elite' respondents, relations between the EU and the Philippines constitutes "(n)ot much at this time"[24] as there "is barely a relationship to speak of the EU."[25] Compared with the US and

---

[24] Mayor, Naga City, Albay in Southern Philippines.

[25] Chief of congressional staff, a District in the Autonomous Region in Muslim Mindanao.

Japan, EU–Philippines relations was noted to be "not as developed"[26] and that perception was based on traditional colonial ties, proximity, and dependency on and familiarity with usual markets. In addition, several comments from the civil society sector revealed that the "EU has not deeply impacted on the economic, political and cultural life of society as ha[ve] US and Japan"[27] and therefore it was "not as significant in terms of trade, investment and development aid".[28] Its presence, however, was manifested "on a second level" based on "human rights and restorative justice."[29]

A more nuanced response originated mostly from the business sector representatives who traced the relative weakness of an EU–Philippine relationship to the "theoretical"[30] nature of the EU's global power. Compared to the US or China, the EU's impact on the Philippines "remains to be seen".[31] Likewise, "Filipinos are not aware of the EU not like China, ASEAN, which are by nature of proximity in our interests."[32] Another consideration stemmed from recognition of the EU as a single entity. That the Philippines is "still dealing with Germany and England (sic)"[33] shed light on the perceived weight of bilateral relations over EU–Philippines ones.

Various responses, though, did reveal an awareness of the possibilities and potential in this dialogue. One of the political elite respondents said that the EU single currency influenced a "partner shift from the US, Japan and China."[34] Possibilities also existed in

---

[26] District representative, District of Quezon, Southern Philippines.

[27] Former Executive Director, OTRADEV (NGO engaged in community based resource management).

[28] Executive Director, of an NGO engaged in rural development.

[29] Project Officer, Ateneo Centre for Educational Development.

[30] President and chief executive officer, real estate firm.

[31] *Ibid.*

[32] Tax Lawyer, French–Philippine law and accounting Office, Makati City, Philippines.

[33] Honorary Consul of the Philippines to Senegal and Trustee, several Philippine banks.

[34] While the US is the country's traditional partner and coloniser, Japan and China, because of proximity show interest in the Philippines. Secretary-General of the Council of Asian Liberals and Democrats (CALD) and former district representative of a district in Northern Mindanao.

"freer"[35] EU migration and labour laws as well as through a more "organised" and "holistic"[36] development aid approach from which the Philippines benefits — "development paradigms have come from the EU such as participatory paradigms, participatory learning, participatory methods and the integrated area development studies".[37] A particular political elite's response summed up the future of this relationship:

> We have a lot of time comparatively with the US and Japan… *With Europe, we have experienced less pain.* But we haven't maximized our relations with Europe… Europe is a boom area. The UK, Italy for instance serves as the place for our labour migrant and health professionals. But there is much to explore…" [authors' italics].[38]

EU as a Great Power

Most frequently, the image of 'great power' was associated with EU collective strength, particularly in its integrated economic and financial institutions like the euro and the European Central Bank. A former Congressman and current Secretary General of the Liberal Democrats in Asia said that this was due to the EU's "integrative power". Business respondents perceived 'great power' as the capability to "mirror common and shared values", to prioritise "collective good", and to achieve a level of "consistency" in one's "legal, socio-legal and political frameworks". To quote a member of several Boards of Philippines' banks, "the union has worked". This perception was shared by a sports media personality who looked at the euro with awe: "Would you believe that they all agreed to use this?"

Across all cohorts though, there seemed to be an understanding that the notions of the EU as a 'great power' went beyond its economic dimension. A congressional chief of staff in a Southern

---

[35] Two local government officials maintain a position that the EU will matter to the Philippines if labour laws of the EU will enable a freer flow of Filipino migrant workers. Vice Mayor of Paete, Rizal; Mayor, Naga City, Albay.

[36] Mayor, San Isidro, Nueva Ecija Province.

[37] President of the Board of Trustees, Foundation of Media Alternatives.

[38] Party list representative of the Philippine Congress.

Philippines province stressed, "more than economic power, it is this idea it has created a level of influence unmatched by the US". Different cohorts also differentiated between economic notions of 'soft' power, and political influence and military power as 'hard' power. To some respondents, integrative power was a source of political strength. One business respondent pointed out that political power "translates a lot of political clout" which was contingent on its power to "lobby in the worldwide stage". For this respondent, a common currency and institutional framework provide a "centralised system [for] imposing [the] will"[39] of the EU.

To civil society respondents, integrative power allowed the EU to act, firstly, as a "counterbalance against the United States"[40] and, secondly, "as means to funnel collective influence on policy decisions such as development aid."[41] Business responses identified "diversity" as a major threat to the "union" and to EU "actorness".[42] As one respondent noted, "the 'actorness' of the EU is still being defined; it is evolving. It depends on its projection on external relations or the ways it acts."

Interviewees partly revealed that 'great power' status is sometimes determined by comparative assessments of EU and US strengths. While comments made by political and civil society respondents revealed a rather realist framing of the EU as a 'power balancer', some comments from local and foreign media instead appeared to view the EU power through the lens of American activities.[43] One media

---

[39] Tax lawyer, Philippine–French law and accounting office.

[40] Director of a research institute.

[41] President of the Board of Trustees, Foundation of Media Alternatives.

[42] President and CEO, real estate firm.

[43] Based on the constructivist and "symbolic interactionist notion" of "looking glass self" which Alex Wendt uses to describe the process of socialization of actors in identity formation. Accordingly while an actor defines his/her identity, this identity is also shaped by others' construction. Interaction is thus seen as an inter-subjective (between selves) exchange of selves and meanings, which results in a seemingly never-ending process of identity formation. See Wendt, Alex, 'Anarchy is what States Make of it: The Social Construction of Power Politics', *International Organization,* Vol. 46, No. 2 (1992), pp. 391–425.

personality, for example, believed that the EU's power is defined "not in the [same] sense that we consider the US as a great power".[44] Another media response reaffirmed that "the US is still up there"[45] with its power of external "intervention".[46] However, there was a perception that inconsistency in US power (in terms of the varying impact of its decisions) has created space for the rise of another actor. One media practitioner noted: "With the US embroiled in so much controversies both domestic and abroad, the EU has been taking lead in resolving diplomatic problems in the international community".[47]

EU as an International Leader

Social constructivists define "actorness" as the ability to act.[48] Respondents to our interviews, on the other hand, defined actorness as the ability to intervene and exercise political leadership in external affairs. Based on this definition, it may be — in the eyes of the Philippines' 'elite' at least — that the EU falls short of being a fully-fledged "international actor".

'Elites' from the business sector generally felt the EU lacked in political and military strength. In addition, the EU was perceived as "structurally" ill-equipped to project itself as a unanimous voice.[49] One respondent pointed to the subordinate role of the EU to NATO over Iraq where the "EU as a body could have thrown its hat into the ring but [it] did not take a stand".[50] As opposed to collective strength,

---

[44] Public relations officer, Public Relations and Communication Office, Ateneo de Manila (formerly features writer in the *Philippine Daily Inquirer*).

[45] Sportscaster, *The ANC Channel*.

[46] Reporter, *Japanese News Agency*.

[47] Reporter, *German News Agency* and Director of the *Foreign Correspondents Agency* of the Philippines.

[48] Kabeer, Naila, *Citizenship and the Boundaries of the Acknowledged Community: Identity, Affiliation and Exclusion*, IDS Working Paper, No. 171 (2002), pp. 1–48.

[49] President and a CEO, real estate firm.

[50] Tax lawyer, Philippine–French of a law and accounting office.

the EU "only individually was able to police their ranks".[51] One remark referred to an apparent lack of a singular EU voice in the Russia and Georgia conflict.[52] Instead, the respondent noted, the ideal "one voice" is subsumed under the voice of the "Commission".[53] In one case, the EU voice was seen to be overtaken by the dominant French interventionist voice in Georgia. Business respondents perceived that this lack of unity stems from the EU's "loose [grouping]" and problems stem from "... a question of a strong national identity separate from community identity".[54] A civil society actor echoed this sentiment:

> The global political clout and significance of the member countries are uneven. Even at the UN, the EU still has to find ways to become a significant power player, apart from the ones being played by its individual members.[55]

Are these inadequacies linked to a perceived lack of EU presence in the Philippines? At least two business respondents referred to Europe as largely "unfamiliar terrain"[56] and as a leader of particular fields or "segment(s)" as opposed to a "world" leader.[57] Two related responses from media respondents underscored the EU's inability to have an impact on the Philippines: "How much of our economy do they dominate?"[58]

---

[51] *Ibid.*

[52] President and CEO, real estate firm.

[53] *Ibid.* The quotable quote is "speaking with a commission voice is not easy".

[54] *Ibid.*

[55] Former executive director, OTRADEV (a community based resource management NGO).

[56] Restaurateur and franchiser 1, Jollibee and Red Ribbon.

[57] Restaurateur and franchiser 2, Jollibee and Red Ribbon. Accordingly, it is stated that the EU is not as aggressive as the United States in terms of products promotion and marketing. Commercial attaches of the US are perceived to more aggressively advance promotional trade fairs and facilitate exchanges in trade and baking technology.

[58] Sportscaster, The *ANC Channel.*

Another one opined that "(t)heir (EU) policies have no consequence for us."[59]

According to Nye, the EU is an economic and normative power.[60] This normative power aspect was recognised by Philippines' political 'elites' who said that "the EU presents a better version of democracy".[61] Two respondents from civil society and media sectors agreed that the EU was a "leader in promoting certain standards" such as standards of "human rights".[62] Alternatively, as an economic power, the EU was also seen a "leader in global economic institutions" and led WTO debates.[63] Unlike the US, characterised by a respondent as a unilateral power,[64] or NATO as a military actor, the EU was perceived to have a naturally economic purpose. Two quotes summed up this vision: "You don't go to war as an EU....It is an economic union..." and "It is not a military power. It is an economic entity. It is not an armed entity".[65]

Relations between the EU and the Philippines

State of Relations

Visions of the state of relations between the EU and the Philippines were mixed. There was a sense that relations were "stable and improving",[66]

---

[59] Public relations officer, Public Relations and Communication Office, Ateneo de Manila (formerly features writer in the *Philippine Daily Inquirer*).

[60] Nye, Jr. , Joseph, 'Soft Power', *Foreign Policy*, <http://www.foreignpolicy.com/Ning/archive/archive/080/SOFT_POWER.PDF>, accessed 8 April 2009.

[61] Chief of congressional staff, a district in the Autonomous Region in Muslim Mindanao.

[62] Convener of the PHILANSA (Philippine Action Network on Small Arms); Reporter, *Japan News Agency*.

[63] President of the Board of Trustees, Foundation of Media Alternatives.

[64] An interview with the director of a research institute states that the EU compared to the US is a normative power. Her quote interestingly captures a tinge of her bias against the US: "If the US bombs Afghanistan... what did they bomb recently?"

[65] Honorary Consul of the Philippines to Senegal and Trustee in several Philippine banks.

[66] Based on the interviews of: Secretary General, Council of Asian Liberals and Democrats; Sr Supt Edwin C. Roque, Armed Forces of the Philippines.

with this vision reflecting the phenomenon of the EU as a migration destination for overseas Filipino workers. Tough migration laws and a "rightward drift of political parties",[67] however, were noted as threats. Alternatively, business 'elite' respondents found increasing Filipino consumption of European goods had resulted in a "heightened level of interest in (their) buyers."

A congressional chief of staff noted that the relationship was "stagnant" because "there is nothing much…while institutions are in place, we have not heard of partnerships." Citing the EU's agricultural policy as a basis of stagnation, an incumbent district representative's staff noted that relations were "not moving because of EU's refusal to remove subsidies in the agricultural sector."

Civil society respondents located EU–Philippine relations around the idea of stability, sourced from the EU's economic performance, role in migration and in development theorising,[68] — and as "worsening" in the area of human rights; in aid, "at best it is not improving" and "stagnant if not worsening"[69] due to shifts in funding to East Timor and transition countries, such as Vietnam, Cambodia and Laos.[70] For some, EU–Philippine relations "do not trickle down", are "inadequate" and are "not improving" primarily due to a lack of "dealings" between the EU and local government because of market dependence on the US. Respondents, however saw "room for growth".[71]

Only political respondents recognised the role of the European Commission Delegation (ECD) and its presence as a source of funding. None of the other local 'elites' saw the relevance of the ECD

---

[67] The response is based on the party list representative's concern for Greece's "return directive" which refers to an order to deport illegal aliens to their home countries.

[68] Project Officer, Ateneo Canter for Educational Development; President of the Board of Trustees, Foundation for Media Alternatives.

[69] Responses include those mentioned above; also the response of Executive Director, Philippine Support Services Agency.

[70] President of the Board of the Trustees, Foundation for Media Alternatives.

[71] Various elite respondents view EU–Philippine relations as a balance between instability/stagnation but recognize areas for improvement. The President and CEO of a real estate firm uses the term "room for growth" to refer to areas for improvement.

to their organisations. Compared with the EU, relations with China, Taiwan, Japan and Israel were seen as far more active. In this context, "the impact on the individual is very strong" and "a multiplier effect"[72] was mentioned in particular.

Euro

Views[73] of the EU as an economic power were reflected in the respondents' views of the euro as a stable currency and a viable alternative to the US dollar. The stability of the euro was seen to add to this "confidence" which was reflected in the "strength of the European economy". To political respondents, the euro has "beaten" or "outperformed" the US dollar. Civil society 'elites' claimed that a shift to the euro "is on the rise": "More and more Filipino elites are converting their money to the euro." In addition, "between the euro and the dollar" one believed that she "will hold on to the euro". In fact, "in some NGOs, they are required to keep [a] euro currency account."

A few respondents viewed the rise of the euro in positive terms for Europe, yet detrimental for Filipino workers and tourists. To US dollar-earning migrant workers, "this translates to reduced buying power".[74] From a business perspective, a very strong euro made trade in goods unfavourable to Philippine businesses: "Europe is not cost competitive...items purchased in Europe are expensive...if quality is good enough, not the best, but good enough then we will go Korea, China and Taiwan."[75]

---

[72] President and CEO, real estate firm.

[73] Responses among elites are aggregated because they represent a consensus on a positive role of the euro as an alternative currency to the USD. There is negative consensus on the euro is a dominantly business perspective.

[74] Party list representative of the Philippine Congress.

[75] The restaurateur of a food chain argues that between European and other brands, his restaurant prefers other Korean brands, because they are cheaper and more accessible. He reveals that trade in baking equipment and technology is increasingly taking place in the Asian market today. Restaurateur and franchiser 1 and 2, Jollibee and Red Ribbon.

Perceptions of the EU's Enlargement

Responses on the impact of EU enlargement on the Philippines were generally divided. Local government respondents tended to see enlargement in a positive light. Enlargement made Europe "take care of their own", although at the same time, threats to the Philippines were perceived as "negligible",[76] except from "communist countries" in Eastern Europe posing "a threat to our [Philippine] democracy".[77]

Because the EU continues to represent universal norms, enlargement was a considered "challenge for (the Philippines) to measure up globally".[78] Referring to EU standards in "environment, trade, human rights", the EU was perceived as a benchmark for global standards as well as for "changing mindsets". Enlargement, too, had an "appeal" derived from its "strict implementation of the respect for human rights."[79] One answer that stood out, however revealed an understanding — admittedly somewhat misguided in view of the reference to the constitution — of the regulatory role of EU institutions and their effect on EU policies:

> I don't think expansion poses as a risk for us because the members have to abide by the constitution and the rules of the EU. If they do not comply or adhere to these, they may be sanctioned or expelled.[80]

Civil society respondents did not share these views and cited overseas migration and development assistance as major casualties of enlargement. Enlargement was equated with "competition in human resource" from countries which "might get preferential option" from the EU. Referring to Central and Eastern Europe, "new states" were viewed as "sources of cheap labour which will hinder export of services" from the Philippines. Civil society responses demonstrated

---

[76] Mayor of Paete, Rizal.

[77] Mayor, San Isidro, Nueva Ecija Province.

[78] Secretary-General of CALD.

[79] Congressional chief of staff, a district in the Autonomous Region of Muslim Mindanao.

[80] District representative, a district in Quezon.

that migration is a nexus for converging negative perceptions on enlargement from civil society and political respondents:

> (t)here might be a shift of attention towards these new Central European states because of the traumatic experiences of the break off of the former Yugoslavia, or Russia… Central Europe is in their gut, in their belly…[81]

Business interviewees' responses provided something of a contrast. Two themes stood out: a market-oriented view of the benefits of enlargement, and a challenge for the EU to get to know Asia through enlargement. Pragmatically, business respondents saw enlargement as a "gateway for migration and for doing business". For them, enlargement corresponded to "freedom to travel" where labour becomes "accessible to other parts of Europe". Associated with a "single legal framework and standards",[82] enlargement was seen to bring "ease of trade" and openings from emergent markets such as the petrochemical markets of the "former Soviet Eastern European bloc" particularly "Ukraine, Russia, Bulgaria, Kazakhstan and Turkey (sic)".[83]

The second strand saw enlargement as a stimulus for the EU to change its behaviour *vis-à-vis* Asia. There is an apparent need for "more delegations [from Europe] coming here [to the Philippines]" and *vice-versa*: "For the Philippines to sell, one has to see what each of these countries needs. These countries are not homogenous as the United States."[84]

ASEM

Respondents were generally unaware of the ASEM process. Those political 'elites' who were aware viewed it as an "intergovernmental

---

[81] Party list representative.

[82] President and CEO, Cathay Pacific Steel Corporation and President of the Chinese Chamber of Commerce in the Philippines.

[83] Quotes are gathered from various business-elite respondents who generally share a positive view of enlargement.

[84] Lifted from the specific responses of: Restaurateur and franchiser 1, Red Ribbon and Jollibee and from the Honorary Consul of the Philippines to Senegal and member of various boards of banks.

forum" with an increased "political, economic and diplomatic reach" which "allow(s) for parallel civil society forums" to discuss free trade agreement drafts.[85] A member of a civil society organisation viewed ASEM as a mechanism providing "…a clearer foreign policy role for EU in Asia". Given Europe's historical relationships with Africa and Latin America an opinion was shared that "European countries are not sure where to place Asia…". A member of a Japanese news agency noted that ASEM is the "only forum that Burma cannot attend" and the same forum that the "EU did not want to deal with ASEAN if Burma is around".

Spontaneous Images of the EU

Sharing their immediate associations about the EU, political respondents presented a variety of images of the Union. Some used metaphors such as "a wall" to signify strength. Other descriptions were of a "multi-polar or supranational democracy", or "liberal democracy", or "community of shared values, cultures and civilisations" (Table 5). Other responses referred to 'big' issues, such as an "emphasis on human rights" and "global warming". As opposed to the image of the 'collective', a frequent mentioning of the "UK, France and Germany" rendered the image of the EU as simply a collection of Member States.

Business respondents also voiced a broad range of images. 'Realists' saw the EU as a "power economic group" or a "bureaucratic" entity. Those images existed side-by-side with 'idealistic/liberal' visions of the Union as a "borderless entity", "symbol of success of a regional grouping" and an institutional framework that promotes "ease of trade and one legal framework."

Civil society respondents included images of 'tradition', for example, the EU in terms of "old culture". One respondent recalled "good public welfare system", for another "Brussels" was a bureaucratic entity. A few responses were norm-oriented, such as "governance", "development paradigm", "protection of human rights", "development aid"

---

[85] CALD and party list representative respectively.

Table 5:   Spontaneous images of the EU

Stakeholders	Images of the EU
Political	Wall Multipolar/liberal democracy Community of shared values, cultures and civilizations Big issues (emphasis on human rights, global warming) UK, France, Germany
Business	Power Economic group Bureaucratic Borderless entity Symbol of success of a regional grouping Ease of trade One legal framework
Civil Society	Old culture One currency Good public welfare system Brussels Governance Development paradigm Protection of human rights Development aid Development assistance Synergy Powerhouse Domination Hierarchy
Media	*Illustrado* Rizal Arts and culture Architecture The flag Union Unity

and "development assistance". Alternatively, 'realist' images listed such visions as "synergy", "one currency", "powerhouse", and "domination" and "hierarchy".

The media respondents described images of an "*illustrado*" (a notion linked to old colonial elites in the Philippines and old Europe).

Related to this was an image of "Rizal" (the Philippine national hero executed by the Spanish colonial regime). In addition, the media professionals came with such 'cultural' images of the EU associated with "arts and culture" and "architecture", as well as 'unity' visions of the entity, namely "the flag", "union" and "unity".

Sources of Information

Commenting on the their sources of information about the EU, political 'elites' generally admitted relying on multiple sources of information listing their jobs connections and direct contacts with the EU in addition to print media, cable news and the Internet sources. In contrast, business 'elites' preferred to rely more heavily on the Internet. Only one civil society actor cited the European Commission Delegation website as a source.

In summary, based on this sample, it was observed that the Philippine decision- and policy-makers perceived the EU as an important actor. Its importance, however, was seen through a 'US' lens — the US was recognised as a major global actor, and the Philippine's ally and friend (based on the countries' previous encounters with each other). The EU, on the other hand, was seen to possess a so-called 'soft' power — a vision based on the Union's integration success, collective institutionalisation and moral ascendancy derived from a profound history and current positioning in world affairs.

Importantly, the EU was often seen as an alternative to the US in the field of foreign policy and a dominant (if not ideal) actor in developmental theory and practice. Such issues as trade, human rights and migration were seen as primary venues for improving and stabilising EU–Philippine relations. However, some stagnation in the relationships between the two was also noted and was mainly traced to the perceptions of reduced EU aid and Europe's general lack of interest or familiarity with the Philippines market and society. Insights into the images of the EU existing among the general public in the Philippines is the focus of the following section of this chapter: what, if any, are the differences between 'elite' and popular visions of the EU.

VIEW FROM BELOW: EU PERCEPTIONS IN THE PHILIPPINE PUBLIC OPINION[86]

EU Partnership with the Philippines

To the question "Which countries or regions, you think, are the most important partners for Philippines?", 38% of the surveyed public answered "the United States". This finding was unsurprising given colonial history, US investment, and ongoing Filipino migration to the US supported by continuing strong ties with relatives left behind. Social network analysis claims that these types of relationships impact on opinions formed by the actors within these social networks.[87] This dense social network with family or friends in the USA reflects the importance accorded to the US as the main partner of the Philippines in this study.

Other important partners in the eyes of the public included Japan (15% of the sample), China (10%) and Canada (6%). Europe/EU was mentioned by only 3% with the same percentage mentioning the UK. In spite of its geographic distance from the Philippines, Europe/EU was considered as an important partner by more respondents when compared to ASEAN (3% *vs.*2%).

When asked to rate the importance of international partners in the future (with 1 being the least important and 5 being the most important), the respondents again selected the USA with an average score

---

[86] A total of 400 Filipino citizens aged 18 and above were interviewed in order to assess the over-all public perception about Europe and the European Union in the Philippines. The sample is relatively young with majority aged 25–34 (32%), 18–24 (26%) and 35–44 (21%). Most common are those with 3–5 years of secondary education (33%) and with completed university degree (33%). Although most frequent were employed full-time (27%), significant also were those who are self-employed (12%), full time home makers (10%) and employed part-time (10%). For those who are employed, most current occupations included unskilled/semi-skilled service type of jobs (29%), followed by those who are small employer/property owner (18%), and in skilled white-collar jobs (17%). The males (52%) slightly outnumber the women (48%).

[87] Ethier, Jason, *Current Research in Social Network Theory*, <http://www.ccs.neu.edu/home/perrolle/archive/Ethier-SocialNetworks.html>, accessed on 31 March 2009.

of 3.98. Interestingly, this choice was closely followed by Europe/EU (3.89) and Russia (3.87). It must be pointed out that even if the USA topped the list, there is also greater variation (SD = 4.89) in the answers compared to the variation of responses for Europe/EU (SD = 1.06) and Russia (SD = 1.10). This indicates that though USA was thought to have the greatest impact on the future of the country, there were also some respondents who thought otherwise. And although Europe/EU only came in second, the lower standard deviation indicates less variation in the assessment of the respondents. Meanwhile, Asia (excluding Japan) only came in fourth (3.78) as the most important region for the future of the Philippines. Its score, however, is still quite close to the top three choices.

Images of Europe

The survey respondents were asked about their images of "the European Union". An overwhelming majority (79%) of the 1,200 different answers was an admission of having no idea about the EU. Just 7% said that the European Union is about 'unity/union'. This answer however might be a case of simple word association as the term union is implicitly contained in the question posed to the respondents.

The pattern above suggests that Filipinos have very little knowledge about Europe in general and the European Union in particular. However, in spite of this limited familiarity, almost half of the respondents (43%) believed that the relationship between the Philippines and the EU was improving while more than a quarter answered that the relationship was steady. Meanwhile, 14% said that the relationship was 'worsening' and 13% did not know how to assess the situation between their country and the EU.

Respondents were asked to rate EU impact on a variety of issues (on a scale from 1 to 10, with 1 indicating no impact and 10 indicating the highest impact). The EU's support for reducing carbon gas emissions within the framework of Kyoto protocol topped the list (with an average score of 9.4). It was followed by the EU's dealings with ASEAN (8.72), and the common European currency, the euro (8.70). This pattern suggests that Europe is perceived by the general public mostly as an environmental actor and as a regional grouping that deals with other regional associations (ASEAN in this case). As discussed above, this corresponds to the media framing of the EU which also highlighted the theme of the EU's involvement in the Kyoto protocol. The importance of the euro (again emphasized in the 'elite' interviews) is understandable considering the importance of remittances sent home by Filipinos working in Europe.

Development Actors and ASEM

Respondents were asked to rank the USA, Japan, China, Australia, the EU and the UN according to their perceived importance as a development actor (on a scale from 1 to 5 where 1 was "very important" and 5 was "not important at all"). The USA came in first with an average ranking of 1.89, with Japan following at 3.04 and China at 3.66. The EU came in last with an average ranking of 4.33. Although there have been substantial development initiatives by Europe/EU, they seem to have been conceived in economic terms rather than development. An analysis of the mass media images and the elites' perceptions of the EU were found to be in parallel with this finding — neither prioritised visions of the EU as a leading developmental actor.

This poor — and ill-informed — ranking of the EU as a development actor was compounded by the majority of respondents (70%) who admitted not knowing about any EU developmental initiatives in the region. This finding confirmed once more that Europe is generally viewed by the Philippine public only as potential labour migration destination and a global economic actor.

ASEM appeared almost non-existent in the consciousness of the general Philippine public. Only 21 of the 400 public survey respondents were aware of ASEM.

Nature of Ties with Europe

The importance of migration in the daily lives of Filipinos is palpable in the nature of connections to EU countries. More than half of the respondents (52%) mentioned having friends, family/relatives (44%)

or people from the Philippines (26%) living in Europe. Of significantly lower frequency were those who reported having professional or business contacts (15%). Only 10% of respondents had actually travelled to Europe. Therefore, the ties of many Filipinos with the region remain primarily familial or personal. This however does not keep the respondents from utilising a variety of sources for information about EU. Television news at 20% remained the most preferred source, followed by newspaper news (11%), internet (10%) and word of mouth including friends and relatives (9%). It is important to underline a discrepancy between the importance assigned to the television news as a source of information about the EU and the virtual absence of the EU in the television prime-time news programmes. Ultimately, by enhancing its presence on Philippines television screens, the EU could also arguably enhance the presence of Europe in the consciousness of the general public in the Philippines.

SO WHAT? CONCLUSIONS AND RECOMMENDATIONS

A focused analysis of EU imagery in the reputable Philippines news media, among national stakeholders and the general public has demonstrated that the EU was not perceived as a very significant actor in the Philippines. This particular finding could be partially explained by the relatively large geographic distance between the Philippines and Europe, and by the stronger influences exerted on the Philippines by the USA, Japan and China. These factors undoubtedly influenced the resulting image of the EU, making the EU appear less significant. These findings suggest that there is significant room left to improve the EU's visibility and the quality of the Union's image in the Philippines.

The evidence-based data gathered seems to illustrate various policy implications that impaired EU imagery could have on EU–Philippines relations. For the EU external relations professionals (and ECD to the Philippines in particular), this research presents several major conclusions. Firstly, the media analysis data indicated an extremely low visibility of the EU in the reputable news media (and especially on national television). Moreover, the research indicated a low motivation by local newsmakers to report on routine EU activities. Unsurprisingly, even when the EU appeared in the coverage, it was presented using external sources of information, predominantly from a neutral perspective and described as an actor acting 'somewhere there in the world'. Encouragingly, a high proportion of the reportage did feature the EU either as a major or secondary actor, thus partially alleviating an otherwise very low visibility profile. Yet, the fact that the EU's developmental, environmental and social actions toward the Philippines received so little acknowledgement in the local press is revealing. The EU's media imagery was stereotypically dominated by the economic themes. Such information should be of value to the local ECD when developing a targeted set of actions on how to interact with the local media. Other conclusions drawn from the 'elite' interviews and the public opinion survey provide the EU with a nuanced understanding of how the Philippine public perceives the process of European integration and its consequences to their own country and their region.

The Philippine government can also utilise various aspects of this research, particularly in the area of foreign affairs. The Philippine Department of Foreign Affairs whose mission it is to maintain functional and effective relations with other countries and regions, as well as the Department of Trade and Industry, could use the 'EU perceptions' data when refining their dialogue with Europe. As a powerful tool for self-reflection, results of this study indicated a general trend across various strata of the Philippine society to disregard the EU as a significant counterpart in the Philippines. This 'invisibility' in the public's eye might have an effect on Philippine government policy towards the EU. For example, the EU's perceived insignificance may mean that many political and economic opportunities with Europe may not be fully exploited. Considering the results of this research, the relevant Philippine institutions could revisit their attitudes and mindsets when it comes to dealing with international partners like the EU.

In summary, this research is an original 'reflection exercise' for the Philippine 'Self' and European 'Other' (or, alternatively, for the

European 'Self' and the Philippine 'Other'). Such exercises are, regretfully, in a deficit in external relations practices, but this 'first step' will hopefully provoke additional, future studies. It can also be seen as a 'springboard' for policy formulation by the EU with regard to the Philippines and *vice versa*. Finally, it provides a number of research insights and opportunities looking to explore various facets in relations between the Philippines and Europe.

Chapter 2

Images and Perceptions of the EU in Vietnam: Media, Elite and Public Opinion Perspectives

Pham Quang Minh, Bui Hai Dang
and Tran Bach Hieu

INTRODUCTION: VIETNAM–EU RELATIONS: PAST, PRESENT AND FUTURE

The relationship between Vietnam and Europe can be traced back to as early as the 17th century and it has been characterised by significant European colonial practices. The first Europeans to make contact with Vietnam were the British, Portuguese, Italian and French missionaries. The British came into formal contact with Vietnam in 1613.[1] However, they left the country after a few years and in 1615, the Portuguese Jesuits Carvalho and Goa Buzoni landed in Tourane (Da Nang) and established missions in Faifo (Hoi An). In 1618, an Italian Jesuit, Cristoforo Borri arrived in Vietnam and published the

---

[1] Lamb, Alastair, *The Mandarin Road to Old Hue-Narratives of Anglo-Vietnamese Diplomacy from the 17th Century to the Eve of the French Conquest*, London: Archon Books, 1970, p. 9.

very first report on the country in a European language.[2] Yet another mission was established in 1629 in Tonkin (North Vietnam) where French Jesuit Alexandre de Rhodes was credited with the conversion of 7,000 people to Christianity[3] and the transcription of the Vietnamese language into the Latin alphabet.[4] The invention of the *Quoc ngu* (National Script)[5] was documented by de Rhodes in his works *Dictionarium* and *Cathechismus* (1651).

However, the local rulers' fear of losing power to the Europeans led to aggravations in the relationship with missionaries. Many European missionaries were persecuted and Catholic books were burnt. Between 1848 and 1851, Kaiser Tu Duc (1848–1883) proclaimed the end to all missionary activities in Vietnam, and even offered a reward for any murdered Europeans. This hostile attitude triggered a violent reaction from French Emperor Napoleon III and in 1858 French military forces landed in Tourane (Da Nang) and began the conquest of Cochinchina (South Vietnam) which fell under total French control in 1867. However, it took another two decades until the French completed their conquest of Annam (Central Vietnam) and Tonkin (North Vietnam), at which point Vietnam became a part of the French empire until Vietnam's independence in 1945.

The two Indochina wars (1946–1954 and 1965–1975) and the 'bipolarity' of the world order induced by the 'Cold War' had a

---

[2] Villiers, John, *Suedostasien vor der Kolonialzeit*, Frankfurt am Mai: Fischer Taschenbuch Verlag, 1995, p. 301.

[3] *Ibid.*, p. 302.

[4] Phan, Peter C., *Mission and Catechesis — Alexandre Rhodes and Inculturation in Seventeenth Century Vietnam*, Maryknoll, NY: Orbis Books, 1998, p. 34. At the beginning of the 20th century, when French colonial government decided to abolish the tradition examinations, the Romanised script, the *quoc ngu*, replaced the old Chinese and Vietnamese characters. Thus, when the Democratic Republic of Vietnam was founded on September 2, 1945, President Ho Chi Minh called for a movement to learn the *quoc ngu* to eradicate the illiteracy among Vietnamese people.

[5] From an erected in 1941 stone monument in Hanoi. See Do Quang Chinh, *La Mission au Vietnam 1624–30 et 1640–45 d'Alexandre de Rhodes, S.J. Avignonnais*, Dissertation, Sorbonne, 1969, p. 102.

significant impact on the relationship between Vietnam and the European Community. In fact, the ideological confrontation became a decisive factor in this relationship, since most of the Community's Member States were closer to the USA's position at a time (including foreign policy stances). As a result, there was no official connection between Vietnam and the European Community before 1990 (although Vietnam did have diplomatic ties with individual Member States).[6]

The reform policy of Vietnam (*Doi moi*) launched in 1986 and the end of the 'Cold War' in 1989 provided an opportunity for both sides to improve relations. On October 22, 1990 — a turning point in the Europe-Vietnam relationship — the European Community established official diplomatic relations with Vietnam. Five years later, on July 17, 1995 the two sides signed a Cooperation Agreement which came into force on 1st June 1996[7] and provided a legal basis for the bilateral ties. Since then, Vietnam-EU relations have enjoyed stability and on-going diversification. Based on the Cooperation Agreement, a new mechanism for regular contact was created to promote open dialogue, introduce initiatives and plan cooperation. Impressive results have been achieved in a relatively short period of time, not least due to the success of the *Doi moi* policy in the Vietnamese society and the "combined efforts of the European Commission and EU Member States."[8]

In the political field, the EU and Vietnam have increased the frequency of their high-level meetings. One of the political 'milestones' was the first-ever Vietnam-EU Summit held in Hanoi before the 5th Asia-Europe Meeting (ASEM5) in October 2004. The President of

---

[6] The first EU member to establish diplomatic relations with Vietnam was the Kingdom of Sweden on January 11, 1969. France was the second EU member which established its relations with Vietnam on April 12, 1973.

[7] Delegation of European Commission to Vietnam, *Vietnam–EU relations — An overview*, <http://www.delvnm.ec.europa.eu/eu_vn_relations/oveview/overview.htm>, accessed 5 September 2008.

[8] Barroso, Jose Manuel, 'Reviewing the Past, Mapping out the Future', in *Delegation of European Commission to Vietnam and Saigon Times Group, Vietnam-EU Relations: 15 Years of Development*, Special Edition, May 5, 2005, p. 4.

the European Commission (EC) and the heads of the EU Member States participated. The two sides have also maintained cooperation within multilateral dialogue frameworks, such as ASEM and ASEAN-EU. Reciprocally, Vietnam's leaders have paid official visits to EU Member States. These frequent meetings have helped both sides to develop a better understanding of each other and find consensus on differing issues in both bilateral and multilateral relations. The EU has praised Vietnam's achievement in economic development, reduction of poverty and its determination to continue the *Doi moi* process. However, views between the two still diverge on issues such as human rights, democracy promotion and freedom of religion.

In the economic field, the EU is Vietnam's leading trade partner, a main source of foreign direct investment and, significantly, a major aid donor. The most important outcomes of economic relations between the two were the granting of 'most favoured nation' status to Vietnam and providing the country with tariff preferences under the EU's Generalized System of Preferences mechanism. Vietnam-EU economic relations have also profited from region-to-region cooperation, especially under the 'Trans-Regional EU-ASEAN Trade Initiative' (TREATI) and the 'Regional EU-ASEAN Dialogue Instrument' (READI). Both programmes were launched in 2003 to promote economic and trade cooperation as well as dialogue and regulatory cooperation between the two organisations. Consequently, trade between the EU and Vietnam has sharply increased. In 2004, the trade volume between the two parties was estimated at €7.5 billion. In 2007, Vietnam's exports to the EU were US$ 8.5 billion, an increase of 19% in comparison with the previous years and constituting 18% of Vietnam's total exports.[9] The EU is also one of the most important investors in Vietnam, accounting for 18% of total invested capital. Supported by the EU, Vietnam became the 150th member of the World Trade Organization (WTO) in January 2007. Responding to the rapid economic development of Vietnam and in accordance

---

[9] National Assembly of Socialist Republic of Vietnam, *The EU Market: Full of Promise for Vietnamese Businesses*, <http://www.na.gov.vn/htx/English/C1330/?Newid=16288>, accessed 7 September 2008.

with the New Southeast Asia Strategy (2004), the European Commission (EC) issued a Country Strategy Paper for Vietnam between 2007–2013 foreshadowing long-term cooperation on the bilateral level. Importantly, according to Ambassador Marcus Cornaro, Head of the EC Delegation to Vietnam, "Vietnam enjoys an exceptionally good level of government-led donor coordination; also, harmonization within the EU and with other major donors have progressed a lot."[10]

Entering the new millennium, Vietnam-EU relations have reached a new level. In 2007, with 27 members and population of 500 million, the EU accounts for 30% of global GDP and 41% of the total value of world trade.[11] The expansion of the EU offered both opportunities and challenges for the Union's external partners. Like other developing countries, Vietnam has been concerned that the commitment of the EU towards its new members might influence its commitment to cooperating with developing countries. Despite these fears, it seems that enlargement has not 'diluted' the EU presence in and involvement with Vietnam. In 2008, the EU was managing a cooperation portfolio of 12 ongoing projects in Vietnam, with a value approximating €78 million. The EU remains one of Vietnam's largest donors of development assistance, allocating €665.22 million in 2008 (including €404 million in grants).[12] In general, it is believed that EU enlargement has created more opportunities for Vietnam–EU relations because the majority of the new EU members had long-standing relations with Vietnam during the Cold War, which present Vietnam with a chance to capitalise on the existing partnerships and expand cooperation. Additionally, there is a large Vietnamese diaspora residing in Europe (approximately 200,000 Vietnamese live in Eastern Europe, with 100,000 in

---

[10] Cornaro Marcus, 'Vietnam-EU Relations: Much Achieved, More to be Done', in *Delegation of European Commission to Vietnam and Saigon Times Group, Vietnam-EU Relations: 15 Years of Development*, Special Edition May 5, 2005, p. 9.

[11] <www.delaus.ec.europa.eu/EU.../Trade.../index.htm>.

[12] <http://www.delvnm.ec.europa.eu/eu_vn_relations/development_coo/develop-ment&coo.htm>.

Germany, 20,000 in Poland, 25,000 in Czech Republic and 5,000 in Hungary).[13] This 'human link' serves as yet another bridge between Vietnam and the expanded EU.

Vietnam remains concerned about the reluctance of EU investors to invest in Vietnamese high-tech, heavy industries, seen as key to the country's industrialisation strategy. On this issue, both sides consented that to generate an increase in this investment, Vietnam should focus on improving regulatory frameworks, fight corruption, reform public administration, restructure the state-owned sector and improve the competitiveness of the Vietnamese economy in the financial sector.

The future for Vietnam-EU relations looks promising. Relations have been built on a long-lasting dialogue which was critically tested during the 'Cold War', but which has persevered as both sides entered a new world order. Though this new partnership was established just two decades ago, it has blossomed in many fields. Yet, despite the fact that official Vietnam-EU relations are flourishing, there is little information about how the EU is perceived and understood in Vietnam by its media, people and decision-makers. The rest of this chapter addresses this oversight and identifies how Vietnam sees the EU by investigating EU images in the national news media and by analysing a variety of opinions among the Vietnamese general public and national stakeholders.

AN ANALYSIS OF EU NEWS IN THE VIETNAMESE MEDIA[14]

The choice of newspapers was guided by a consideration of the targeted readership. The first of the three selected newspapers, *Tien Phong,* is published by the Ho Chi Minh Youth Union, but is popular

---

[13] Science Activities Reviews, *The Role of Overseas Vietnamese Intellectuals in Developing Human Resources for Vietnam Sciences and Technology,* <http://www.tchdkh.org.vn/tchitiet.asp?code=444>, 22 February 2009.

[14] We would like to express our sincere thanks to Prof. Charles Waugh from Utah University for his reading and comments on this part of the chapter.

among a wide audience, distributed nationwide and boasts the largest circulation.[15]

The second newspaper chosen was *The Vietnam Economic Times* (*Thoi bao Kinh te Vietnam*, also known as *VNET*) with its focus on economic and business issues. The *Vietnam Economic Times* reflects the interests of Vietnam's business community and is considered one of the most reliable sources of information for conducting business in Vietnam.[16] The readership of this paper includes entrepreneurs, policy makers, and those who take an interest in economic issues domestically and internationally. In addition to the printed version, there is an online version in both Vietnamese and English which attracts up to 3 million readers.

The third newspaper selected was an English-language newspaper the *Vietnam News*. It has been published since 1991 by Vietnam News Agency and has become one of most popular English-language newspapers in Vietnam.[17] Each day the *Vietnam News* provides comprehensive coverage of the latest domestic and international developments in politics, economics, business, social affairs and sport. There are also special pages containing comment, analysis, and reports on the environment, science and technology, lifestyle and key social issues. The readership is mainly foreigners and Vietnamese who want to improve their English. The circulation as of July 1st 2008 was 6051.[18]

Vietnam Television (*VTV*) broadcasts from Hanoi and as the national broadcaster of the Socialist Republic of Vietnam it is the only nation-wide television network in Vietnam. Founded on September 7th, 1970 by the "Voice of Vietnam" Radio Network, *VTV* became an independent entity in 1976. However, it took until April 30, 1987 before *VTV* could be broadcasted nationwide. As a government institution, *VTV* is supported through the state budget. The news channel chosen for this study was Vietnam Television 1 (*VTV1*) which has

---

[15] Information from Editorial Board of the *Tien Phong* newspaper.

[16] <http://www.mondotimes.com/2/topics/2/business/1/12099>.

[17] <http://vietnamnews.vnanet.vn/showarticle.php?num=ABOUT>.

[18] Information from Editorial Board of the *Vietnam News* newspaper.

a national outreach and is the premiere channel in Vietnam, with a viewership in the millions for the 7pm News.

Volume of Coverage

In the period January–June 2008, a total of 228 news items which referenced the term 'European Union/EU' (as well as 'European Central Bank/ECB', 'European Parliament/EP', 'European Commission/EC', 'European Court of Justice/ECJ', and 'Asia-Europe Meeting/ASEM') were identified. The English-language newspaper, *Vietnam News* accounted for 159 items (69.85%), and the *Vietnam Economic Times* followed with 29 items (12.7%), *Tien Phong* had only 19 items (8.3%) and *VTV1* had 21 news items (9.2%.)[19]

June was the month with 'peak' coverage (66 news items). The typical events reported in June included the EU's relations with Russia in general and the EU's warning to Russia on breaking the peace of Abkhazia; the threat by the US and the EU to impose an embargo on Iran; the introduction of the EU's sanctions affecting the manufacture of shoes in Vietnam; the EU ending its embargo on Cuba; Ireland's rejection of the Lisbon Treaty; and Vietnam-EU discussions on boosting trade.

The *Vietnam News* featured the highest volume of EU news during the six months of monitoring. Arguably, this was for several reasons. Firstly, the *Vietnam News* is a physically larger newspaper and thus can allocate more space to cover global events. Secondly, the paper extensively uses international news agencies, such as *Reuters*, *Agency France Press* (*AFP*) and *Associate Press* (*AP*). Thirdly, the newspaper's mandate is to cover diverse fields of information from economics, politics, society, culture and international affairs. Conversely, the *Tien Phong* focuses primarily on domestic issues and limits its sources of information primarily to its own reporting, while

---

[19] At this point we would like to express our sincere thanks to Ms. Nguyen Ngoc Van, a staff member of the *VTV1* for her great help in collecting and providing the news on the EU for this study.

VNET prioritises business-type news and *VTV1* has only one hour to cover all news during prime-time.

Sources of EU News

News items were categorised according to their sources — from a local Vietnamese journalist, an international source (such as an international news agency) or where the source was unattributed. Figure 1 presents the results of this analysis. Overall, 68% of EU news in Vietnamese newspapers came from local sources (144 items), with 32% from international wires and foreign correspondents. In comparison to the other newspapers, the *Vietnam News* had a higher volume of EU news from international wires while all three monitored newspapers explicated a similar share originating from international sources (*Vietnam News* — 30%, *Tien Phong* — 36%, *VNET* — 28%. *AFP* comprised 30.26% with 69 of 228 news broadcasted, *AP* had 11.84% with 27 of 228 news, *Reuters* had 29 of 228 news, thus accounting for 12.71%. The other sources accounted for 45.2% with 103 of 228 news. *VTV1* reported a very small number of EU news and of those, sources were never cited clearly.

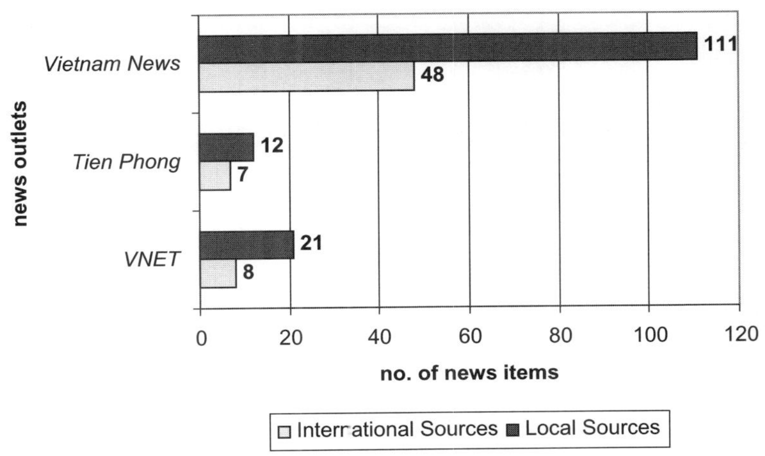

Figure 1:   **Sources of EU news**

Focus of Domesticity

Figure 2 describes the focus of domesticity of EU news items: overall the 'EU' focus was the largest comprising 43.7% (111 items); the 'third party' focus was second with 42.1% (107 items) and the 'local' focus was last with 14.2% (36 items). This profile suggests that the Vietnamese media tended to largely ignore the EU's local relevance and instead represented the Union as an important actor in European discourses and acting in world affairs, where it was engaged with many international partners, arguably reflecting its multilateral approach to foreign policy.

Examining this perspective through the individual media outlets revealed significant differences. The 'third party' focus was dominant for *Tien Phong* (50%) and especially for the *VTV1* (68.2%). In contrast, in the *Vietnam News* and *VNET*, the 'EU' focus was dominant (49% — 88/180 items and 50% — 16/32 items) respectively. It would appear from this that 'popular' sources of news ('popular' newspapers and nation-wide television news broadcasts) present the news differently to the 'business' and English-language papers. For the two former outlets, a general nature of news was more important than specifically focusing on a distant subject like the EU

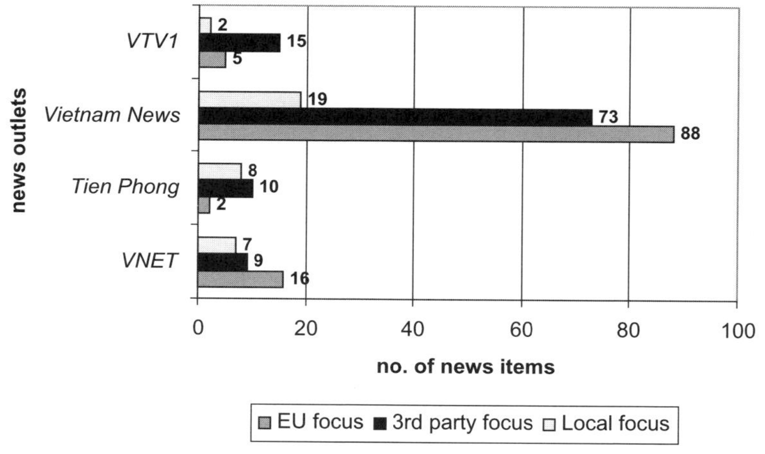

Figure 2:   Focus of domesticity of EU News

as was stressed in the two latter papers. Importantly though, none of the monitored outlets prioritised EU reporting in the 'local' (i.e. Vietnamese) context — a framing which possibly indicates a perception by local newsmakers of a certain degree of distance and irrelevance of the EU's actions.

Degree of Centrality

In contrast to the distribution of volume and the foci of domesticity, the distribution of the degree of centrality in the chosen newspapers and the *VTV* channel was very similar (Figure 3). The news items which presented the EU as the primary focus in the coverage were very modest accounting for 14.5% (33 items) of the total news. Conversely, news in which the EU was only a minor focus dominated with 54.8% (125 items), followed by representations of the EU as the secondary focus with 30.7% of total news (70 items).

Arguably, the low number of news stories presenting the EU as the leading focus of the news items indicate that much of the Vietnamese news media information on the EU was not very detailed about the EU itself. Rather, it tended to portray the EU either indirectly or in a largely superficial manner.

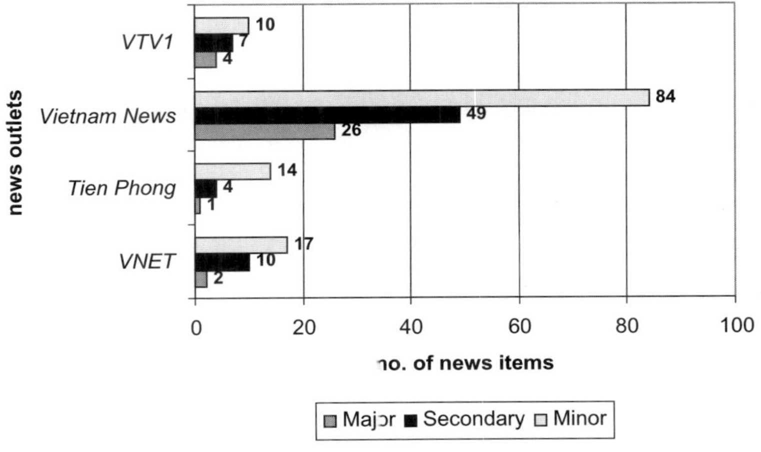

Figure 3:   Centrality of the EU in Vietnamese news media

The Most Visible EU Actors

In terms of the various EU institutions, the EC was the most visible with 30 appearances, perhaps because of the greater number of political news stories (as discussed below). The heightened profile of the EC was reflected in the reporting of many European internal political issues, for instance, the Lisbon Treaty agreement among Eastern European Member States, such as Slovenia, Hungary and Bulgaria, and the reports about the Irish rejection of this Treaty. The EC was also seen in news concerning the recession in the European economy or in the coverage of the EC's decision to issue sanctions against Microsoft. The EC was also profiled as an active actor in helping the typhoon victims in Vietnam, as well as in removing trading embargoes imposed on Cuba.

The second most visible institution was the European Central Bank (ECB) with 17 appearances. Unsurprisingly, it was often reported in articles about EU financial regulations and EU antitrust legislation. For example, the ECB was described as withdrawing money from eurozone markets; mulling over interest rates and expecting to hold those rates steady; and intriguingly, the ECB governor was reported as quoting Bob Dylan in relation to inflation!

In terms of specific EU representatives (Figure 4), the Vietnamese media covered EC President José Manuel Barroso most prominently (with 17 appearances), generally in stories about the negotiations between the EU and others during the Doha round and the ratification of the Lisbon Treaty. He was also presented discussing the effects of the global recession on the euro-zone economy. In the news touching on EU–Vietnamese relations, Barosso was reported as participating in a conference with Vietnam Prime Minister Nguyen Tan Dung in which the latter was reported to be highly appreciative of the active support from the EC and the Member States for Vietnam's efforts to reform its society and integrate internationally, especially in terms of Vietnam's entrance to the WTO. The head of the ECB, Jean-Claude Trichet, was the second most visible actor with eight appearances across four outlets monitored. He was reported as repeatedly emphasising the ECB's focus on preventing short-term

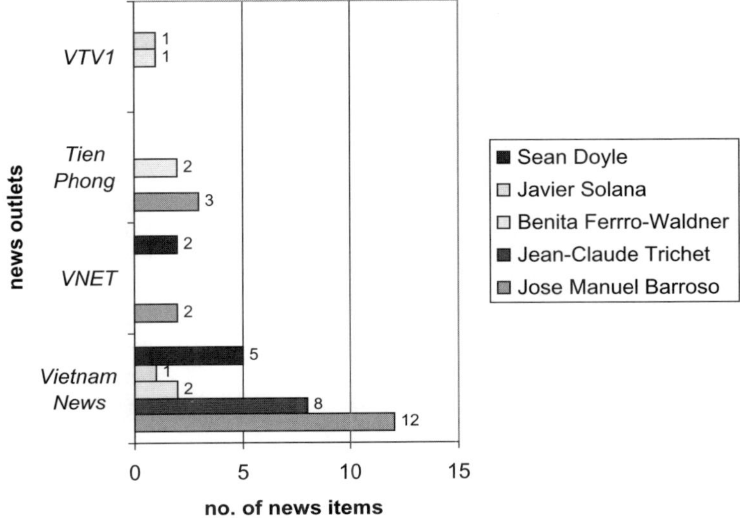

Figure 4:   Visibility of the EU officials

price pressures from increasing commodity prices and thus causing longer-term inflation problems.

Of the 27 EU Member States, the EU's 'big three', Germany, France and the United Kingdom (UK), occupied the top three most visible positions (Figures 5 and 6) with France leading. Taking into account the historical connections between Vietnam and France, this preference was expected. Additionally, 30.26% of news sourced from international wires came from the French wire, *AFP*. France, and its President Nicolas Sarkozy, were reported in many instances, such as in France and Spain's united reaction to the actions of ETA, the Basque separatist movement; French measures to strengthen migration control; Sarkozy's statement regarding the prioritisation of energy issues during a French EU Presidency; Sarkozy's rejection of a proposal to extend the working week; France's military deal with Algeria; Sarkozy's reaction to the Irish 'no' vote to the Lisbon Treaty in the context of the forthcoming French Presidency of the EU, and so on. Germany (and Chancellor Angela Merkel) came second.

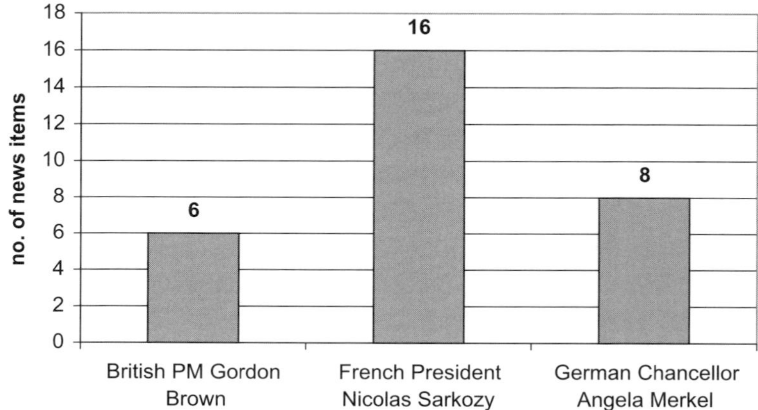

Figure 5:   Visibility of EU member states officials

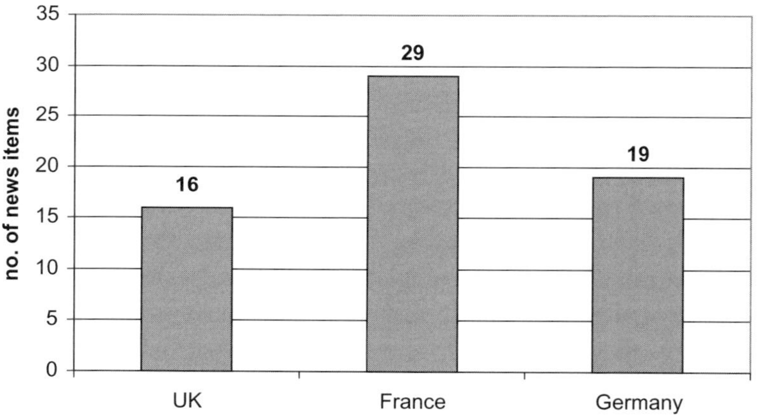

Figure 6:   Visibility of EU member states

The Vietnamese media reported Germany's reaction to the Irish rejection of the Lisbon Treaty; its involvement with EU-US bid to cut red tape and boost trans-Atlantic trade; Merkel's participation in the meeting between the EU and Latin American leaders; and Merkel's reaction to EU-Russian relations. The UK (and Prime Minister Gordon Brown) came third. Coverage included the UK government's reaction to the new European treaty; Brown's visit to Brussels to dispel the anti-EU image; and the UK government fending off calls for a referendum on the EU's controversial new treaty.

EU News Frames

The EU news items were categorised according to five frames: politics, economy, society, environment and development. Figure 7 presents the breakdown of this analysis. As can be seen, the results of the EU's framing across the four media are very different. The *Vietnam News*, the *Tien Phong* and *VTV1* presented the EU mainly as a political actor with 60% (96/159), 63% (12/19), and 66% (14/21) of their stories about political issues. Since the *Vietnam News*, *Tien Phong* and *VTV1* tend towards political coverage in general, they were expected to prioritise this frame. Economy was the second largest frame in the *Vietnam News* with 28% (44/159). In contrast, in the *VNET*, 79% of the news featured the EU as an economic actor (23/29), and political actions were less visible. In the four outlets, the EU was very rarely featured as an environmental, developmental or social affairs actor.

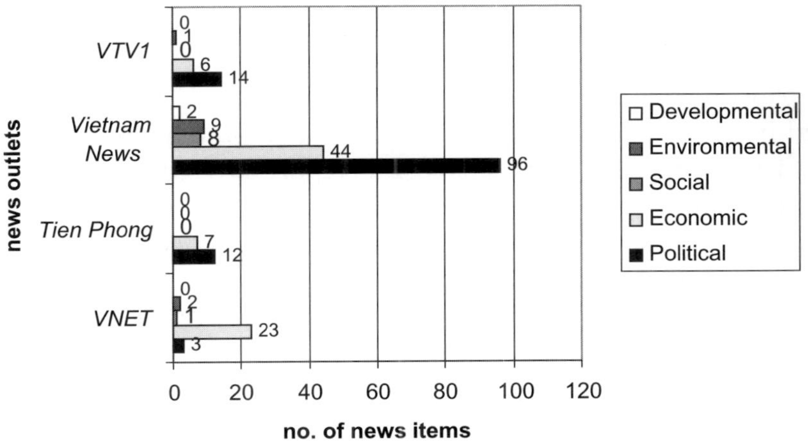

Figure 7:   **Primary frames of the EU**

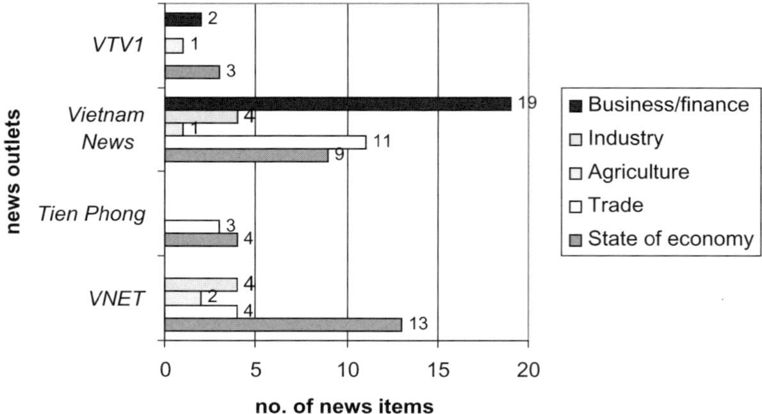

Figure 8:   Economic sub-frames

Examining the content of the political and economic frames further helps to identify the specific areas in which the EU was seen to be involved.

Five economic sub-frames were identified: the state of economy in general, trade, agriculture, industry, and business/finance. As shown in Figure 8, news reporting the state of the EU economy accounted for the largest proportion of the reportage in the economic frame. The main issues discussed within this sub-frame news were (in order of importance): the EU's economic growth and EU trading relationships with countries such as the USA, Japan and Vietnam. Business and finance covered topics such as EU action on the global financial market or the ECB. For example, one report covered the meeting of European leaders in London to discuss how to respond to the global financial turmoil and to reassure that Europe's economy would survive the crisis. Any EU economic influence on Vietnam was presented as very important. For example, the *Vietnam News* noted that

the value of trade between VN and Europe will surge this year, but the European market will still present challenges for Vietnamese traders, according to VN's Ministry of Industry and Trade. The department said Vietnamese enterprises should enhance participation in market research

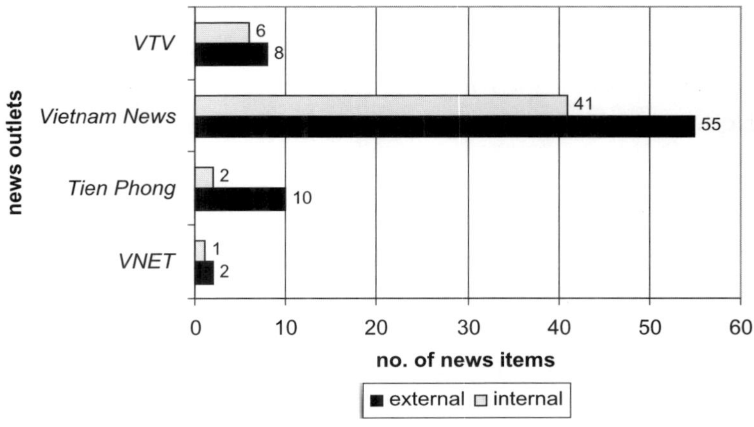

Figure 9:   Political sub-frames

delegations and trade fairs in order to establish permanent partners, open new markets and develop new export products.[20]

In the politically oriented EU news, two sub-frames were identified: internal EU affairs and external political affairs (Figure 9).

EU news pertaining to *external affairs* occupied 60% of the monitored political coverage, with *internal affairs* reports accounting for the remainder, confirming that the EU was presented most frequently in the role of an international actor. Within the *external political affairs* sub-frame, the most frequently reported topic was the EU's role in the Balkans in general and its interactions with Serbia in particular. The next most reported topics dealt with the EU's role in Africa, especially in Chad; supporting poor countries, and also relations between the EU and other 'big players' such as Russia, China, Japan and the USA. Most of the *internal political affairs* sub-frame stories focused on the ratification of the Lisbon Treaty. It was interesting to note that the EU's interactions with Vietnam and other South East Asian countries were not very visible. However, when there were news reports on EU-Vietnam relations, the image of the

---

[20] 'Vietnam's EU trade to raise', *Vietnam News*, May 13, 2008, p. 17.

EU was very positive, possibly due to the dominant perception that the official relationship between Vietnam and the EU is seen to be strengthening and improving and that the EU's development assistance efforts are appreciated.

Evaluations

Finally, the findings clearly showed that when reporting the EU, Vietnam's media presented the news in a predominantly neutral way, with 89% of monitored newpaper items being neutral and 100% on *VTV1* (see Figure 10). The *Vietnam News* was the only outlet to present any volume of positively evaluated news, with stories about the EU committing $962 million in aid to Vietnam; or about Germans approving EU treaty. There was almost no negative coverage, but those negative terms which did appear featured stories relating to internal EU affairs, such as Ireland rejecting EU treaty or the need for the EU to improve social welfare spending.

Summary

In summary, EU images created by the Vietnamese news media appeared to be fairly diverse, although the political and economic

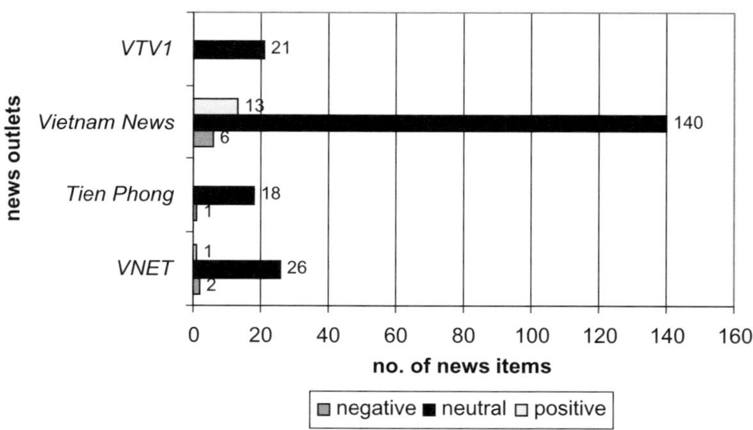

Figure 10:   **Evaluation of EU news items**

attributes of the Union were stressed and social, environmental and developmental representations actions tended to be underplayed. The 2008 media portrait of the EU included such images of the EU as an international actor performing mostly in Europe or around the word, but not interacting extensively with South East Asia in general, or Vietnam in particular. Indeed, the 'local' focus in reporting the Union was minimal. Intuitively, this framing appears inconsistent with the sources of EU news — each press outlet monitored in this study relied on international 'wires' for just one-third of its EU coverage, with the rest written by Vietnamese authors. It seems in this case that the local media does not prioritise the EU, especially in comparison to the other higher levels of EU news found in Indonesia and the Philippines, as described elsewhere in this volume. Moreover, the majority of the news stories reported the EU from a minor perspective, indicating that the EU was often presented to Vietnamese audiences in a marginal manner. Finally, the Vietnamese news media preferred to report the EU from a predominantly neutral position, arguably indicating not only a cultural norm of politeness and harmony, but also a certain degree of indifference towards the EU on behalf of local newsmakers. This low, muted media profile of the EU seems to be a paradox with the political reality of EU-Vietnam relations which has gone from strength to strength. To determine whether this media imagery of the EU was reflected in the opinion of the Vietnamese people, this chapter now considers the analysis of public opinion and the views of the national decision- and policy-makers.

STAKEHOLDERS' PERCEPTIONS OF THE EU

As discussed above, the present-day Vietnam-EU relationship is stable and quickly developing, but the fields of co-operation are limited and appear to be primarily anchored in economic co-operation. Unsurprisingly then, an image of the EU as an economic power dominated the perceptions of the Vietnamese stakeholders explored in this section. The following results are drawn from 33 in-depth interviews conducted with Vietnamese 'elites' (eight representatives from the political sector; nine civil society representatives, eight business people and eight media practitioners).

The Importance of Different Overseas Regions to Vietnam

The interviewed stakeholders were asked about their perceived importance of the EU to Vietnam. In comparison with other 'big players' in the world arena — namely, the USA, China, Japan and Asia as a whole — the EU was seen by the Vietnamese respondents as less important. Only some business stakeholders considered the EU as important as Japan and more important than Russia. This vision was understandable — while Russia's influence on Vietnam has been gradually declining, Japan has grown in importance recently.

When comparing the importance of the EU to Vietnam in the present and in the future, most stakeholders believed that the EU's importance would increase over time. The future importance of the EU to Vietnam was rated as "5" (very important) by eight respondents and "4" by 13 others. In contrast, only 6 respondents rated the EU' present-day importance at "5" and nine who gave it "4" (see Figure 11).

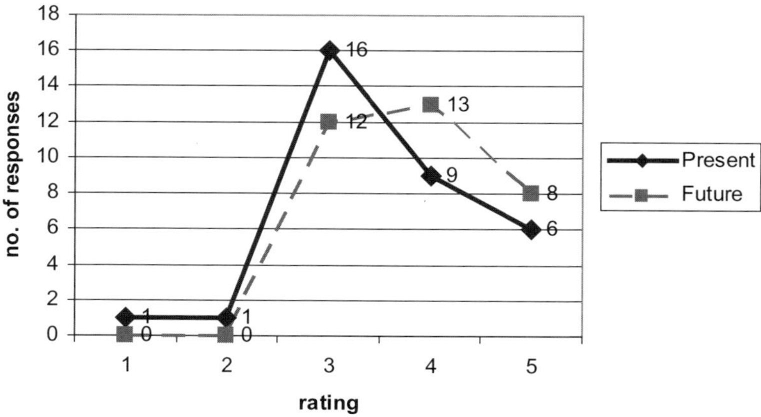

Figure 11:   The importance of the EU to Vietnam in present and future

The EU as a Global Power and an International Leader

Since its inception, the EU has achieved considerable success in its 50 years of economic and political integration. These achievements have encouraged some scholars to view the Union as an emerging supranational power, although this role and profile in the international arena is still widely debated. To investigate what international images of the EU dominated the perceptions of the national decision-makers, the Vietnamese stakeholders were asked if they saw the EU as a global power and an international leader.

Two-thirds of respondents perceived the EU as a global power in terms of economy and diplomacy (Figure 12). For example the Deputy Director of a well-known fashion enterprise in Ho Chi Minh City, stated:

> The EU has developed from 6 to 27 to become the third strongest economy all over the world. Therefore, any changes in the EU will probably have effect on every field of the international environment.

However, a third of respondents considered the EU as a union of 27 individual members, not a united actor. A comment by a respondent

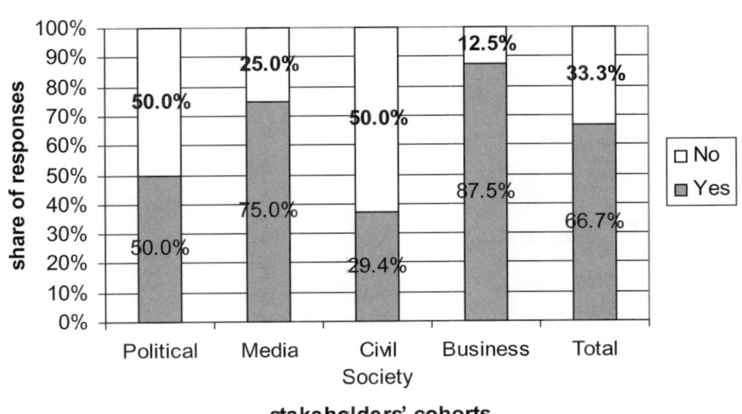

Figure 12:   The EU as a global power

from the Vietnam Ministry of Justice illustrated this point: "the EU as an alliance of European countries, such a blend of many different countries; therefore, EU couldn't be regarded as a global power".

Assessing the EU as an international leader, many interviewees agreed that the role of the EU in international politics has sharply increased. Yet, around half of the respondents did not consider the EU as a political actor in international relations, and this vision was explained in various ways. For example, respondents commented on the EU's status as 'not a nation state', but just a union of European countries in which members do not always agree on international issues. The conflict in Kosovo and the War in Iraq were specifically brought forward as the most compelling evidence of such dissonance. The second reason was that the EU has no common voice on a wide range of issues and was shackled by an inefficient Common Foreign and Security Policy (CFSP). On this note, the Deputy Director of the Institute for Strategy and Foreign Policy at the Vietnam Diplomatic Academy remarked, "Although the EU has been trying to adjust itself, it has not been a leader in the world politics. The EU has a Common Foreign and Security [Policy], but it is just for reference". Finally, despite the fact that the EU has been seen playing an important role in the world politics nowadays, most respondents believed that the USA remains the only international leader. As one political respondent asserted, "although the EU is now attempting to be a counter-balance with the United States, there is no entity that has capacity to threaten and compete with the USA at this moment".

Vietnam–EU relations

A stronger presence of the EU in Vietnam undeniably affects Vietnam–EU relations. Correspondingly, this study investigated the dominant perceptions of the state of relations between the two partners and asked respondents to describe the relationship between Vietnam and the EU. Most (over 90%) considered the relationship to be stable and improving in all fields of cooperation. The 1995

Cooperation Agreement was specifically noted as a key factor in this dynamic. Only one-quarter of business sector stakeholders (which constituted 8% of the total sample), described the relationship negatively. This particular vision arguably reflects the fact that the EU began its anti-dumping measures against Vietnamese shoe products in July 2005. Unsurprisingly, this conflict in EU–Vietnam relations influenced business people's views making them feel dissatisfied and unsure about the EU.

The overall perception of the growing importance of the EU to Vietnam shared by the respondents (as discussed above) constitutes another facet of a more positive vision of the EU–Vietnam relations. In addition, the high number of Vietnamese now living in EU Member States was seen as an important link in the relationship between the two. The EU enlargement in 2004 included ten new countries, many of whom were Vietnam's traditional 'Cold War' partners. These new EU countries attracted many Vietnamese in the past and this fact contributes to a special relationship in the present. This peculiar population migration was one of the reasons for the large proportion of interviewed stakeholders having personal contacts with the EU (Figures 13 and 14). Also, in comparison with the the Vietnamese public (discussed below), the percentage of stakeholders who registered professional contacts with the EU was much higher.

The perception of the state of Vietnam–EU relations can be further refined by analysing those issues listed by respondents as

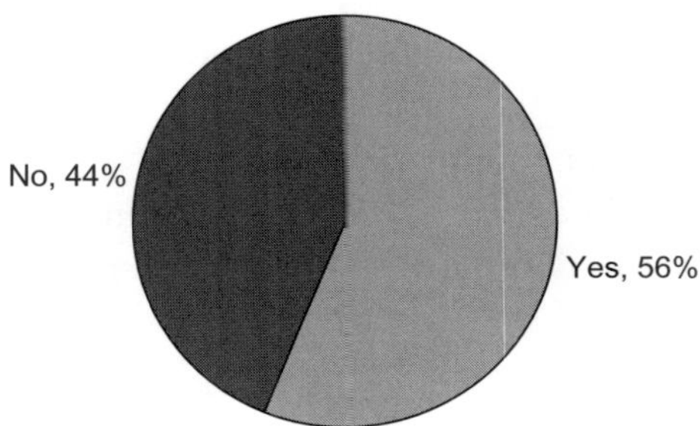

Figure 13:   Stakeholders' professional contacts with the EU

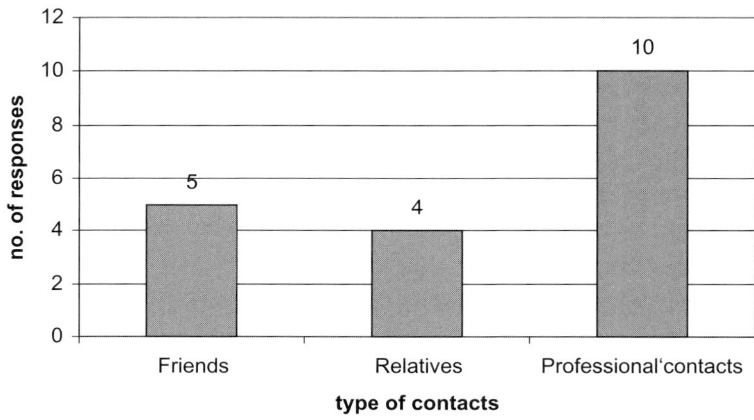

Figure 14:   Stakeholders' contacts with the EU in details

having an impact on Vietnam. Four dominant issues were repeatedly outlined: human rights, the economy, political and diplomatic influence, and culture. For most of the interviewed stakeholders, Vietnam–EU economic relations were the main concern. In particular, respondents mentioned the quality of Vietnamese products exported to the EU as a measure for promoting economic cooperation. In their view, Vietnam must pay attention to the quality of its products due to the high standards of the EU market.[21] It seems that in the eyes of local decision-makers 'sensitive' issues such as the promotion of democracy and human right were no longer significant obstacles for further cooperation, but rather were considered opportunities for furthering the dialogue.[22] The human rights issues were predominantly seen as still having an impact on the relationship, but this impact was recognised as being less than those from political, diplomatic and cultural issues.

The interviewed stakeholders also gave suggestions on how to promote the Vietnam–EU dialogue further. Among these were improvements in the quality of Vietnamese export products

---

[21] Civil society respondent.

[22] Civil society respondent.

(mentioned four times); the EU's influence on the development of Vietnam's market economy; EU regulations with regard to tax barriers including issues of and fairness in economic relations (each mentioned twice). Other issues mentioned only once were: EU diplomatic actions, the Common Agricultural Policy (CAP), culture, trade policy, the influence of specific European countries and intellectual property rights.

Focusing on the perceived impact of EU enlargement on Vietnam, this analysis showed that 44% of respondents saw enlargement as an opportunity for Vietnam (Figure 15). As mentioned above, several former socialist countries, such as the Czech Republic, Poland, Hungary, Bulgaria and Romania, as well as former USSR republics of Estonia, Latvia and Lithuania, have traditionally been Vietnam's external partners. A smaller group of respondents (36%) saw the EU enlargement as both as an opportunity and challenge. As a business sector interviewee[23] noted,

> Vietnam will surely face with new challenges when the EU has more member states. Therefore, Vietnam has to adjust itself for the relations in economic, political and cultural exchange because it is also the opportunity for Vietnam to have a great export market.

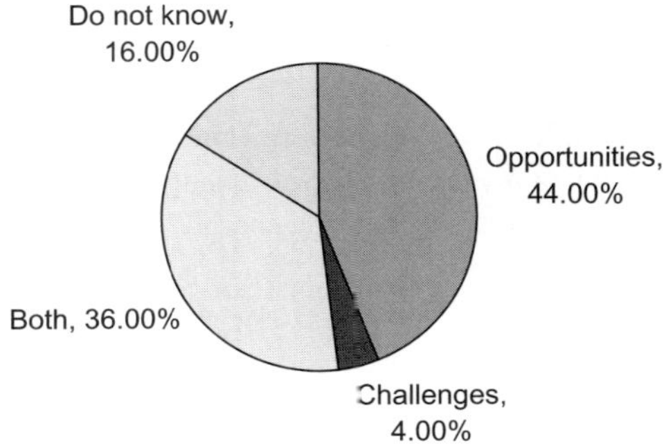

Figure 15:   Impact of EU enlargement to Vietnam

---

[23] Director of Thu Quan Company (student service).

The common belief was that Vietnam would have a bigger export market on the one hand, but would have more difficulties in meeting the requirements to export its products to these countries on the other. The director of the Institute for European Studies commented:

> As weighing up the pros and cons, we can see that new EU Member States have had traditional relationship and friendship with Vietnam. They will consider Vietnam as a bridge in order for them to reach Asia. In return, we are suggested to regard them as a bridge to the EU. Vietnamese community in foreign countries is also a connection between Vietnam and new EU Member States in particular and EU in general. On the other hand, old EU Member States would give preferential treatment to new ones. As a result, they are not able to pay more attention outside the Union, from that, Vietnam would also be influenced. In addition, after the EU's participation, new Member States must comply with the EU's regulations and common policy so that they also require high standards from Vietnam's products exported to their markets.

Finally, the relationship between Vietnam and the EU was seen by the interviewees to be partially influenced by the use of the common currency. The euro was seen as a successful example of the EU's monetary policy and has become a symbol of the EU competing with the US in the monetary field. In this study, 44% of respondents thought that the euro was stronger than the US dollar, while 40% did not think so. However, paradoxically, the euro was considered less popular than the US dollar. For example, a business respondent,[24] commented,

> The US dollar is still very important and much more popular than the euro. However, many of my friends recently change to buy and use the euro and gold as its exchange rate keeps rising sharply.

A political respondent also noted that the rise in value of the euro has reflected the strength of the EU's economy in comparison with the US economy, but felt that the US dollar would probably regain its high value as soon as its economy recovers.

---

[24] Deputy Director of Azony Co.

ASEM and Vietnam

'Elite' respondents were also asked about their perception of the ASEM process, a prominent inter-regional forum intended to further strengthen the relations and cooperation between European and Asian countries. If APEC is seen as the channel that the USA uses to promote its influence in Asia, ASEM has become the parallel forum for the EU to promote its presence in Asia. From the onset of its operation, ASEM has played an important role in boosting cooperation between Vietnam and the EU. Assessing the impact of the ASEM process on EU–Vietnam interactions, most respondents (60%) believed that the ASEM process had had a positive impact on Vietnam. However, when evaluating the specific effects of ASEM6 in Helsinki in 2006 under half of the respondents (48%) saw a positive impact on Vietnam, while the other half saw no impact.

Spontaneous Images of the EU

To identify a range of stereotypical visions of the EU held by national decision- and policy-makers, the interviewees were asked about the first three images that came to mind when they heard the term the 'European Union'. The answers revealed six dominant images, namely: EU as an economic power, a model of regionalism, a great culture, the balancer of the USA, Vietnam's partner and the euro. Associations that were economy-related led — 'EU as an economic power' and 'euro' were mentioned 28 times (41% of all responses) and 6 times (9%) respectively (Table 1).

Sources of Information

Finally, stakeholders were asked where they sourced their information about the EU and which specific media they used to access it. Most of the respondents mentioned getting information about the EU from local government offices, as well as EU Member State embassies

Table 1:   The EU's spontaneous images

Images	Percentage
Economic Power	41.1
Great Culture	22.0
Regionalism Model	20.5
Euro	8.8
Vietnam's Partner	4.4
The USA's Balancer	4.4

and consulates in Vietnam. The most preferred media for EU information were newspapers and the internet (both 27%) (Figure 16).

The European Commission Delegation (ECD) could be considered to be a significant source of information on the EU. However, its role in Vietnam was not perceived as prominent, even though 41% of repsondents in this study evaluated its activities in a positive way. Such positive comments, for example, included:

> The Commission Delegation has a good relation with my Department. It works actively to push up Vietnam–EU relation. As a result, thanks to its contribution, Vietnam becomes one of the founding members of ASEM.[25]

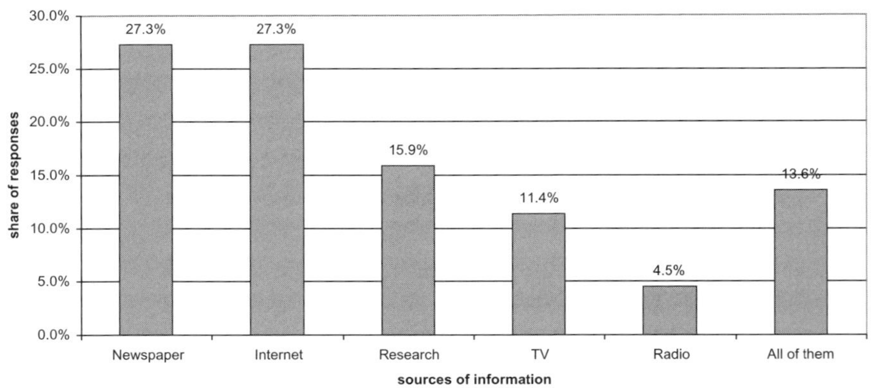

Figure 16:   Preferred sources of information on the EU

---

[25] Head of Law division, Vietnam Ministry of Justice.

Another stakeholder from civil society sector added,

> "I also know the Delegation and have exchanged information, communicated and cooperated with them. I think it's an important bridge to maintain and develop the relationship between Vietnam and the EU."[26]

However, 25% of stakeholders did not understand the ECD's role in Vietnam, and one-in-three did not know about the ECD at all. One stakeholder from business sector, for instance, noted, "I do not know about this Delegation because the Delegation is not very…popular in Vietnam".[27]

Summary

In the perceptions of Vietnamese policy- and decision-makers, the Vietnam-EU relationship has been not only stable, but developing rapidly since the Framework Co-operation Agreement was signed in 1995. However, the role of the EU was recognised to be of less importance to Vietnam than the roles of other international counterparts, such as the USA, China, Japan and Asia as a whole. Encouragingly though, the EU was considered to be more important to Vietnam than Russia, and the EU's importance was seen to be growing in the future.

This importance, however, was considered to be mainly in the area of economic relations and there was potential seen for further growth in this area, for several reasons. Firstly, the Vietnamese economy is not yet fully developed or strong enough to attract a large amount of capital and investment from the EU (however, since Vietnam joined the WTO, EU foreign direct investment has increased). Secondly, EU investors have yet to concentrate their attention on semifinished products (a quickly developing field for Vietnam that is undergoing industrialisation and modernisation). Thirdly, Vietnamese commercial law still lacks transparency. With these

---

[26] Director of the Institute for American studies, Vietnam Academy.
[27] CEO of School materials joint-stock Company.

issues considered to be the most visible in the EU–Vietnam dialogue, it is not surprising that for most interviewed stakeholders the dominant image of the EU concerned the Union's importance for economic development.

VIETNAMESE PUBLIC OPINION

In this final section, how the EU was seen in the eyes of the Vietnamese public is examined, to determine whether there were any differences in EU perceptions between the Vietnamese stakeholders and the general public. A nation-wide survey was conducted with 400 Vietnamese respondents the findings of which are presented below.

The Importance of Different Overseas Regions to Vietnam

Respondents were asked to rank the importance of the EU against other international counterparts to Vietnam. When comparing it with China, the USA and Japan, the Vietnamese public considered the EU to be a less important partner for Vietnam (Figure 17): China was seen as the most important partner, the USA came second with Japan

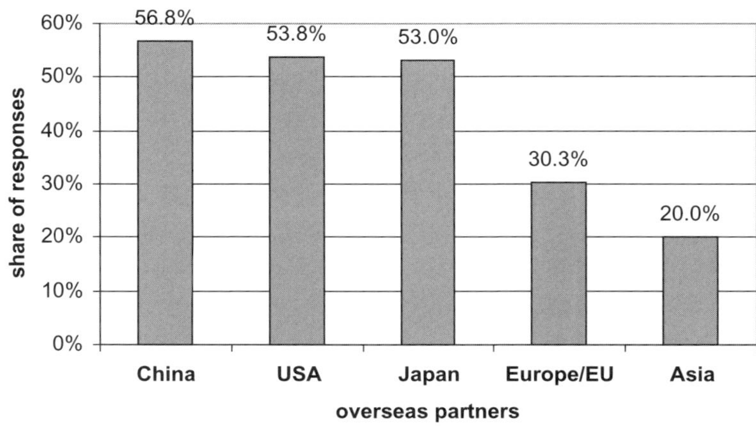

Figure 17:   Top five important partners for Vietnam in the present

slightly behind in third place. The EU was ranked fourth with only three-out-of-ten respondents indicating this preference. The EU's 'big three' — France, Germany and the UK — individually received 17.8%, 14.5% and 7.8% of responses respectively.

The choice of China as the most important present-day partner for Vietnam was expected and was typical for both the general public and the national 'elites'. China's perceived importance stems not only from the ubiquitous 'rise of China', but also from the ongoing debate on the East Sea issues. Thus the public opinion survey arguably constitutes a 'snap shot' reflecting the state of Vietnam–China relations in 2008.

The Vietnamese public was also asked to rate the future importance of these regions and states for Vietnam, using the scale from 1 to 5 where 1 was 'least important' and 5 was the 'most important'. China was again ranked as the most important partner for Vietnam with an average rating of 4.4. The next ranked three were Japan (4.39), the USA (4.36) and Asia as a whole (4.14). The EU was ranked 5th — slightly lower than Asia with the average rating of 4.1 (Figure 18). Thus, there was a little perceived difference concerning the current and the future importance of the big international 'players' for Vietnam in the eyes of the surveyed public. Importantly,

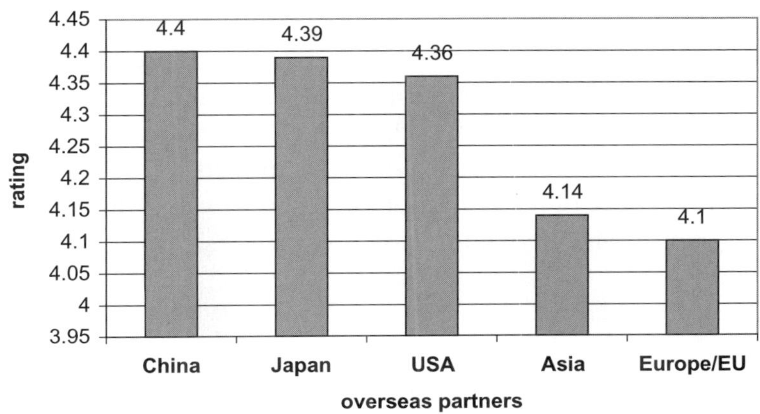

Figure 18:   **Future importance of overseas regions and countries for Vietnam**

the EU was ranked as the fifth most important partner both in 2008 and in the future, thus remaining constantly on the periphery of perceived importance when compared with other international counterparts.

The respondents were then asked about the various EU actions and initiatives that they were aware of. Revealingly, nearly three-quarters of respondents confessed to having no knowledge of what the EU was involved in, while one-in-nine said they knew about EU development aid and a handful were aware of environmental issues raised by the EU. It is clear from this that the Vietnamese public is not well-informed about the EU in general, its international agenda or its presence in Vietnam. Consequently, this limited awareness offers an explanation of why the Union was perceived as such an unimportant partner for Vietnam. It was encouraging, however, that some respondents acknowledged the EU as a provider of aid and supporter of environmental protection.

The survey asked respondents about the most important developmental actors for Vietnam (rating the importance on the scale from 1 to 5, where 1 was "not important at all" and 5 was "very important"). Interestingly, Australia emerged as the most significant with the average rating of 4.68. The United Nations (UN) came next (4.13), with the EU in third place (3.61), followed by China, Japan, and the US respectively (Figure 19). It seems that the Vietnamese public were aware of and appreciated the contributions to Vietnam's development from a peaceful larger power (Australia), from an international institution (UN), and an integrated politico-economic entity (the EU). The recognition of Australia as the 'No. 1' developmental actor was arguably due to its increasingly visible role in such areas as educational cooperation, developmental scholarships and many other Australian aid programmes in Vietnam initiated recently.

Vietnam and the EU

The perceived peripheral importance of the EU in Vietnam when compared to other international partners can be partially explained by the fact that most information about the EU consumed by the

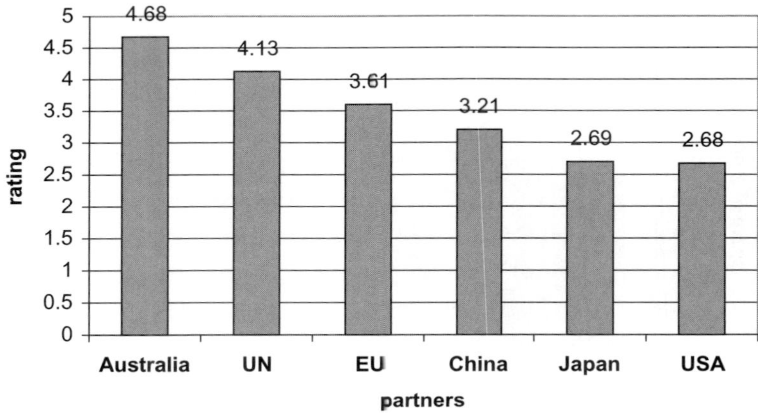

Figure 19:   Most important developmental actors for Vietnam

Vietnamese mostly comes from the mass media such as newspapers, television, radio or the internet (discussed below). As discussed above, the media in Vietnam does not fully represent the volume or range of EU activities in local projects or initiatives. Unsurprisingly then, public opinion was also found to be largely ignorant of these activities. Despite this lack of detailed knowledge, some 77% of respondents believed that the relationship between Vietnam and the EU had improved. In contrast, only 2.8% of respondents saw this relationship worsening (Figure 20). Such a perception paralleled the views on the relationship held by Vietnamese stakeholders and could be instrumental for the EU and Vietnam when developing collaboration and cooperation in the future.

However, despite the high percentage of respondents noticing an improvement in the relationship, they also commented on a number of issues requiring attention when the Vietnamese government develops its future policy towards the EU. The answers featured a wide range of opinions. Specific programmes and campaigns drew the most attention with 17% of responses. However, 14% admitted to not having any idea about what policies should be developed towards the EU. For 11% of respondents EU economic support was the most important consideration for the formulation of policy. Other issues

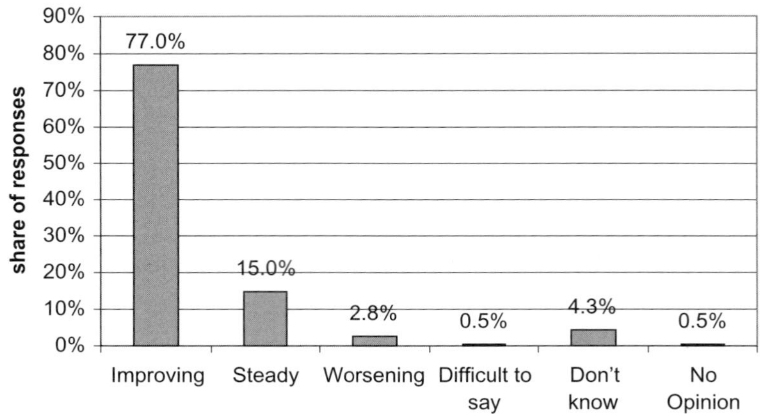

Figure 20:   State of relationship with the EU

like trade tax reduction and general trade/business issues were noted
by 7.5%. Notably, most of the issues mentioned were economic in
nature. Issues such as human rights, democracy, and politics and
governance were mentioned in less than 5% of responses. Similarly,
the most visible issues in the Vietnamese stakeholders' survey were
reforming Vietnam's economic structure in order to create a more
attractive business environment.

The public were also asked to rate the impact of the above-men-
tioned issues on Vietnam–EU relations in the near future (using the
scale of 1 to 10, where 1 was 'little impact' and 10 was 'great
impact'). Again, the focus was on the EU's economic growth as the
issue impacting Vietnam the most (with an average score of 8) as was
the EU's actions as a world trade power in dealings with the
WTO (7.95). With ASEAN being considered another success story
of regional integration (and one involving Vietnam), the impact of
EU-ASEAN relations on Vietnam was placed third scoring at 7.87.
The next three prominent issues seen to have an impact on Vietnam
were the EU's actions as a development aid donor (7.67); the EU's
advocacy of human rights and democracy (7.53) and EU support for
reducing carbon gas emissions (Kyoto protocol) (7.44). Despite the
disinterest shown by their media towards the subject, the Vietnamese

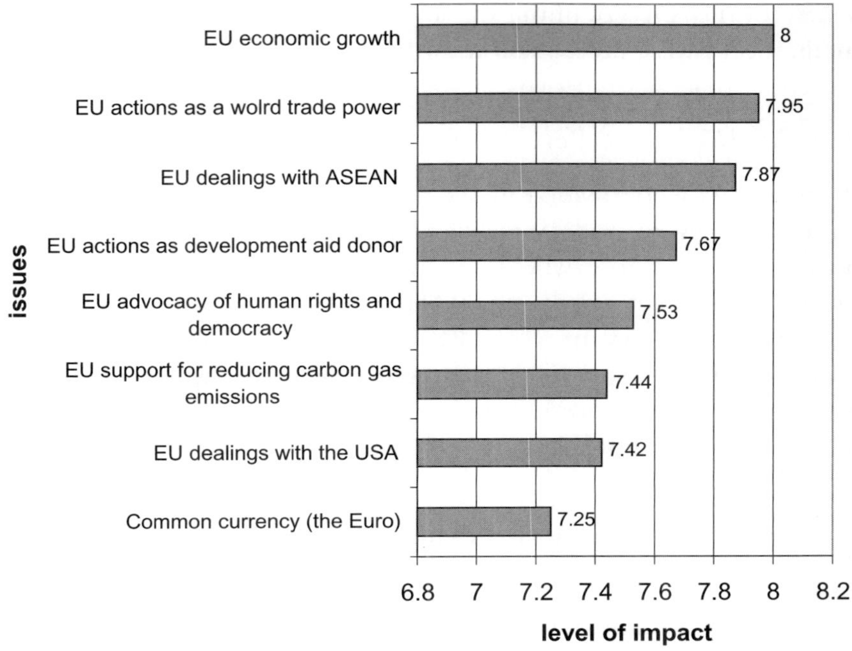

Figure 21:   EU-realted issues seen to impact Vietnam in the near future

public seem to be increasingly aware of the EU as a vanguard of environmental protection (Figure 21).

Spontaneous Images of the EU

Similarly to the 'elite' respondents, the public were asked to list the first three spontaneous thoughts that came to their minds when they heard of the term the 'European Union'. The EU as the symbol of unity (union) was noted by a quarter of respondents. The next most visible image was the EU as a monetary and economic power (17.5%). The common currency (euro) was the third most noted image with 13%. The EU's involvement with Vietnam featured in only a tiny fraction of the immediate associations — the EU's role as an aid donor featured in only 4.3% of responses, and EU relations with Vietnam was noted in a mere 0.9% of responses. Arguably, this creates a stereotypical picture of the EU as a successful model of institutional integration with a united market with a common currency.

The ASEM in the Perceptions of the Vietnamese Public

Respondents were divided in their awareness of the ASEM process, with 50.5% aware, and 49.5% claiming to have no knowledge of the forum. Among those who were aware of ASEM, 40.6% rated the impact of the meeting process on Vietnam–EU relations as either very important or important. Only 4.8% said it was not important or not important at all. From this we can see that when Vietnamese people are aware of the process, they consider it to be important to the EU–Vietnam relationship.

Sources of Information on the EU

In contrast to the findings for the interviewed stakeholders, television news was named by the general public as the most popular medium for information about the EU (34.3% of respondents: see Figure 22). The printed press came next with 23.5%, other (non-news) television programmes and the Internet were fourth and fifth

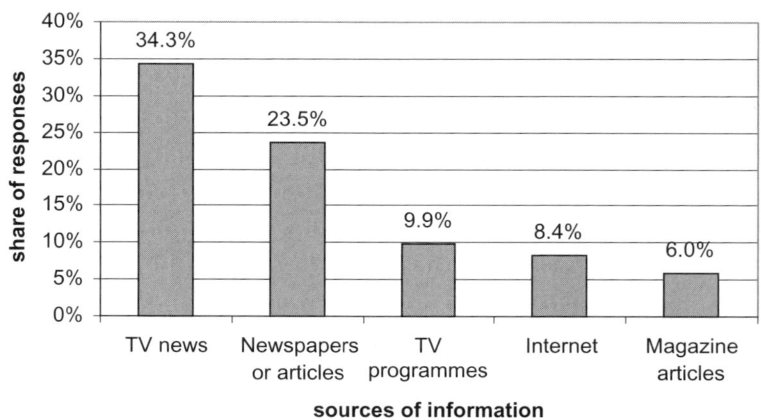

Figure 22:   Source of information about the EU

places respectively with both used by under 10%. Cumulatively, television sources accounted for 43.2% and its suggested that better utilising television could be an effective way of enhancing the EU's profile in Vietnam.

The general public's personal and business ties with the EU were also explored. France was the EU country that Vietnamese respondents had the most extensive personal or business ties with (19.5%). This can be explained in many ways, including the obvious historical and long-term bilateral relationship between the two countries. Austria was second (14%) and Germany third (12.8%). Only 2% of respondents named the UK as a place that they had personal or business ties with. As many as 65.8% selected other countries not listed in the questionnaire, signifying that the survey participants had diversified ties with various European countries. When asked about their type of links with the EU, 40% of respondents replied that they had family or relatives living in EU countries and 23% had friends residing there. Virtually none had business ties with EU partners. Such intense personal connections could be instrumental for enhancing Vietnam–EU relations in the future.

Summary

Although the relationship between Vietnam and the EU has been rapidly improving and the presence of the EU in Vietnam has been increasing, the Vietnamese public still do not highly regard the role of the Union for Vietnam. The relationship between the two was not comprehensively understood, with most perceptions limited to economic aspects of the EU's profile. The economic relationship between the EU with Vietnam has had some problems in recent times, and this fact may have contributed to the perception of the Union as a less important partner for Vietnam in comparison with China, Japan, the USA and Asia as a whole.

CONCLUSION

This chapter has investigated how the EU was represented in the popular Vietnamese reputable news media, as well as in the views of national stakeholders and the general public. The results of this tri-partite study seem to reflect the existent dynamics in the rapidly developing Vietnam–EU relationship.

In the news media analysis, a relatively low output of EU-related news was identified, however, in contrast to the findings in the other countries under investigation, almost two-thirds of this coverage was produced by local Vietnamese sources. Despite this, however, the majority of the EU coverage showed the Union as active outside the local Vietnamese context and only referenced it in a fleeting, minor way. None of the monitored outlets grounded the EU in local, Vietnamese situations, thus projecting an image of the EU as a relatively distant and somehow irrelevant partner to Vietnam. Perhaps encouragingly, most of the EU news was presented without an explicit evaluation, however this could arguably indicate a sense of indifference towards the Union by Vietnamese newsmakers. Despite the economic importance of the EU relationship, the Vietnamese news media preferred to profile the political aspects of the Union, although economic framing was the second most common representation. Importantly for the EU, as it strives to become a global leader in these areas, issues relating to its social, environmental and developmental actorness were almost invisible.

In contrast to this policised media framing, the Vietnamese stakeholders instead perceived the EU to be a primarily economic power of importance, and most did not view it as a significant global political leader. While all interviewed Vietnamese stakeholders acknowledged the EU's importance to Vietnam presently and its growing importance in the future, this importance was considered to be less than that of the USA, China, Japan and Asia as a whole. Interestingly, most respondents felt that the onus was on Vietnam to help improve its economic relations with the EU in the future, particularly in terms of ensuring and promoting the quality of its export products.

The general public of Vietnam seemed to support the perceptions of the interviewed stakeholders. The majority of survey participants also viewed the EU to be lower down the 'food chain' of importance for Vietnam, although most also felt that the relationship was likely to improve in the future. The key focus of the relationship, in the eyes of the Vietnamese public, was economic issues, and it was these that they felt their government should prioritise in its future engagement with the EU.

It is clear, then, that there are more similarities than differences between EU images and perceptions detected in the Vietnamese media, among national stakeholders and the general public. The future progress for Vietnam–EU bilateral relations requires expanded efforts from both sides. Arguably, it also requires considerable diversification, and the two partners should promote their cooperation in fields other than the economy, such as collaborations in the political, cultural, educational and social sectors. For a country like Vietnam that has a long tradition and respect for learning, a focus on education would be particularly important. Secondly, the study found that there was an overwhelming tendency in Vietnam to identify the EU with its Member States, especially with France, Germany and the UK. Yet, this image of the EU has a chance to transform in the eyes of Vietnamese, if the EU acts more actively in Vietnam as a unique but common voice on the one side, and a powerful supranational interlocutor within multilateral dialogues such as ASEAN-EU cooperation, ASEM and other international forums, on the other. Finally, this study revealed that for the Vietnamese public and 'elites', television and reputable newspapers are still important sources of information on the EU. Yet, with the low volume of EU news featured in these outlets, EU information and cultural offices attached to the ECD could become a more informative source for providing a more sophisticated and first-hand knowledge of the EU. In this way, the ECD can contribute to fostering a deepening of mutual understanding and can serve as a bridge between peoples.

Chapter 3

EU Images in Indonesia

*CPF Luhulima, Edward ML Panjaitan
and Anika Widiana*

INTRODUCTION

Historically, Indonesia has experienced extensive colonial ties with several European countries, notably the United Kingdom (UK), Portugal and the Netherlands. With the end of colonisation, these relationships have changed, but not ceased. In particular, the economic development of Indonesia has become a responsibility associated with the European Union (EU). Indonesia is classified as a developing country and has a specific and very special relationship with the EU in this context. In terms of its demography and politics, Indonesia is the third largest democratic country (after the United States of America and India), and constitutes the world's largest Muslim society, providing the important example that Islam and democracy are not mutually exclusive ideas. Economically, Indonesia has abundant natural resources, economic growth is positive and supports a population of 225 million. Indonesia also plays a leading role within the Association of South East Asian Nations (ASEAN). It is the only ASEAN country to be a member of the G20, making Indonesia the best bridge for EU-ASEAN relations in general.

The Asia–Europe Meeting (ASEM) established in Bangkok in 1996 provides an additional cooperation forum between the Asian region and Europe. The aim of ASEM is to strengthen cooperation across three pillars (1) politics and security, (2) economy, trade, and investment, and (3) cultural and social sectors.[1] For Indonesia, the ASEM forum plays an additionally important and beneficial role because through open dialogue, both Asia and Europe can share ideas promoting win-win trade and investment. The pressure on developing countries can be minimised and transparency increased.[2]

Although the initial expectations for the political pillar of ASEM were not that great, gradually the political dialogues have developed to become the main element in the ASEM process. This positive development has occurred despite informality; the political dialogues have regularly covered sensitive and controversial issues, for example, human rights, democracy, the rule of law and good governance. Meanwhile, the dialogue on security has also developed well, not only on international terrorism, but also concerning global threats and environmental issues. Even though criticised by some to be superficial, this growth shows that ASEM cooperation has progressed in general.[3]

Economic Relations

Currently, the EU is reforming its trade relations with poor and developing countries and it is the leading trade partner for the world's poorest developing countries. According to an EU report, in 2003 79% of developing countries' imports to the EU entered either tax-free or with reduced tax and Indonesia has experienced increased

---

[1] Pangestu, Mari Elka, *10 Tahun ASEM: Dinamika Hubungan Ekonomi Asia-Eropa.* Deplu RI, 2006, pp. 12, 15.

[2] *Ibid.*

[3] Wirengjurit, Dian, *Pilar Politik ASEM: Sebuah Tinjauan Kritis.* Unpublished MA dissertation, 2006.

opportunities to export to the EU. In 2003, 63% of developing countries' total exports were absorbed by the EU and in the agricultural sector the EU took 70% of the total. Under the EU's Generalised System of Preferences (GSP) (for the period 1999–2003), developing countries' share of the EU market increased from 33% to 40%. Since 2001, the EU has provided more than half of the world's development funding, amounting to €750 million per year.[4]

Trade relations between Indonesia and EU have been significant for both parties. Up until the end of the 1970s, EU policies to assist Indonesia were largely economic and trade mainly focused on forestry; from the 1980s, the focus changed to rice sustainability, and then to trade and investment in the new millennium.[5] Since the Indonesian economic crisis in 1998, trade between Europe and Indonesia has been recovering its dynamism. For example, in the period 1999–2003 EU imports from Indonesia increased at an average of 3.3% per annum, while exports from Indonesia to the EU increased by 5.7%. Consequently, Indonesia experienced a trade surplus. The average bilateral trade balance between the two partners over these five years was a surplus of €7 million per year in Indonesia's favour.[6]

Although the bilateral trade balance between the EU and Indonesia in the 1998–2003 period was beneficial for Indonesia, there were a number of external trade policies implemented by the EU which had less benign effects. One example is the GSP policy which gives the EU unilateral discretionary power: not all Indonesian commodities were included in GSP. Another example concerned the implementation of the EU's General Food Law with its Rapid Alert System for Food and Feed (RASFF) mechanism. In September 2005, Indonesian fishery products — tuna, marlin fish and shrimps — were

---

[4] Widiana, Anika, 'Kebijakan Perdagangan EU terhadap Ekspor Indonesia dan Pola Ekspor Indonesia', *Journal Ekonomi & Bisnis*, Vol. 9, No. 2, 2007, p. 119.

[5] Aruli, Abdul Manna, 'Economic and Trade Relations Between the EU and Indonesia', *Jurnal Kajian Wilayah Eropa*, Vol. 1, No. 1, 2005, pp. 30–1.

[6] European Commission in Indonesia, 2003, <http://ec.europa.eu/news/archives_en.htm>.

refused entry to the EU market because they were suspected of containing chemical residues such as chloramphenicol and nitrofuran which are harmful to humans.[7] This resulted in the loss of significant foreign exchange for the Indonesian fishery sector. Since then these problems have been overcome through EU financial support for training and for the improvement of fishery laboratory facilities throughout Indonesia to ensure that fish products exported to the EU are free from harmful chemicals. Lastly, in the context of the 2008 global financial crisis, it is potentially harder for Indonesia to enter the European market. The prospect of renewed protectionism is particularly worrying for the textile and garment industry in Indonesia which saw an opportunity to export to the new Central and Eastern European countries after 2004.

European Union Programmes in Indonesia

Typically, relations between developed and developing countries struggle to implement the principle of partnership: economic disparities pose a challenge to the equality of benefits even where there is no intention to exploit trade partners. Ideally, relations should be beneficial for both (in terms of gains from trade) on the basis of an equal partnership which is comprehensive and non-conditional. In the case of Indonesia, the EU needs to import Indonesian products, while Indonesia needs the EU both as an export market and for technology transfer, and to develop human resources through education and training.

The development cooperation between the EU and Indonesia has grown since the *reformasi* (reform) of 1998. EU development policy embraces the Millennium Development Goals (MDGs) with the aim of eradicating global poverty.[8] Further, the EU's own treaties require it to promote economic and social development and to integrate developing countries into the global economy. Indonesia and the EU

---

[7] Paramitaningrum, 'Penolakan UE Terhadap Ekspor Ikan dari Indonesia', *Jurnal Kajian Wilayah Eropa*, Vol. 2, No. 2, 2006, pp. 92–93.

[8] European Commission, 2005, <http://ec.europa.eu/news/archives_en.htm>.

have a number of agreements governing bilateral cooperation and development. Most significant is the European Commission's Framework Agreement for Economic and Development Cooperation and the 1982 technical and administrative project implementation procedures. Under the European Commission Communication 2000, the cooperation programmes between the EU and Indonesia were reorganised to enhance their focus and contemporary relevance. The European Commission's Country Strategy Paper (CSP) on Indonesia outlined the 2002–2006 assistance available with a focus on natural resources, good governance (particularly in state administration, health, education), and economic cooperation.[9] The CSP included a National Indicative Programme (NIP) for the 2002–2004 period with budget allocations. The total Commission grant for the 2002–2004 NIP was €150 million divided into €58 million for 2002, €46 million for 2003 and €46 million for 2004. The NIP Memorandum was signed in Jakarta on 19th November 2002 by the Ambassador of European Commission and it provides support for the following activities:[10] East Kalimantan National Resources Planning Management Project; Good Governance in health division in Jambi, South Sumatra and Papua; Small Project Facility for Economic Cooperation; Trade Related Technical Assistance (TRTA); Micro Projects for economic cooperation; Forest Law Enforcement Governance and Trade (FLEGT) Programme; and, Support to Improve Judiciary, Decentralisation and Local Democracy.

The CSP was extended for the 2007–2013 period. Education, trade and governance were to become "the main areas of intervention".[11] According to EU calculations for 2007–2013, the Indonesian economy needs to grow at 6–7% annually to absorb its annual population growth of 2.5 million new members of the labour force. Currently, approximately 52% of Indonesia's population live on just US$2 daily and are the focus of the MDGs. To compound the

---

[9] European Commission, 2002, <http://ec.europa.eu/external_relations/indonesia/index_en.htm>.

[10] European Commission in Indonesia, 2004.

[11] *Ibid.* 'The EU's Relations with Indonesia — Overview'.

challenges faced by Indonesia, there has been serious degradation of its environment, specifically in forestry, air quality, clean water and sanitation. Good governance is also still a major problem and poor governance has a negative effect on the country's economic performance. Corruption and weak law enforcement also remain significant problems.

The EU provides further assistance under the Development Cooperation Instrument for 2007–2013. This prioritises education, then trade and improved investment to foster economic growth, followed by improving governance through justice and the rule of law. Hence, education, trade and investment promotion will be needed to foster economic growth and the rule of law. To make this financial assistance more effective, cross-cutting issues are to be promoted specifically the environment, conflict prevention, human rights, gender equality issues and good governance.

This is the reality of the EU-Indonesia relationship. But, as discussed in the Introduction to this volume, there is a lack of information about the perception of that reality in Indonesia. How is the EU framed in the Indonesian news media? What do the Indonesian public and 'elite' think about the European integration project and do they think that it has any relevance for their daily lives? In order to address some of these questions, and to examine the nature and content of relations between Indonesia and the EU underpinning the formal arrangements, the representations of the EU in the Indonesian media, as well as the perceptions of the EU by the Indonesian public and 'elite' stakeholders are discussed below.

THE EU IN INDONESIAN NEWS MEDIA

General Profile of Media in Indonesia

The 1998 political reforms in Indonesia have resulted in the promotion of democracy, including freedom of the press. The Indonesian Government issued the Media Act No. 40/1999 to replace the Media Core Act No. 11/1966 and junto No. 21/1982. The latter act had led to the government regulation "Peraturan Pemerintah" which proclaimed that the power to control the media belonged to the government's Department of Information, and under this regulation, the Minister of Information could withdraw the publishing permits according to *Permen* (Ministry Regulation) No. 1/1984.[12] In the legal framework after the reform, the Indonesian media became free to express their opinion.[13] On the basis of Press Act No. 40/1999, the Government cannot intervene or control the media in Indonesia (including no power of imprisonment of journalists on the basis of their work). Consequently, the role over journalists in society is becoming more prominent, and the local media is enjoying a renaissance.

The present-day media landscape in Indonesia is characterized by a variety of styles, and diversity of the targeted readership means that a wide scope of local, national and international topics are reported. This research chose four media outlets for monitoring, each featuring a unique profile: the two local-language monitored dailies were a 'popular' paper, *Kompas*, and a 'business' paper, *Bisnis Indonesia*; the English-language newspaper was the *Jakarta Post*, and the prime-time news bulletin chosen was the national channel *TVRI*.

The *Kompas* daily (first published in 1965) is the nation's leading independent morning daily.[14] The paper was chosen due to its profile as the largest paper in terms of circulation (509,000 copies on weekdays and 800,000 copies on Sunday) and as the daily with the widest national outreach (it is distributed in Java, Sumatera, Kalimantan, Sulawesi, Bali and Papua). This newspaper is known for its balanced news reporting and it traditionally features two editorials (one on domestic issues and the other one on international affairs) and covers

---

[12] Batubara, Leo, 'Revisi UU Pers atau Hak Konstitusional?', *Kompas*, 29 June 2007, p. 6.

[13] According to Media Act No. 40/1999 which is a breakdown of Article 28 UUD 1945 (original) and Act 28 F Amendment II UUD 1945.

[14] <http://www.kompas.com>.

such broad themes as politics, economics, international affairs, social affairs, welfare, culture, sports, and public figures. In addition, *Kompas* has special inserts for children and youth. The paper is also known for its neutral and objective reporting style, journalistic integrity and credibility and multicultural staff[15] employing approximately 400 news writers, including five international affairs journalists. Its readership is mostly male white-collar, university-educated middle- or upper-class readers aged between 25–60 years old (among those government officials, academics and entrepreneurs). Since 2005, *Kompas* has adopted a new style, namely brief, simpler and more compact news reporting divided into such sections as general news, business, economy and advertisements. This new format proved to be a success adding to the paper's circulation and its earnings.

Bisnis Indonesia is a national leader in the coverage of business and economics news in Indonesia.[16] A daily with a circulation of 85,000 copies, it is the biggest business newspaper in the country. First published in 1985, *Bisnis Indonesia* is owned by Cahaya Pelangi Persada and the biggest shareholders are Ciputra Group and Anthony Salim. The newspaper covers such topics as trade, transportation, banking, monetary, finance, economy, industry and agribusiness. It employs 100 journalists, including those posted to Batam and the USA. The distribution areas of this newspaper are Jakarta and Greater Area (Jabodetabek). With the editorial policy prioritising insights into the national economy, *Bisnis Indonesia* also reports on the international economic developments taking place in the EU, Japan, the USA, China and other major economic hubs. The paper is popular among decision-makers in economic and business circles both in government and the private sector, as well as business people with a wider international outlook. The readers of the newspaper are typically university educated middle- and

---

[15] Although this newspaper belongs to Kompas Gramedia Group (KGG) affiliated with the Catholic groups, it employs practitioners of various religious backgrounds, such as Muslims, Buddhists and Christians.

[16] <http://www.bisnis.com>.

upper-class individuals between 30–40 years old (of which approximately 30% are women).

The *Jakarta Post* is a well-known English-language daily with circulation of 50,000 copies.[17] Established in 1983, it belongs to the Kompas Gramedia Group and is distributed in Java and Bali. The *Jakarta Post* employs 60 journalists, three of whom are international journalists reporting from Yogyakarta, Bandung, Batam, Medan and Bali. The readership of this newspaper features well-educated wealthy urban-dwelling locals (among those, businessmen and private sector employees), as well as expatriates residing in Indonesia who look for current information on the local economy, politics and social-cultural aspects in English. The newspaper reports news on politics, economy, international relations, social welfare, culture, sports and leisure news, focusing on local events in order to inform and educate the expatriate readership. Similar to *Kompas*, the *Jakarta Post* revamped its style in 2001 increasing the number of pages, providing shorter news items and writing in simpler language. A digital edition of the newspaper has existed since 1999.

TVRI is a state-owned television channel established in 1962.[18] With its 27 transmitters reaching even remote areas of the country, *TVRI* has been particularly effective in informing the Indonesian community on national and international topics. The viewership is approximately 12 million people covering all educational levels and professional backgrounds, in major urban centres, small towns and rural areas. The channel features three news broadcasts daily. Since 1962, the *TVRI* has presented a prime-time news programme *Dunia dalam Berita* (World in the News) reporting current world affairs from economic, political, legal cultural, social and security perspectives and from various geographical destinations (such as the EU, the USA, Japan, China and Russia and other international 'players'). This is the news bulletin which was monitored in this study.

---

[17] <http://www.thejakartapost.com>.
[18] <http://www.tvri.co.id>.

Results of Media Monitoring

Volume of Coverage

In six months of monitoring (January 1–June 31, 2008), the three press outlets observed had a relatively balanced distribution of EU news when compared with the two other media cases in this volume. *Kompas* and the *Jakarta Post* published the most EU news (252 and 239 articles respectively), while *Bisnis Indonesia* accounted for 155 articles. *TVRI* broadcast 50 news items on the EU (Figure 1).

The leading position in the EU's coverage by *Kompas* can be explained by the fact that this 'prestigious' national daily takes pride in presenting diverse information (including news on external relations) catering for an educated readership. Similarly, the English-language *Jakarta Post* also targets 'elite' audiences, including expatriates, who are interested in international affairs, yet this market is much smaller than *Kompas*'s national outreach. *Bisnis Indonesia* focusing on economy and business news serves a very specific and limited market of news consumers who are usually interested in a more narrow perspective on the EU, i.e., business and economics. Arguably, these readership profiles influence the overall output of EU

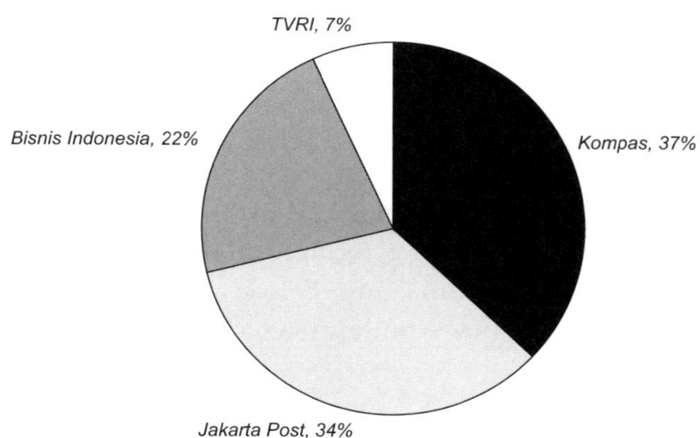

Figure 1:   **Distribution of EU news in the four monitored outlets**

news in each outlet. It is worth noting that the *Dunia Dalam Berita* programme observed here provides balanced attention to many international actors (such as the USA, China, ASEAN, NAFTA, East Asia, and the EU).

Sources of News

When it came to sourcing EU news, the three press outlets in the study showed different preferences. The *Jakarta Post* exhibited the highest share of EU news originating from the international wires (*Reuters, AFP, Bloomberg* and others) — at almost 90%. *Kompas* presented a more balanced distribution of sources (58% were international). In contrast, *Bisnis Indonesia* preferred local sources in reporting the EU, either writing from inside Indonesia itself, or posted overseas (only 10% were internationally sourced). *TVRI* reportage of the EU was heavily dominated by the foreign sources. Interestingly, 100% of this foreign-sourced news came from one wire, *Reuters* (Figure 2).

Financed by wealthy media groups, both *Bisnis Indonesia* and *Kompas* have sufficient funds to place their journalists in foreign locations (*Kompas*, for example, has five international journalists

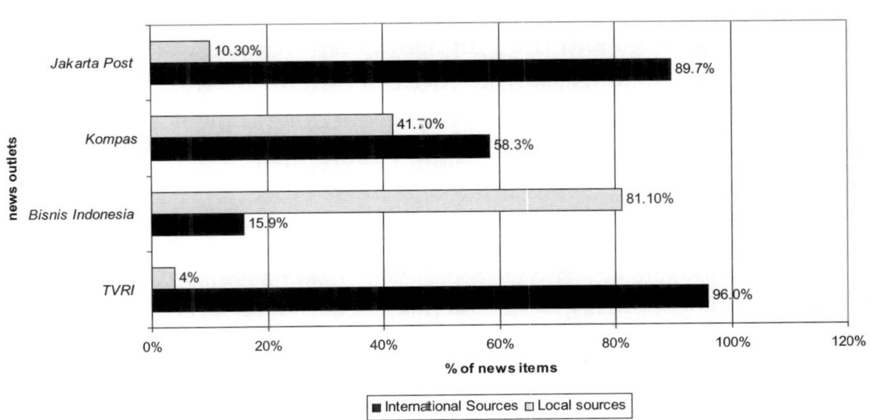

Figure 2:   Sources of EU news

reporting from the USA and Europe). The *Jakarta Post* uses international sources mostly to satisfy its readers — expatriates and educated 'elites' — who look for news from the international wires. An exclusive sourcing of the *TVRI* news from *Reuters* is due to the fact that the station has enjoyed a special relation with the agency (as well as with the *BBC*). Such heavy reliance on international sources could also be explained by cost-cutting imperatives — posting reporters overseas is expensive, while sourcing news from the wires is relatively affordable.

Degree of Centrality

Evaluating the intensity of the EU's media representations, it was noticed that out of the three chosen press outlets, the 'business' paper *Bisnis Indonesia* had the highest share of news presenting the EU as a *major* actor (31%). In contrast, the 'popular' paper, *Kompas*, had the lowest share when reporting the EU (6%) from this perspective, instead prioritising the EU as a *minor* angle. The lowest share of *minor* representations of the EU was observed in the English-language *Jakarta Post* (17.6%). *TVRI* almost evenly split its reporting of the EU between the *secondary* and *minor* perspectives (44% and. 42% respectively) (Figure 3).

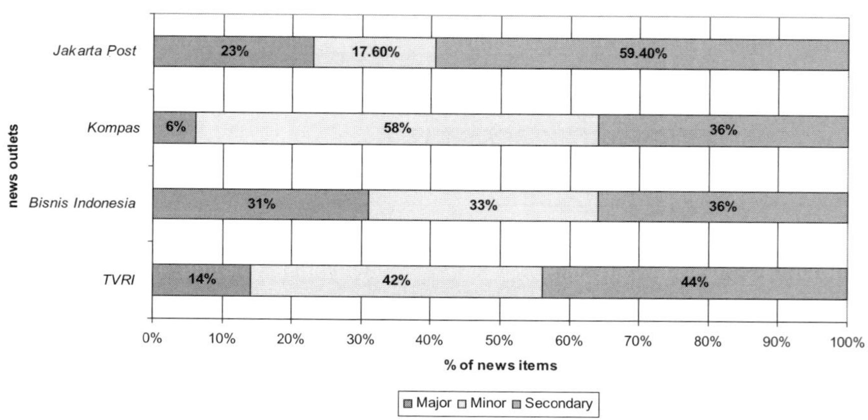

Figure 3:   Degree of centrality of EU media representations

With the focus of *Bisnis Indonesia* on the EU's business and economic developments in general and the euro-zone in particular, a *major* role assigned to the EU in such reportages is self-explanatory. The general diversity of topics typical of *Kompas*'s reporting style is partially accounted by the dominant *minor* intensity in the EU's representations in this paper. International sourcing of EU news by the *Jakarta Post* often resulted in profiling the EU as an actor who acts *on par* with other international actors, and hence the dominance of the *secondary* degree of centrality. *TVRI*'s *Dunia dalam Berita* philosophy of presenting a balanced reportage on as many international actors as possible results in a profile similar to the *Jakarta Post*'s; that is, the EU as a *secondary* actor. To summarise, most of EU news in the four reputable media outlets (43% of the sample) presented the EU from the secondary perspective, meaning that the EU is presented as a complementary rather than as the main actor for Indonesian readers and viewers.

Focus of Domesticity

Assessing whether the EU was presented as a locally relevant actor, the study discovered that again the three press outlets had completely different preferences in their EU framings. The 'popular' *Kompas* was the leader among the three papers in framing the EU in the context of a third country (neither the EU nor Indonesia) (39% — see Figure 4). The Union was portrayed acting 'somewhere out there in the world' and this depiction conveyed a message of the EU not being directly relevant to local events or people. Yet, in this outlet, the regional angle of grounding the EU was also the highest among the three papers (almost 7%). In contrast, the 'business' paper *Bisnis Indonesia* revealed the highest share of locally-grounded EU news (46.5%). Uniquely, the *Jakarta Post* preferred to report the EU in its own internal contexts. This particular framing is understood to appeal to the paper's readers — expatriates and educated elites — looking for specific, EU-related information. In the television medium, the EU was framed predominantly as an actor in the European context (66%) — a profile expected given the preference of international news

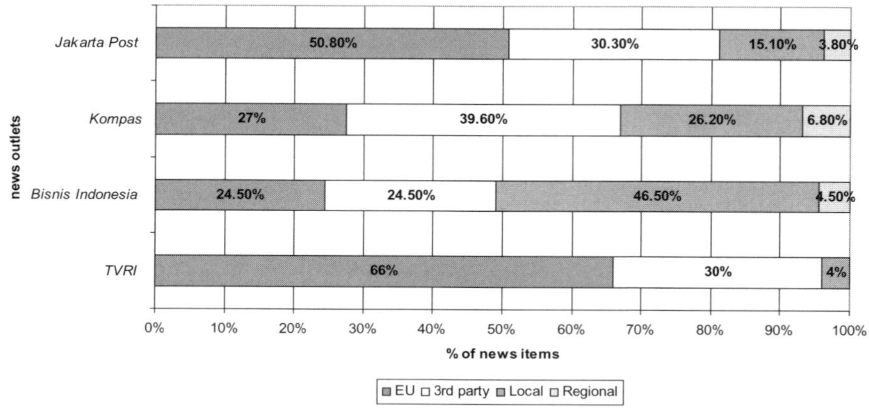

Figure 4:   Focus of domesticity of EU media representations

sources by this network. When this EU-focus was combined with the 30% of news covering the EU in the context of third countries on the television news network, it left almost no available space for reporting the EU as a locally or regionally relevant actor.

A local grounding of the EU in the 'business' paper was expected — one of the goals of such outlets is to inform its readers on the activities of foreign partners which directly affect the locality in question. However, it should be remembered that the readership of this paper is specialised and not sizeable, when compared with the more 'popular' news media. Additionally, the 'regional' angle in reporting the EU's activities was the least visible overall. This observation specifically relates to the coverage of ASEM which was minimal (discussed below). Arguably, the ASEM forum's informal structure and floating agenda does not raise the EU's profile in the regional context in the Indonesia news media.

The Most Visible EU Officials and Institutions

The European Commission was the most visible EU body in the monitored reportage (mentioned 90 times — see Figure 5). The President of the European Central Bank, Jean-Claude Trichet and

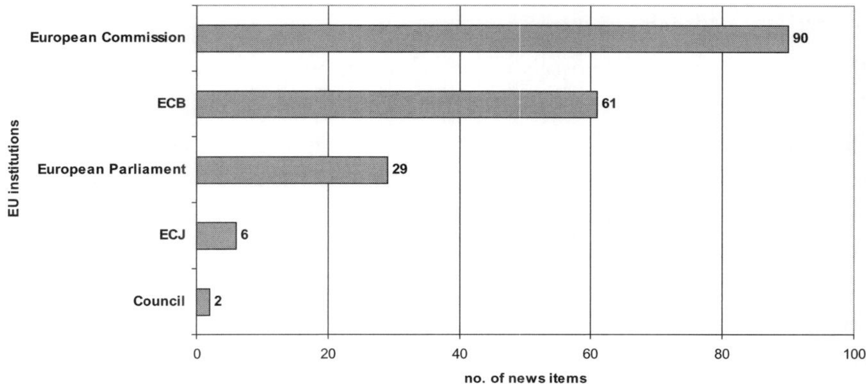

Figure 5:   The most visible EU institutions

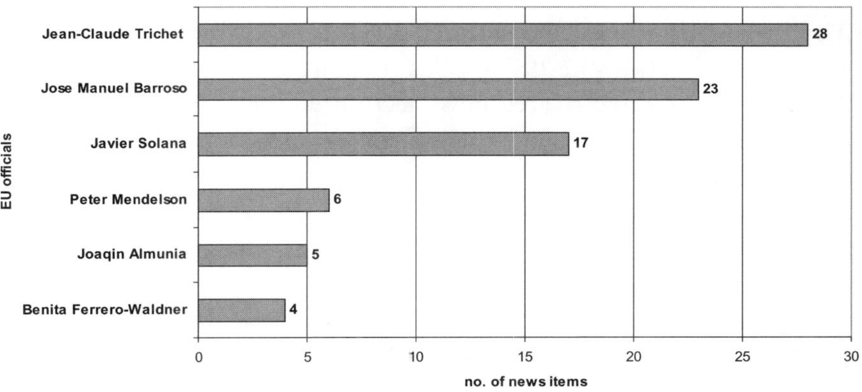

Figure 6:   The most visible EU officials

Commission President Barroso were the most reported EU officials (mentioned in 28 and 23 articles respectively — see Figure 6).

A heightened visibility of the European Commission was partially due to its function of executing policies that directly affected EU citizens — a topic of interest for the Indonesian newsmakers. The transformation of the euro-zone (namely, the accession of Malta and Cyprus into the zone in January 2008) significantly raised the visibility of Jean-Claude Trichet.

'Framing' the EU

Currently, Indonesia enjoys close relations with many individual EU Member States — among those, the Netherlands, the UK and France. However, whether "the awareness of a European country is expected to become European collective awareness"[19] remains a question. Arguably, Indonesia needs to update itself on understanding its traditional European partners in the context of EU27, and the news media could be instrumental for developing this awareness. On this basis, the thematic representation of the EU in the news — the EU as a political, economic, social affairs, environmental and developmental actor — was investigated.

EU as a political actor

Over the six months of monitoring, the four news outlets profiled the EU's political actions in 297 articles (making it the second most visible frame). Economic-related news accounted for 320 news items. All other themes (social, environmental or developmental affairs) were less visible.

Each outlet observed in this study had a slightly different share of political news in their samples, and various shares of the sub-frames — external *vs.* internal EU political news (Figure 7). *Kompas* focused its political reportage on the EU's involvement in problem areas around the globe, namely the Israeli-Palestinian conflicts in Gaza, elections in Russia and riots in Armenia. Similar themes attracted attention of the *TVRI* newsmakers. Arguably, the two most 'popular' news outlets in the country highlighted the international actions of the EU due to a greater emphasis such news producers place on conflict and drama. The *Jakarta Post* was the only outlet that devoted a significant share of its coverage to internal EU issues.

For several months, the political coverage was dominated by Indonesia's reaction to the EU's decision to ban all Indonesian

---

[19] *Dirjen Perhubungan Udara Dephub Budhi Muliawan Suyitno.*

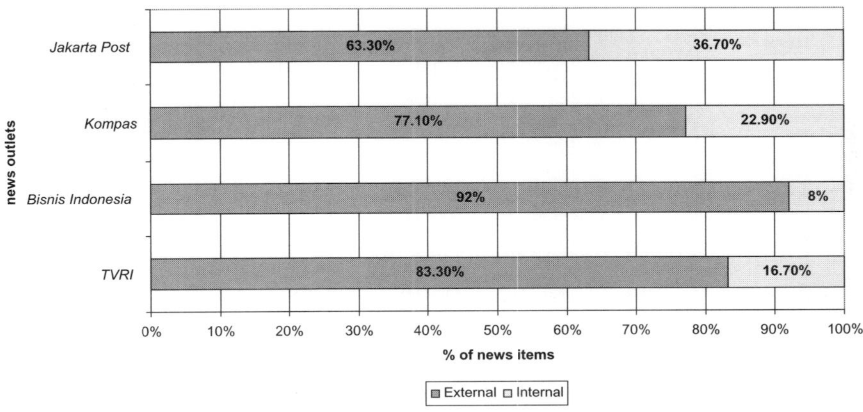

Figure 7:   Distribution of external vs. internal political news on the EU

flights from entering the Union's airspace[20] because of low flight safety standards of Indonesinan airlines which had led to crashes in 2006–07. This ban was reported from both political and economic angles since it impacted on Indonesia's strategic economic sectors and tourism. Most of this news reported from an economic angle appeared in *Bisnis Indonesia*, while politically-coloured reporting surfaced in *Kompas*.

Economic issues

Predictably, most of the news about the EU's economic perform-ance was located in the 'business' daily *Bisnis Indonesia* (78% of its coverage was economic in focus). The *Jakarta Post* followed with 40.6% and *Kompas* had 38.6% of its sample devoted to this theme. The *Bisnis Indonesia* reportage produced the following dis-tribution of issues — trade (43%), business (42%), industry (8.8%) and agriculture (5%) (Figure 8). Surprisingly, agriculture, which was expected to receive more attention from Indonesian news-makers,

---

[20] European Commission, 'Updated Airline Blacklist', <http://ec.europa.eu/ireland/press_office/media_centre/july2008_en.htm>.

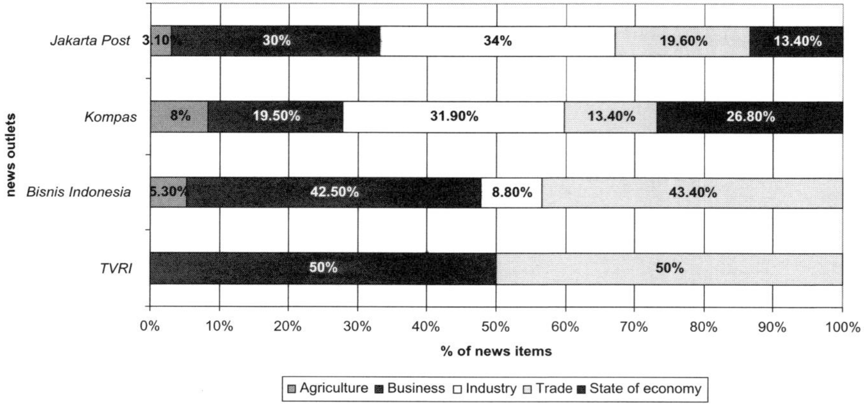

Figure 8:   Distribution of themes within the frame 'EU as an economic actor'

was peripheral in all outlets. When reported, such news was dominated by insights into the implementation of General Food Law RASFF and the mechanism for fishery products (such as shrimp, tuna and marlin).[21]

As Figure 8 illustrates, EU-Indonesia trade relations received extensive coverage in all observed media outlets. The issues discussed included non-tariff trade constraints such as export dumping from Indonesia to the EU (specifically, the export of chemical products), eco-labeling and quality certification. The media often conveyed the message that the EU's regulations were increasingly restraining Indonesia's trade with Europe.

The second most visible issue reported was EU investments. Surviving the 1997 financial crisis in Asia, Indonesia has worked hard to attract foreign investors. Foreign Direct Investment has been particularly sought after. The Indonesian news media reported a relatively high interest among EU investors towards Indonesia, yet Indonesia's regulation constraints on the one hand, and procedural vagueness on the other, were seen as counterbalancing this interest.

---

[21] The implementation of this law means that all fishery products from Indonesia have to be chloramphenicol-and-nitrofuran-free ones.

For most European investors, the key for future cooperation with Indonesia are guarantees of investment's safety and clear and standardised operating procedures.

The exchange rate between the euro and US dollar (as well as some other foreign currencies) also attracted close media attention. The prominence of this issue was due to the exchange rate's impact on Indonesia's trade, investment and tourism. During the period of monitoring, the US dollar had an unfavourable exchange rate with other currencies, including the euro. Some assigned this to the USA's growing budget deficit caused by its military sector's expenses in Iraq and Afganistan.[22] A perception of the weakening US dollar on the one hand and stability of the euro-zone on the other added to a greater appreciatiation of the euro by the local news media.

Social affairs

Th EU's actions in the social affairs sector were reported in only 45 news items and the majority of these appeared in *Kompas*. Such topics as migration, healthcare, education, culture, human rights and lifestyle were reported, but not extensively. Most of the 'social affairs' news reported by *Kompas* featured sports reports and articles on multicultural diversity in the EU (Figure 9). The *Jakarta Post* presented discussions on diversity, social legislation and welfare. *Bisnis Indonesia* only featured a tiny fraction of the EU social affairs news (under 2% of its sample), and this focused on diversity and entertainment. Notably, all three newspapers were interested in reporting the diversity of the Union in cultural and linguistic terms. Migration reportage often focused on the Union's internal migration as a consequence of enlargement, and rarely had a local Indonesian 'flavour' to it.

TVRI, which sourced its news from the international wires, also prioritised the topics of diversity and immigration in its reports on the EU's social affairs. One event that caught attention was a tragedy

---

[22] Aby the Liberal, 'Euro *vs* Dollar — The War of Currencies', <http://www.abythe-liberal.com/business-finance/euro-vs-dollar-the-war-of-currencies>.

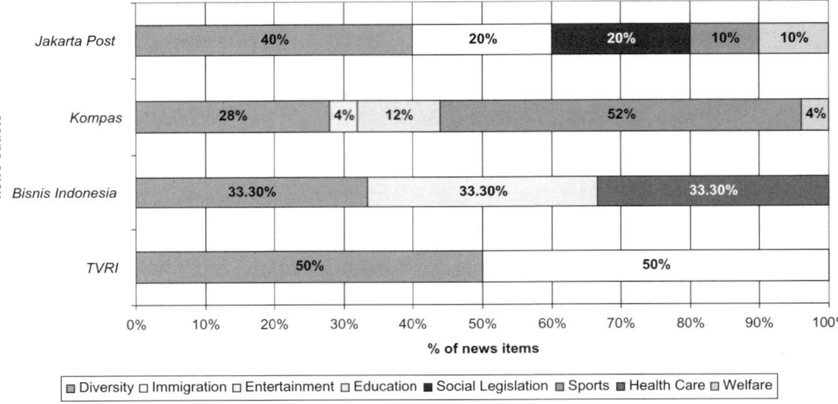

Figure 9:   Distribution of themes within the frame 'EU as a social affairs actor'

about illegal migrants from Myanmar and the EU's response to this. In this reporting, the EU was presented as an actor whose actions mattered locally and regionally — Myanmar is Indonesia's neighbour and a member of ASEAN. Other news with a 'regional' taste extensively presented on television was the news about the EU's intention to boycott the opening ceremony of the Olympic Games in Beijing in response to the violation of human rights in the China-Tibet conflict.

Environment and development

Only 22 news items over six months across all outlets discussed the EU's actions on the environment. Half of these presented the EU as an actor performing inside the Union, and the other half were EU actions in the global context. The only exception was the *Bisnis Indonesia* reportage where all monitored news items in this frame concerned the EU's international actions in the environmental field (Figure 10). This extremely low volume of reportage mostly focused on forestry destruction and global warming. Indonesia's forestry is being rapidly depleted (in the last 50 years the country lost 64 million

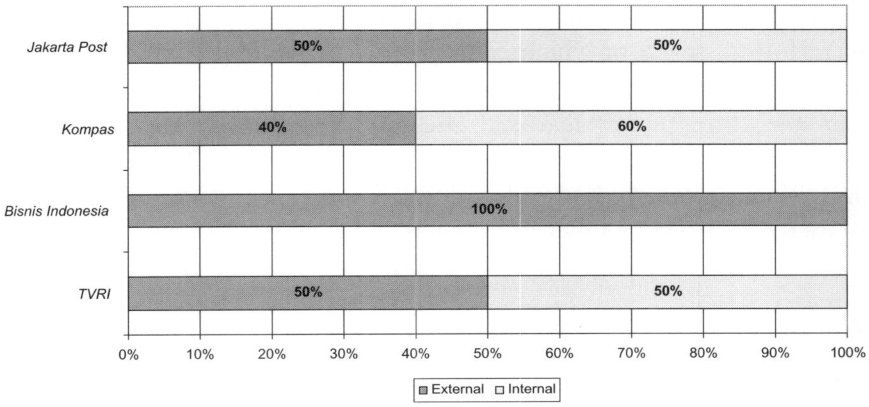

Figure 10:   Distribution of environmental news

hectares).[23] The reports mentioned the EU's reaction to this problem. The issue of deforesterisation was also closely linked in the news to the existence of wood-based Indonesian exports. Another example of environmental news[24] was the European Commission's proposal to speak against climate change and to increase renewable energy.[25] Through this proposal, cooperation between Indonesia and EU was anticipated given that Indonesia is the biggest crude palm oil (CPO) exporter in the world.[26] This cooperation was presented as being beneficial for both sides.

---

[23] Depdagri, 'Dalam 50 Tahun: Luas Hutan Indonesia Berkurang 64 Juta Ha', <www.depdagri.go.id>.

[24] Memerangi perubahan Iklim, 'Meningkatkan Energi Terbarukan', *Against Climate Change, Improving Renewable Energy, Kompas*, 19 Maret 2008, p. 40.

[25] This package covers one instruction regarding the use of renewable energy through Renewal Energy Directive (RED) programme issuing the objective tying European, to use 20% renewable energy source from all energy consumption and minimum objective at 10% to use biofuel energy in the transportation sectors in 2020 (European Commission, 'Rurality — Environment — Development', <http://ec.europa.eu/geninfo/query/resultaction.jsp>).

[26] CPO exports from Indonesia per year reach 15 juta ton. Lexregis, 'RI Ingin Harga CPO-nya Bisa Jadi Harga Acuan Internasional', <www.lexregis.com>.

Only 11 news reports on the EU's role as a developmental actor were found, seven of which came from *Kompas.* All of these covered aid administered by the EU to Indonesia and other countries. For example, one report featured the aid provided by the European Commission to eradicate the avian flu in Indonesia. The *Jakarta Post* and *Bisnis Indonesia* had only miniscule coverage of the EU's developmental actions (2 news items each in six months!).

Evaluation

Assessing the tone of EU reporting, it was found that *Bisnis Indonesia* featured the highest share of positively-coloured EU news (59% of its sample), while the three other outlets had a somewhat lower share of such news (around a third in each case). On average, the share of positive news across the four outlets was 45%. The share of news which represented the EU from a negative angle averaged 27%, while the neutral category was at 34% (Figure 11). This dominance of the positive and neutral assessments of the EU on average suggests that the local media present a relatively favourable picture of the EU to their audience, possibly reflecting that relations between Indonesia and the European Union are constructive and on-going.

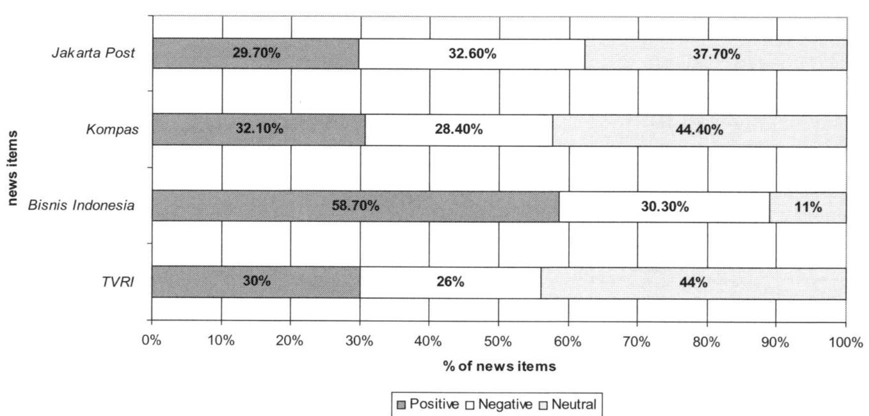

Figure 11:   Evaluation of EU news items

In summary, the analysis of the four reputable news outlets in Indonesia indicated that the EU's economic and political portrayals are almost equally visible to the news audiences, with the EU's external political actions (either in the context of the third country or the EU itself) being the most reported within the political frame. However, local and regional angles were de-prioritised. Moreover, the EU's actions in social affairs, environmental and developmental fields were almost invisible. Yet, these are areas which seem to have the most immediate links to the audience's human interests. The identified framing of the EU was arguably creates an overall impression of a geographically- and personally-distant entity. With most of the reportage coming from minor or secondary perspectives, it also conveyed an image of the EU as 'not yet a main actor' in the eyes of the Indonesian newsmakers. Yet, encouragingly for the EU's presence in Indonesia, the dominance of positive-to-neutral assessments in the EU's reportage indicates a potential for increasing the awareness of the EU in Indonesia and initiating a public discussion of mutual benefits in the EU-Indonesia dialogue.

The news media is believed to influence the general public's opinion on foreign counterparts more than it does for the respective views of national 'elites'. The latter group typically has more first-hand experience with foreign partners, is more educated and internationally travelled, while the former group tends to rely on the mass media to learn about current international reality. Respectively, the next section explores if the media imagery of the EU was echoed in the opinions held by the national stakeholders and the general public.

EU IN THE EYES OF INDONESIAN 'ELITES' AND THE GENERAL PUBLIC

'Elite' Opinion

In this short overview of Indonesian 'elite' opinions, the focus is on several key questions. First, was the EU seen as a global power? Remarkably, 92% of the respondents saw the EU as a global power.

Yet, the EU was not perceived as the most important partner for Indonesia. The USA was assigned the 'No. 1' ranking by 62% of respondents (43% picked the EU). Japan and China followed with 18.5% each. Thus, in the eyes of the interviewed Indonesian decision- and policy-makers, the EU was perceived as their country's second most important overseas partner — a promising perception for furthering the EU-Indonesia dialogue in the future. As one business 'elite' respondent noted, "the EU is important for Indonesia when it comes to trade, and it is followed by politics in order to balance the US influences".

Second, the interviewees were asked about their perception of the euro *vis-à-vis* the US dollar. The views on the former were very positive — 88% agreed that the euro could replace US dollar in the future, with two-thirds believing that the euro could be stronger than the American dollar. However, this extremely positive opinion should be placed in context — between January and June 2008 (the period when the interviews took place), the US dollar substantially depreciated against the euro and other currencies (a development resulting from the growing budget deficit in the USA).

Third, the respondents were asked if the EU's enlargement was seen as an opportunity or a threat for Indonesia. While 64% of those interviewed saw EU enlargement as an opportunity, 32% considered it a threat to Indonesia (the rest were undecided). This view, leaning towards the positive end of the perception continuum, was explained by the respondents in terms of the EU's image as a 'soft' power — an entity spreading its ideals of democracy, market economy and law enforcement. These ideas were seen as attractive for the countries on the European continent, thus their desire to join the Union. Interestingly, these ideas were also seen as appealing around the world, including Indonesia. The new Member States from Eastern Europe were seen as important markets given their population size and developing economic potential. Another consideration, however, was that East European products were seen to be similar to those of Indonesia and could constitute competition. This was viewed both as an opportunity and a challenge for Indonesian exporters.

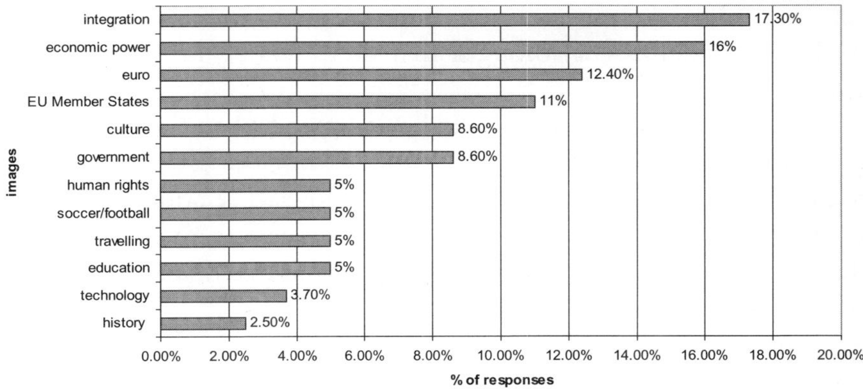

Figure 12:   Spontaneous images of the EU in the eyes of Indonesian 'elites'

Positive images also surfaced when the 'elites' were asked to list their three spontaneous associations when they head the phrase "the European Union". The image of 'European integration' was the most visible (17.3% of all listed associations). The EU as an economic power' was second with 16%, and the euro as a symbol of economic success as well as of economic and political integration was the third with 12.4% (Figure 12). A political respondent noted:

> I actually respect the European Union ... We clearly see the advantages of the European Union, because the Union has helped us solve our big and even small problems in Indonesia a lot. The second one is that European Union members can agree on key political, economic and trade issues. The third one is that people's mobility in Europe has become easier since the birth of the European Union. Prior to this, in the 1990s when I visited some European countries, I had to change some currencies according to the countries I visited with typical bureaucratic procedures. Now, however, with the euro, it's great.

When asked about their preferred sources of information on news about the EU, the interviewees chose the Internet first (30% of responses). Newspapers and magazines followed (23% each). Importantly, contacts (personal and professional) were mentioned in 17% of responses. Significantly, 39% of the interviewed 'elites' perceived EU-Indonesian relations improving, and only a small number of the respondents (7%) thought that there was no improvement in the relationship.

When asked what issues should be addressed when the Indonesian government develops its official dialogue with the EU, 29% of the respondents mentioned furthering EU-Indonesia relations on development. The need to continue political dialogue was noted by 19% of the interviewees. The same percentage commented on Free Trade arrangements between the two partners.

When asked about their perceptions of ASEM, most of the 'elite' respondents noted that they did not care about ASEM, and they did not think that the process had any effect on Indonesia-EU relations. Such low awareness of the process was succinctly summed up by one civil society respondent, "I don't know much about ASEM".

Public Opinion

Turning to the results of the public opinion analysis, in parallel with the 'elite' interviews, the survey respondents were asked to name the most important international partners to Indonesia both in the present and future. The USA led in the perception of present-day importance with 53% of responses, Japan followed with 32% (Figure 13). While China (19%), Asia as a whole (16%), Australia (15%) were mentioned next, the EU was recognised as currently the most important partner by only 8.9% of respondents. Looking to the future, the USA, Japan, Asia (excluding China and Japan), and China took the top four positions, with the EU seen as only the fifth most important future interlocutor for Indonesia.

This distribution of perceived importance is somewhat predictable — the USA still possesses the status of 'super power' in the world, while Japan is the Asian country which has consistently provided Indonesia with substantial financial support in the past. Asia in general, China in particular, and Australia were seen to be important geographically. China's rapid economic growth and Australia's extensive financial support of Indonesia's various training and educational programmes possibly contributed to this particular ranking in importance. Yet, the

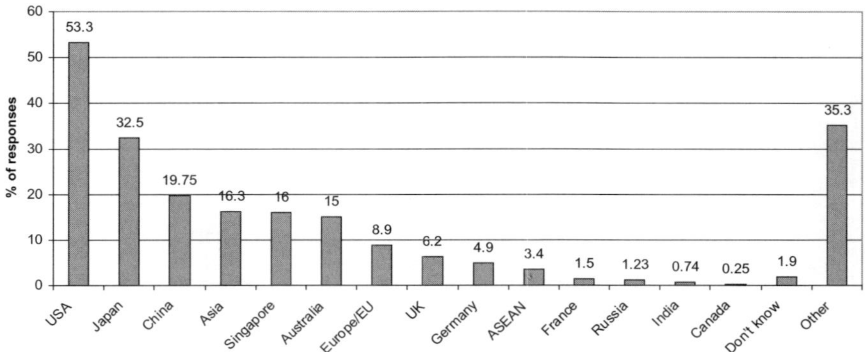

Figure 13:   **Most important partners to Indonesia in the present**

perception of the EU's importance is in contradiction to the reality. In the last ten years, the role of the EU has strengthened in Indonesia: for example, by 1998, the EU was Indonesia's second most important trading partner (after Japan), and the EU was the main export area for Indonesia's non-oil products.[27] Despite being such an important trading partner and a generous financial supporter, the EU was not recognised as such possibly due to its geographic remoteness.

Respondents were further asked to rate the state of the relationship between Indonesia and the EU. The survey's 48% of respondents agreed that the relationship has been steady, and 40% noted that relations need to improve for both parties. Elaborating what issues should be stressed by the Indonesian government in its future dialogue with the EU, respondents mentioned the economy (22% of responses), development cooperation/relations (17%) and trade (14%).

Several EU-related issues were identified by the general public as impacting on Indonesia. Among the top three choices were the dialogue between the EU and ASEAN; the EU as a world economic/ trade power and its performance at the WTO forum; and the EU's

---

[27] Gunaryadi, 'EU Visibility in Indonesia,' *Asia Europe Journal*, 2005, p. 49; retéché, Jean B. 'EU-Indonesia Stronger Partners-Stronger Partnership,' *Jurnal Kajian Wilayah Eropa*, Vol. 1, No. 1, 2005, p. 14.

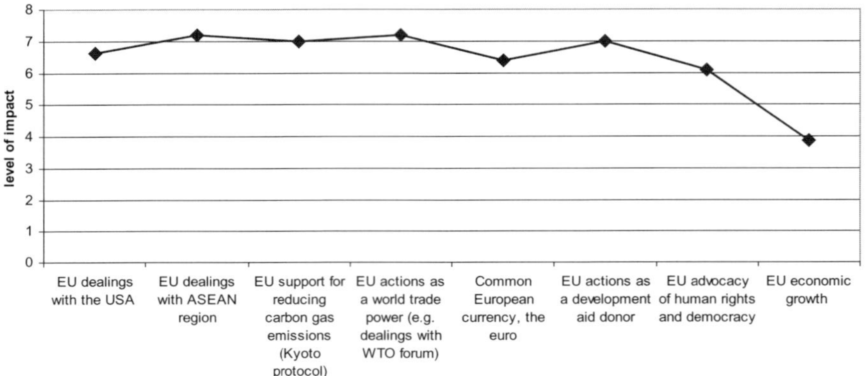

Figure 14:   EU-Indonesian issues impacting on Indonesia

support of Indonesia in the field of environment while implementing Kyoto protocol regulations (Figure 14). When asked to rate the importance of various development actors to Indonesia, the general public ranked the EU second after the UN (ahead of Australia and the USA). It is suggested that the general public recognised the EU's assistance to Aceh (both immediately after the 2004 tsunami disaster and in establishing peace between the Indonesian Government and the Aceh Freedom Movement). The respondents also noted the EU's role in administering aid and financial support, as well as in investments and trade.

When asked about their personal/professional connections with individual EU Member States, the top three countries mentioned by the respondents were the Netherlands (27% of respondents), Germany (18%) and the UK (12%). The Netherlands was arguably the 'No. 1' spot because Indonesian CPO commodity exports are traditionally shipped via Rotterdam, and historically Indonesia was a Dutch colony. 30% of those respondents with contacts in the Netherlands mentioned having friends living there, having family/relatives there (27%), or having travelled there themselves (19%).

When asked to list the three spontaneous images of the EU that came to their minds, the public survey respondents registered stereotypical visions of the EU which reflected its economic integration

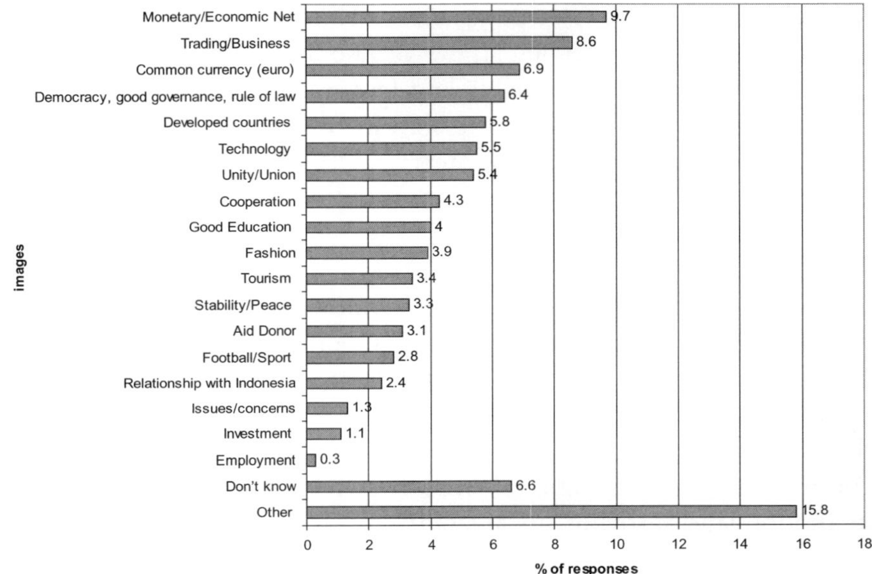

Figure 15:   Spontaneous images of the EU

(including its monetary union) (Figure 15). Unsurprisingly, the relationship between Indonesia and the EU was predominantly seen in an economic light, with priority assigned to trade. Yet, notably, a significant number of respondents did not have any spontaneous images of the EU, possibly indicating a low level of public awareness of the Union.

In terms of age profile, 25–34 year-olds were the most aware (32%) of the EU, followed by those between 34–44 years-old (23%) with only 18% of the youngest cohort of 18–24 year-olds acknowledging an awareness of the EU. It would seem from this that there is only partial public interest in the EU, a distant geographic location from Indonesia. Educationally, respondents who were familiar with the European Union were Junior and Senior High School leavers (3–5 years secondary school at 48%) followed by university-degree graduates (24%) and Primary Education leavers with fewer than 3 years secondary education (11%). In terms of ethnicity, 49% of

Javanese knew of the EU, Batavianese (17%) and Sundanese (10%): for gender, 51% of women knew of the EU, with men at 49%. However, the finding for women and Javanese are partly explained by the fact that they represent the mid-income levels and 3–5 years secondary education of these groups.

CONCLUSIONS

Current relations between the EU and Indonesia have been guided by two consecutive documents — the Country Strategy Papers of 2002–2006 and 2007–2013. The latter document specifically highlighted the need for cooperation between Indonesia and the EU in the fields of good governance, environmental matters, health, social-cultural issues and education. With its key foci on eradicating poverty in Indonesia, improving sustainability in economic growth through trade and investments, and stressing good governance and security through better law enforcement, the current Country Strategic Paper is expected to enhance the dialogue between the two partners and facilitate a more meaningful relationship. This chapter has indicated that the main directions in the interactions between the two partners outlined in the Country Strategic Paper, and the focus on developmental issues and FTA in particular, were reflected in the opinions on the EU as expressed by national stakeholders and the general public. Moreover, the perception that current relations between Indonesia and the EU have been stable and are improving seemed to be confirmed by the results of the study, and was reflected in the news media observed in this research.

Yet, despite this existing awareness of the priorities in the Indonesian-EU dialogue and the stability in the relationship, the EU was not viewed either by the ordinary citizens or national 'elites' as the most important partner for Indonesia. Indeed, the USA, Japan and Asia as a whole were perceived as more important partners. Undoubtedly, the USA's status as a 'superpower', Asian players' geographical proximity (including Japan's generous financial support to Indonesia and the growing economic power of China and India) are important factors that explain why both the 'elite' and pubic respondents did not prioritise the EU.

A more pronounced interaction by the EU with the USA and Japan and an assertion of its position in these dialogues may contribute to the EU's shifting profile in Indonesia. In addition, the ASEM forum offers a powerful potential for raising the EU's presence and recognition in Asia. Finally, a more effective engagement with the Indonesian news media on the ground could be instrumental in disseminating information about the Union among the Indonesian public and lifting the awareness of the EU's actions in local and regional discourses. The EU's message on democracy promotion, law enforcement and market economy has an intrinsic value to Indonesia and arguably deserves better explication.

Chapter 4

Assuming Superpower Status? Evolving Asian Perceptions of the EU as a Political and Economic Actor

Martin Holland[1]

"Here in the United States I hear 'who is Europe, where is Europe? They are looking for China and for India. Europe is increasingly fading away beyond the horizon ..."

Joschka Fischer, 30th March 2007

As the former German Foreign Minister suggests, the EU faces a global relevance challenge. Its unique attributes (consensus, soft-power, rule of law and regionalism) are often difficult for outsiders to interpret or value appropriately: too often these characteristics are seen to imply complexity, ineffectiveness and delay. Only since the turn of the 21st century has Europe begun to ponder quite how it is viewed externally and what the consequences of its international

------

[1] The author would like to acknowledge the research assistance undertaken for this project by the following ESiA colleagues: Dr. Natalia Chaban, Dr. Jessica Bain, Lai Suet Yi, Ma Shaohua, Chung Yoongu, Rachanirom Raveepaopong, Zhang Shuangquan, Yeo-Jung Seo and Eijiro Fukui.

image might be (both for domestic European reasons as well as for influencing international issues). A special issue of the journal *European Foreign Affairs Review* in 2007 underlined the past missed opportunity to investigate "not just why and how the EU behaves differently because of its different configuration..." but "if such a distinctiveness is likely to feed back into the EU's internal and international credibility, and possibly also into the self-identification of the Europeans as a political group".[2] The absence of any empirical evidence upon which to evaluate these ideas was also noted as was the unique exception of the "research team focusing on perceptions in the Asia-Pacific region",[3] members of whom have authored the chapters in this volume.

And yet another recent report has suggested that EU citizens themselves support a stronger, single EU global role. In a poll conducted in June 2007, close to 90% of respondents called for the EU to take on greater responsibility on the world stage.[4] In particular, 84% wanted a greater EU aid contribution to assist development initiatives, 74% called for the EU's trade competences to be better used as a mechanism for influencing third country behaviour and 68% wanted to see higher levels of EU troops committed to international peacekeeping missions. These findings broadly confirmed what has been evident in *Eurobarometre* results over the last decade: European citizens value the EU's global role and are often more progressive than the EU's official intergovernmental position on key international issues by calling for 'more Europe' not less.

This newly discovered interest in the EU's global role among academics and practitioners is welcome, albeit long overdue. The analysis presented in this publication continues to be ground-breaking and complements the limited existing empirical assessment of how the

---

[2] Lucarelli, Sonia, 'The European Union in the Eyes of Others: Towards Filling a Gap in the Literature', *European Foreign Affairs Review*, Vol. 12, No. 3, 2007, pp. 249–270, p. 268.

[3] *Ibid.*, p. 258.

[4] For full details see the German Marshall Fund of the USA publication *TransAtlantic Trends 2007* <http://www.transatlantictrends.org/trends/index.cfm?lang=eng>

EU is perceived in Asia (and should be read in conjunction with the first volume). The individual country chapters in this volume have presented a rich array of empirical data, nuanced and specific to each geographical context, examining how the media represents the European Union and how this is translated into the images and perceptions held by citizens in Asia towards the EU. The aim of this chapter (and the following one by Natalia Chaban) is to highlight some of the broad themes that emerge through a comparative analysis. To what extent did the different Asian societies and media share similar perceptions of the EU? To what extent could regional differences be identified? And, what factors helped differentiate 'Asian' responses? The focus for comparison in this chapter is on two specific frames — the EU seen as a political actor and the EU seen as an economic actor. As the previous chapters have already hinted, the twentieth century belief that the EU was predominantly just a global economic player has to be modified: the EU's twenty-first century political role is increasingly being reported and recognised and while not perhaps a 'giant', Asia no longer disregards the EU for being a political 'dwarf'.

Before turning to the findings, the EU's economic and political development since the Maastricht Treaty needs to be explored in order to provide a relevant contextualisation for interpreting both the media and public perceptions. What, then, was the 'reality' of the European Union's formative years? First, while the European integration process turned fifty on the 25th March 2007, the European Union is a comparatively new construct as it was only legally recognised on 1st November 1993 with the final implementation of the Maastricht Treaty. Less than two decades is perhaps a short period to develop brand awareness, especially where the brand fails to convey a consistent image or gain wide audience appeal.

Maastricht — or to give it its official designation, the Treaty of European Union — did, however, mark substantive changes to Europe's common economic and political competences even to the extent some may argue (and to the horror of the EU's intergovernmentalist Member States) of laying the foundations for a future federal EU construction. The introduction of Economic and

Monetary Union (EMU) including the Euro (building on the success of the Single European Market), the establishment of the Common Foreign and Security Policy (CFSP) and the binding commitment to global development and poverty alleviation in the Treaty's defining Articles all signalled a European ambition that went beyond past rhetoric and facilitated the emergence of a new enhanced EU global role. Matching these ambitions in some areas has been problematic, most notably in executing CFSP in the former-Yugoslavia and in Iraq, but these headline disappointments should not detract from the evident progress and impact the EU has come to exercise in foreign affairs. The EU together with the Member States provides over half of all global development aid and the United Nation's Millennium Development Goals have now been incorporated into the EU's own development policy. The EU has matured from a state of political infancy into a recognised and needed political actor in the post-Soviet world. The fledgling Euro has also confounded the early sceptics and within its first five years has appreciated some 30% against the US dollar and is increasingly used as a foreign reserve currency (especially in Asia and the Middle East). This new phenomenon coupled with the EU retaining its place as the world's largest trader and finally addressing the vagaries of the Common Agricultural Policy for third countries, has consolidated the EU's reputation as an economic powerhouse.

Developments since the turn of the millennium have further enhanced the EU's international significance. First, the introduction of the 'High Representative for CFSP' has considerably raised the EU's external profile and the 'single face' of Javier Solana has almost become emblematic of EU foreign policy. The launch of the European Security and Defence Policy (ESDP) has gone a long way to addressing the soft-power limitations of Europe's previous foreign policy mechanism, European Political Cooperation. The ESDP mandate is to provide for autonomous action in both decision-making and in the means to act and as such appears to be at least a potential competitor with NATO (North Atlantic Treaty Organization). Within the first seven years (2003–9) of operation, some twenty-three ESDP missions have been deployed covering conflict and reconstruction missions as far afield as Aceh, Darfur, the Democratic Republic of Congo, Georgia and the Palestinian Territories.[5] The complementary developments of EU Battlegroups (currently numbering thirteen consisting of 1,500 troops each), a common Defence Agency to enhance interoperability, a European Gendamerie, military policy-making structures, the "2010 Headline Goals" as well as the EU's formal 2008 Security Strategy Paper, have considerably added to the EU's international standing. While still bound by the rule of law, effective multilateralism and a respect for international institutions, the EU of the twenty-first century has developed into a credible international actor, albeit one that rejects unilateralism and seeks consensus and compromise rather than confrontation.

While it would be foolhardy to suggest that in any sense the EU is a military superpower, it can perhaps claim that moniker in terms of its development policy and trading prowess. Whether this new reality is reflected in the media or has penetrated public and elite opinion has been a focus in this volume. In the following section some of the comparative themes that are evident in the nine individual case-studies are highlighted and it is to this data that the chapter now turns.

COMPARATIVE RESULTS

The Media[6]

First, the dataset involving the nine media studies is presented in Table 1 listing the newspapers and television channels monitored in the analysis in this collected volume. The first item in each case is a popular daily with the largest public circulation; the second newspaper listed is the leading business daily; and the third item is an English-language daily printed in each area (largely read by elites);

---

[5] For full details see <www.ISS.Europa.eu>.

[6] All the data presented in this collection is from the ESiA research project. The full datasets can be made available to ASEF partners on request.

Table 1:   The thirty-five news outlets monitored in nine locations[7]

	Popular Daily	Business Daily	English-Language Daily	TV News
2006				
Mainland China	*People's Daily*	*International Finance*	*China Daily*	*CCTV*
Hong Kong SAR	*Oriental Daily*	*Hong Kong Economic Journal*	*South China Morning Post*	*TVB Jade*
Japan	*Yomiuri*	*Nikkei Shimbun*	*Japan Times*	*N/A*
South Korea	*Chosun Daily*	*Maeil Business*	*Korea Herald*	*KBS*
Singapore	*Lianhe Zaobao*	*Straits Times*	*Business Times*	*Channel 8*
Thailand	*Thai Rath*	*The Manager*	*Bangkok Post*	*ITV*
2008				
Indonesia	*Kompas*	*Bisnis Indonesia*	*Jakarta Post*	*TVRI*
The Philippines	*Philippines Daily Inquirer*	*Business World*	*Manila Bulletin*	*GMA 7 24 Oras*
Vietnam	*Youth*	*VNET*	*Vietnam News*	*VTV1*

[7] The project conducted in 2006 covers the period from 1st January to 31st December 2006, with the exception of Japan. The data for Japan only covers the printed media for the period 1st July — 31st December 2006. Besides, the 2006 data from television news excluded the month of January. In 2008, data of all news outlets covers the period between 1st January and 30th June 2008.

Table 2:   Overall distribution of EU news items across 35 media outlets

	TV	Popular	English	Business	Total
2006					
China	131	686	596	564	**1,977**
Hong Kong	13	745	454	952	**2,164**
Japan	n.a.	247	92	493	**832**
Singapore	14	684	1,009	675	**2,382**
S. Korea	30	342	183	387	**942**
Thailand	16	76	610	156	**858**
2008					
Indonesia	50	248	236	154	**688**
Philippines	1	55	126	72	**254**
Vietnam	21	19	159	29	**228**
Total	**276**	**3,102**	**3,465**	**3,482**	**10,325**

and finally, the most popular prime-time news television broadcast in each country is given.

Table 2 presents the overall findings for the twelve months of 2006 across five Asian locations of South Korea, mainland China, SAR Hong Kong, Singapore and Thailand. Data presented here only covers the second half of 2006 for Japan, and for Indonesia, the Philippines and Vietnam the period of analysis was 1 January–30 June 2008. During this period there was a total of 10,325 articles or news reports that mentioned the EU either as a minor factor or major topic. Given this figure represents thirty-five media outlets, the extent of EU coverage appeared remarkably limited overall. The most striking finding is given in column one, television. Less than one item a day involving the EU appeared on all of the eight prime-time news broadcasts.[8] Not only was the EU virtually invisible on the Asian television news, the data where it existed, was dominated by China with 131 news items — more than 60% of the 2006 sample and equivalent to the EU featuring on prime-time Chinese television roughly three times a week. Similarly, in the 2008

---

[8] The sample period for the 2006 prime-time television news broadcasts only covered eleven months — from February to December.

data, near 70% of the EU's appearance on TV news was in Indonesia. Elsewhere on Asian prime-time television the EU was never mentioned more than four times a month! The levels of EU coverage in the popular press were at comparatively similar, if low, levels for mainland China, Hong Kong SAR, Singapore, South Korea, Japan and Indonesia with under an average of two items a day appearing in these most widely read papers — *People's Daily, Oriental Daily, Lienhe Zaobao, Chosun Daily, Yomiuri Shimbun* and *Kompas.* In striking contrast, in three out of five Southeast Asian countries — Thailand, the Philippines and Vietnam — the popular press rarely covered the EU. Consequently, for citizens who rely predominantly on television news and the popular press across Southeast and Northeast Asia, finding information on the EU is generally difficult with a significant number of people likely to have at best just a passing and obscure understanding of the importance of the EU internationally.

If we assume that each county's influential elites are also likely to be high consumers of both English-language and 'business' newspapers, then arguably a more reassuring conclusion may be drawn. However, the overwhelming level of EU reporting in Thailand's English-language *The Bangkok Post* (representing 71% of all EU news in Thailand), *Vietnam News* (responsible for 70% of all EU news in Vietnam) and Philippines' *Manila Bulletin* (accounting for 50% of all EU news in the Philippines) also suggests that such readerships may well be expatriate rather than local in nature. Turning to the 'business' dailies, remarkably, *Nihon Keizai Shimbun* reported 60% of all EU news in Japan (by far the greatest percentage of all EU stories reported for each location), followed by the *Hong Kong Economic Journal* and Korea's *Maeil Business* which account for 44% and 41% of all EU News in each location respectively.

Notably, regional differences are apparent. While the EU was found most often in the 'business' dailies in North East Asia, (except in mainland China), English-language dailies dominated the reportage of the EU in South East Asia, (with Indonesia as an exception). Interestingly, China and Indonesia shared a very similar pattern: relatively high visibility of the EU in popular news media (popular daily and television news) and a lower coverage in the business press.

Overall, the modest level of reporting raises serious issues about the EU's visibility and identity in Asia: if newspapers are still important for conveying international news images (and in technologically advanced societies this may not be the case for much longer), it is hard to be secure in concluding that the EU has an undisputed and transparent presence. Opaque may be a better description. However, if people prefer to access television for international news, the conclusion is even less sanguine with significant public diplomacy implications. Other than in China and Indonesia, the EU was rarely seen on prime-time news. Moreover, press coverage was low in volume (especially in the case of South Korea, Thailand, the Philippines and Vietnam).

The analysis in this chapter considers just two comparative aspects of this wider dataset — the presence of the EU as both a *political* and as an *economic* actor as presented in the media across nine locations. The following chapter focuses on the *social, developmental* and *environmental* nature of the EU's actions. Together, such a focus can provide an initial estimate of the broad public exposure and awareness of the EU among Asian citizens. Table 3 provides the complete dataset from the nine locations and all media outlets. The overwhelming

Table 3:   Overall distribution of frames across all media outlets

	Political (%)	Economic (%)	Social (%)	Environment (%)	Development (%)	Total
2006						
China	38	43	14	2	2	1,977
Hong Kong	25	53	14	7	1	2,164
Japan	43	47	7	2	0	832
Singapore	35	45	14	3	2	2,382
S. Korea	31	48	18	2	1	942
Thailand	39	42	15	2	2	858
2008						
Indonesia	42	46	6	3	2	688
Philippines	28	53	6	9	4	254
Vietnam	53	37	4	5	1	228
Overall	35	46	13	4	2	10,325

description of the EU used in the Asian media surveyed characterised the EU in either economic (46%) or political (35%) terms, with some evidence of a more nuanced EU global role as both a social and environmental reference point. While the economic importance of the EU is hardly surprising, the emergence of the EU as a recognised political actor is an interesting development: the traditional criticism of the EU suffering from an "expectations-capability gap" in its international relations may need to be rethought.[9]

The EU as a Political Actor

As shown in Table 3 depictions of the EU as a political action were commonly found in all of the nine locations, while Vietnam was unique in this being the dominant frame (although these 120 news items were largely reflected through the English-language press as noted above); elsewhere the economic frame was the main focus of EU reporting. Hong Kong SAR recorded the lowest level of political

Table 4:   The EU as a political actor: internal and external frames

Countries	Internal	External	% of External News
China	130	642	83
Hong Kong	157	386	71
Japan	100	261	70[10]
Singapore	205	652	75
S. Korea	65	230	78
Thailand	41	304	87
Indonesia	75	217	72
The Philippines	16	57	78
Vietnam	40	81	66
Total	829	2,830	76

---

[9] Hill, Christopher, 'The Capability-Expectations Gap, or Conceptualizing Europe's International Role', *Journal of Common Market Studies*, Vol. 31, No. 3 (1993), pp. 305–28.

[10] This data has been modified from that used in the chapter on Japan in Volume I which recorded a 68%–32% internal/external split.

news both in absolute terms (538 items) and as a percentage of all EU news stories (25%).

A closer examination of those reports where Europe was presented as a political actor unearths a significant common perspective: around three-quarters of these news items related to an external view of the EU in the world compared with less than one-quarter focused on internal European questions. This emphasis was particularly clear for Thailand and China where 87% and 83% of reports respectively, involving the EU as a political actor were externally focussed.

This similarity found across the different Asian contexts extended to the dominant EU international involvements that were reported. In general, while these topics obviously reflect the international events of 2006 and 2008, it is noteworthy that the EU is now being presented in the Asian media as an international political actor.

In 2006, some 57% all such external political news stories across the region concerned just three EU actions: the EU's intervention in the Iran nuclear issue (654 items), involvement in the Middle-East (excluding Iran; 445 pieces of news) and EU-China relations (296 stories). There was a clear pattern of priority among the media in China, Hong Kong, Singapore and Thailand as illustrated in Table 5. For Singapore, Thailand and China over 25% of their coverage of the EU's external actions were related to items on Iran (with Hong Kong SAR at 24%). For the Middle East, coverage in Singapore (21%) and Thailand (22%) outstripped the others and not surprisingly, EU-China relations were most frequently covered by the Chinese mainland and SAR media (25% and 18% respectively).

South Korea, together with Japan and Thailand to a lesser degree, were exceptions to this topical consensus. Rather than Iran, South Korea's nuclear concerns were understandably focussed much closer to home and the EU's mediation in this issue was the most widely covered story involving EU foreign affairs. These concerns were seemingly shared also by Japan but largely missing elsewhere. Interestingly, EU-China relations were a topic widely ignored by the Korean and Japanese media (just 6 items out of 230 identified in the external political frame in Korea; 7 items out of 261 in Japan). Attention to EU policy towards the Middle East and Iran were the

Table 5:   Ranking of leading external political news items

	No. 1 (n)	No. 2	No. 3
2006			
China	Iran (201.5)	Home (159)	Middle East (107.5)
HKSAR	Iran (92)	China (68)	Middle East (42)
Japan	Iran (65)	Middle East (54)	North Korea (15)
S. Korea	North Korea (38.5)	Middle East (36)	Iran (34.5)
Singapore	Iran (184.5)	Middle East (138)	China (55)
Thailand	Iran (77.5)	Middle East (67)	Sri Lanka (17)
Leading topics	**Iran (655)**	**Middle East (444.5)**	**China (296)**
2008			
Indonesia	Kosovo/Serbia (57)	Middle East (29)	Home (28)
Philippines	Kosovo/Serbia (13)	Home (10)	Iran (5)
Vietnam	Home (16)	Kosovo/Serbia (12.5)	US (10.5)
Leading topics	**Kosovo/Serbia (82.5)**	**Home (54)**	**Middle East (31.5)**

second and third most commonly cited news topic in South Korea. In addition, the Thai media chose to look at EU's monitor mission in Sri Lanka. But overwhelmingly, the EU's external political action is clearly located in Middle East in the eyes of Asian media.

The 2008 landscape is quite different from that of 2006. In all three cases the EU's involvement in the Kosovo/Serbia conflict was prominent, followed by each of the three countries' concerns regarding their own political relations with the EU rather than elsewhere in the world. This focus of the EU's political actorness 'at home' was rarely found in the six locations in the 2006 data. Coverage of EU external action in the Middle East was minimal in the Vietnamese news media, which was more interested in EU-US relations. On the other hand, Indonesia did focus attention on the EU-Middle East stories, especially the Israel-Palestine conflicts. In the Philippines, the Iranian nuclear issue received more attention than any other issue.

Remarkably, three themes stood out among the various political stories reported in the nine Asian locations: the EU as a key negotiating party in the Iranian nuclear issues; EU-Russian relations; and

EU-US relations. These were found in all nine locations monitored. Furthermore, the EU's political involvement in ASEAN (Association of Southeast Asian Nations), China, Georgia, Middle East, Montenegro and NATO were all reported by eight out of nine locations (EU-ASEAN relations was absent in South Korea; Sino-EU relations and EU-Middle East stories were absent in Vietnamese news; EU's involvement in Georgia was ignored in Thailand; EU-Montenegro relations was not found in the Philippines; and the EU's participation in NATO was neglected in Indonesia).

Turning to the smaller of the two political frames — those stories internal to the EU itself — the leading theme common to the nine locations was EU enlargement (which represented one-in-five of the 829 intra-EU political news items analysed). There were two distinct groups camouflaged by this average figure: over one-third of the internal EU political news items in Singapore were about enlargement; coverage of this issue in Hong Kong SAR, mainland China and Japan, was more than one-in-five. And when the Asian media reported on enlargement, the focus was not on the 2004 process, or on Romania, Bulgaria and Croatia, but generally about Turkey!

Additionally, the 2006 and 2008 data witnessed the process of the failed Treaty of European Constitution 'transformed' into the Lisbon Treaty, with 9% of the total EU-internal political news. Singapore, Indonesia and Vietnam gave relatively high attention to the Constitution/Lisbon Treaty and often placed this in relation to the new ASEAN Charter.

In support of the media emphasis of the EU as a political actor in other parts of the world, it was not surprising (albeit a relief to those still trying to construct a single EU international personality) that in all regions the dominant political face of the EU was Javier Solana, the High Representative for CFSP. Among 3,590 political-framed news items, Solana was featured in 390, much more frequently than the 'runner up', President of the European Commission José Manuel Barroso (120 news items). Turning to institutions, the Commission was the most visible representative, with 304 pieces of news referring to it. However, the EU Council presidency was rarely featured.

More positively, the press is now comfortable in using the acronym EU without any explanation that this refers to the 'European Union', putting Europe on par with the commonly accepted substitution of 'USA' for the United States of America, for example. This may sound like a trivial point, but the fact that the term 'EU' has been accepted as a self-explicit acronym is indicative of a wide-spread public awareness. No longer is the EU confused with either trade unions or insurance unions! Interestingly too, in the media the term EU3 (France, UK and Germany) is often taken as synonymous with speaking for the EU (a reflection perhaps of the 2006–8 interaction with Iran, where it was the EU3, not the EU Council presidency Troika that led).

However, this potentially reassuring response to Henry Kissinger's now 37 year-old question "who speaks for Europe?" has to be somewhat moderated by the continuing presence of key Member States (the EU3) within news reports about the EU's international political character.[11] While theoretically it might be sustainable to argue that this Janus quality to the EU's international image is an accurate reflection of institutional and treaty realities, it does nothing to clarify or promote the EU as a single actor in the eyes of the Asian media.

The EU as an Economic Actor

While the emergence of the EU as a global political actor in the Asian media is a welcome sign of multidimensionality in EU news reporting, as noted already, traditional perceptions have not waned totally, with the EU still presented as primarily an economic actor in almost half (47% in 2006; 45% in 2008) of all EU news reports in the monitored Asian media. Table 3 provided the geographical breakdown revealing comparatively modest variations. While Hong Kong and the

---

[11] The much cited reference to Henry Kissinger's complaint about foreign policy under the European Political Cooperation procedure of the early 1970s remains a useful shorthand for criticising the EU's multiple personalities in external political relations.

Philippines (both 53%) had the highest volume of EU economic stories, last placed Vietnam still had a high level of coverage (37%) of the EU as an economic player in its EU news items. This general preoccupation with the EU as a mercantilist entity matches the trading realities for all our analysed locations. At worst, the EU was a country's fourth most important trade partner (Indonesia and Philippines) and at best first (China) for both imports and exports. To what extent, then, does the Asian media reflect these general trends in its coverage of the EU?

First, an obvious but important observation: in each of the individual media studies (television, popular, English-language and business press), the business press recorded the highest volume of EU items with an economic focus. While this was most dramatically the case for Singapore and for China, the average for all six business papers monitored in 2006 was a remarkably high level of 66%. In the 2008 data, EU economic news accounted for 77% of the volume of the three business dailies. Here the regional similarity ends, however: in five cases the English-language press are in second place (*China Daily*, *The Japan Times*, *Korean Herald*, *Bangkok Post*, *and Business World*), in Hong Kong it is the popular newspaper *Oriental Daily*, whereas television was the second most important source of EU economic news stories in Singapore (albeit based on a particularly small number of news bulletins). In Indonesia, the EU was featured as an economic actor in about 40% of the news in both *Bisnis Indonesia* and *Jakarta Post*.

Within the dataset two separate economic themes are clearly apparent: the EU as a trading partner and the EU in relation to business and finance (see Table 6 for details). These two topics combined accounted for over two-thirds of all news stories on the EU as an economic actor (over 80% in Hong Kong SAR and Japan; over 70% in mainland China and Singapore; over 65% in the Philippines and Vietnam; over 60% in South Korea and Thailand; 56% in Indonesia). Under the heading of *trade*, the issues discussed in relation to the EU covered bilateral trading issues, the WTO Doha Round, anti-dumping duties, Free Trade Areas and trade protection. For example, in Thailand the majority of all *Thai Rath* stories (the most widely read

Table 6:   The EU as an economic actor — the most visible themes

	Trade (%)	Business/ Finance (%)	Industry (%)	State of Economy (%)	Agriculture (%)
China	50	23	20	5	2
Hong Kong	33	50	3	12	2
Japan	29	51	14	4	1
Singapore	37	35	15	8	1
S. Korea	37	24	14	22	0
Thailand	42	19	23	8	7
Indonesia	26	31	24	15	5
Philippines	31	35	11	11	10
Vietnam	38	27	11	18	5

Thai popular daily paper) that framed Europe as an economic actor dealt with trade restrictions or anti-dumping measures that the European Union had imposed on Thai exports.

News reports on the Euro, European interest rates, merger regulation and competition rules, foreign direct investment and taxation predominated in the *business and finance* category. Within these topics there was a diversity of positive stories (trade surpluses, strong economy, economic cooperation) and negative ones (trade restrictions, lack of progress at Doha, energy crises, problems with the European economy) presented. From a European perspective what is quite remarkable is the striking disinterest in the EU's Common Agricultural Policy (CAP), a topic which has historically been something of a media favourite (critically) within the European media. Even in the Philippines and Thailand which have experienced agricultural disputes with the EU, this subject only accounted for 10% and 7% of the coverage of the EU as an economic player respectively. In contrast to consistent *Eurobarometre* findings on European attitudes, for Asia, the CAP seems no longer newsworthy.

Notably, in mainland China, Thailand and Indonesia, *industry* was the third most frequent sub-frame in the EU's economic reportage. These stories included the EU's action in various industry sectors, including plans to diversify energy production and rules on aviation industry inside the EU. In South Korea and Vietnam, the *state of economy* and depictions of how strong/weak the economies of the member states were, was the third most visible economic EU story.

The face of Europe in economic affairs was less clear-cut than that for the political arena where Mr. Solana — representing the Council — dominated. The media used both the Governor of the European Central Bank (ECB), Jean-Claude Trichet, and the former Commissioner for Trade, Peter Mandelson, to symbolise the EU as an economic entity (and thereby extended the institutional complexity and opaqueness of the EU). In total, Trichet was cited in 306 news items among the 4,807 pieces of economic-framed EU news, while Mandelson was mentioned in 292 news items. Turning to the supra-national institutions, remarkably, both the ECB and EC were featured in 1,027 pieces of news, a number much higher than the third most visible institution in economic reporting (the European Parliament mentioned in only 79 news items). The profile given to the ECB was particularly high in Hong Kong's media, which alone accounted for 501 Central Bank citations.

Consequently, both the ECB and DG Trade were the leading institutional bodies mentioned in these news reports, with the more usual addition of the European Parliament appearing through its Community budget oversight responsibilities. The terms 'euro' and 'euro-zone' were regularly used to complement EU brand awareness. However, once again these common EU symbols were in conflict with the ever-present Member State presence: just as was found in the analysis of the political frame, France, the UK and Germany were frequently used to moderate the EU's collective economic message.

The use of metaphors within the economic frame revealed different categories being used. Examples covered metaphors from the natural world, from transport and of movement. However, the most prevalent metaphor related to the human body, actions and emotions. The EU was typically described as either in "sickness", "death" or paradoxically in "revival"; emotionally the EU was often seen to be disappointed, worrying or even in grief, although images of "pleasure" and "optimism" were also to be found. But in the area of human action metaphors, the dominant language was less ambivalent: in such metaphors the EU was general described as "at war", "under pressure", "challenged", "tension" with the process of economic and monetary integration viewed as a "game" and a "gamble". Metaphors do matter when individuals are interpreting complex messages, but their appealing simplifications may deceive as well as illuminate.

To summarise, the media in the Asian region surveyed — the eight television prime-time news broadcasts, the twenty-seven press (popular, business and English-language newspapers) — published or broadcast 10,325 EU news items over the whole year in 2006 and half year in 2008 demonstrating that coverage of the EU is unquestionably modest. Where the EU was reported, it predominantly described Europe as an economic global power and as an external political actor elsewhere in the world and not as necessarily locally relevant to bilateral issues in the region. While the television and press marginally favoured describing the EU in economic terms, the comparative closeness of the findings for two frames (politics and economics) was striking and demonstrated that the EU is no longer presented as a monolithic bloc but its different roles are beginning to become effectively differentiated by the media. The EU's economic prowess is still recognised, but this is now balanced by recognition of an active emerging political international role, even when that role is with a third country elsewhere. Against these common themes regional differentiations were also evident with mainland China the most noteworthy case given its distinctive coverage of the EU on the television media.

So, if the EU is largely peripheral in the media is that necessarily problematic? There are certainly risks that can be associated with inaccurate or inappropriate perceptions generated through the media. The data suggest that there is a potential expectations deficit: if the EU is not given prominence and its role in the region is under-reported, reduced expectations of Europe's involvement may be an inevitable consequence. A self-fulfilling logic — lower demands leading to reduced media interest leading to lower demands — could ensue. Given that the EU is a significant economic partner for all the regions covered in this research and has growing political and security relationships, misperceptions based on media choices pose significant policy challenges, such as a possible undervaluing of the EU-ASEAN/ASEM[12] relationship and an over-valuing of say EU-MERCUSOR or EU-India relations.[13] Any such downgrading runs the risk of missed opportunities for both the EU and Asia. While under-reported, the positive development unearthed by the findings is the emerging perception of an EU that is more economically and politically balanced: Europe's image is no longer just that of Fortress Europe; rather the EU as an international, hopefully benign, international actor is being observed and reported more often and more accurately. Provided that this media trend continues (and the EU's global role continues to expand) new opportunities for matching Asian needs and objectives with what the EU might be in a position to provide are possible.

So what then do the citizens of China, Japan, SAR Hong Kong, Singapore, South Korea, Thailand, Indonesia, the Philippines and Vietnam think about the EU? Does the low level of EU coverage distort perceptions? How is the EU seen through the eyes of Asians — if seen at all?

---

[12] The Asia-Europe Meeting (ASEM) is an informal process of dialogue and cooperation. It brings together Austria, Belgium, Brunei, Bulgaria, Cambodia, China, Cyprus, Czech Republic, Denmark, Estonia, Finland, France, Germany, Greece, Hungary, India, Indonesia, Ireland, Italy, Japan, Laos, Latvia, Lithuania, Luxembourg, Malaysia, Malta, Mongolia, Myanmar, The Netherlands, Pakistan, The Philippines, Poland, Portugal, Romania, Singapore, Slovakia, Slovenia, South Korea, Spain, Sweden, Thailand, United Kingdom, Vietnam, the ASEAN Secretariat and the European Commission. See: <http://aseminfoboard.org>.

[13] The ASEM process seems to have been largely ignored by the Asian media: over the whole year of 2006, across six locations in Asia, there were only 205 ASEM stories identified in the survey's media outlets. This figure was boosted somewhat after the holding of the ASEM 6 Summit in Helsinki September 2006 (see Chapter 6 by Suet Yi Lai and Natalia Chaban in this volume).

Public Opinion[14]

Cultural assumptions — especially those imported from Europe — are to be avoided when assessing public opinion: civil society, the ideal "civic culture"[15] and democratic expectations taken for granted in Europe do not necessarily travel well. Indeed, the very notion of 'public opinion' is a Western invention based around an informed, literate and globalised citizenship presumed to be an essential democratic attribute. In newly industrialised societies, democratic values are recent transplants and literacy levels while rising are still incomplete. Importantly, individuals in such Asian societies often tend to identify more strongly with their local identity and political context than with the State let alone the external world. From the Berlaymont Building on Rue de Loi in Brussels the EU may appear a Colossus striding the world: in Hanoi, Bangkok or Shanghai public opinion might be more concerned with events closer to home. Consequently, participants were asked to give an indication of how often they accessed international news and their preferred media. Before examining these findings a methodological note is necessary: the relatively small sample size (total $n = 3,605$) means that the survey results need to be interpreted only as indicative of general trends and certainly no direct causality between media effects and public opinion are being drawn.

Bearing in mind that respondents in six out of nine countries participated in the survey online (with Indonesia, Vietnam and the Philippines as an exception) and therefore would have an unimpaired technological access to foreign news, the results were quite surprising. In none of these six countries did half of the respondents access international news on a daily basis; when "daily" and "several times a week" were combined into a composite score then at least over 70% of surveyed mainland Chinese, South Koreans, Thais and those from Hong Kong achieved a reasonably regular level of awareness of

---

[14] The surveys ($n = 400$) used stratified online panels in China, Japan, SAR Hong Kong, Singapore, South Korea, Thailand; telephone interviews in the Philippines and Vietnam; and face-to-face interviews were conducted in Indonesia) conducted in November 2006 and November 2008. See the Introduction for further details.

[15] Almond, Gabriel Abraham and Sidney Verba, *The Civic Culture*, Boston: Little Brown, 1965.

Table 7:   Regularity of accessing foreign news (% of respondents)

	Daily	Several Days a Week	Combined ("regular")	Once a Week	Rarely/ Never
China	46	38	84	9	8
Hong Kong	43	29	72	14	14
Japan	31	36	67	11	22
Singapore	46	22	68	12	20
S. Korea	33	40	73	13	13
Thailand	45	31	76	9	15

Table 8:   Preferred media for accessing foreign news (% of respondents)

	TV News	Newspapers	Internet	TV Programmes	Radio
2006					
China	98	97	82	40	31
Hong Kong	99	98	49	31	29
Japan	95	78	48	28	7
Singapore	98	98	59	27	24
S. Korea	98	92	55	35	18
Thailand	95	93	69	20	9
2008					
Indonesia	53	39	13	32	8
Philippines	62	35	30	26	19
Vietnam	90	62	22	26	4

foreign news. Conversely, 22% of our Japanese sample and 20% of those from Singapore admitted to virtually never accessing foreign news!

The preferred news medium for accessing international news at least confirmed the methodological assumptions underpinning this research: namely that television news and newspapers remain the primary sources for individuals to learn about foreign affairs. A minimum of 95% of respondents across the surveys conducted in 2006 listed prime-time television news, with the exception of Japan where the figure fell to 78%. The data do reveal two unexpected findings: first, the continuing relative importance of radio for foreign news delivery (used by around one-in-four respondents in China, Hong Kong and Singapore); second, the growing use of the internet. These figures, however, may well over-represent this phenomenon given that the survey in six locations was itself conducted online through the internet and may therefore have biased the sample on this specific variable. Importantly, the three survey results from 2008, differed markedly from those of 2006. In both Indonesia and Philippines, the usage of TV news and press to access foreign news was low compared with other locations; whereas in Vietnam, TV news was much more popular as a source of foreign news than newspapers. Nor did radio seem to be a preferred media for foreign news for Indonesians and Vietnamese. The reliance on internet was significantly lower in the three Southeast Asian countries.

Turning to the perceptions of the EU held by the sample, an estimation of the actual importance of the EU to each country was investigated. As noted above, the EU is among the top three economic partners for seven of our selected areas, the fourth most important to Indonesia and the Philippines. Table 9 provides the summation of perceptions of the EU's comparative bilateral importance. Remarkably, only respondents in China had an accurate perception of the importance of the EU to their own country, with the Japanese, Singaporeans and

Table 9:   Perceptions of the most important foreign partners: now and in the future

	Current Perception 1st Place	EU Rank	In Future 1st Place	EU Rank
2006				
China	USA	2nd	EU	1st
Hong Kong	China	4th	China	4th
Japan	USA	6th	**China**	**4th**
Singapore	China	6th	China	**4th**
S. Korea	USA	4th	**China**	4th
Thailand	China	5th	China	4th
2008				
Indonesia	USA	7th	USA	5th
Philippines	USA	5th	USA	2nd
Vietnam	China	4th	China	5th

Indonesians undervaluing the role of the EU the most dramatically (the first two placed the EU as only the sixth most important partner, while Indonesians placed the EU as the seventh). A possible explanation here is the comparatively high profile of the EU on *CCTV1* influencing perceptions (as well as China's official pro-EU policy). When current and future primary partners were investigated, Indonesia and the Philippines were the exceptional cases: for Jakarta and Manila, the importance of the USA remained constant (ranked first now and in the future); in contrast, while mainland Chinese respondents also considered the USA China's most important current partner, America was replaced by the EU in the future scenario. For all other locations in the survey, the growing importance of China was clearly visible in the respondent's perception and expectations.

Putting the accuracy of the respondent's ranking of the EU to one side, when asked what were the most important issues to be kept in mind in bilateral official relations with the EU there was clear priority given to economic issues in the majority of areas with over 70% of Thai respondents, around 60% of respondents in South Korea, Indonesia and Vietnam identifying this as the priority with over one-third ranking trade similarly highly in China, Hong Kong, Singapore and the Philippines (Figure 1). Once again, the odd-man-out was

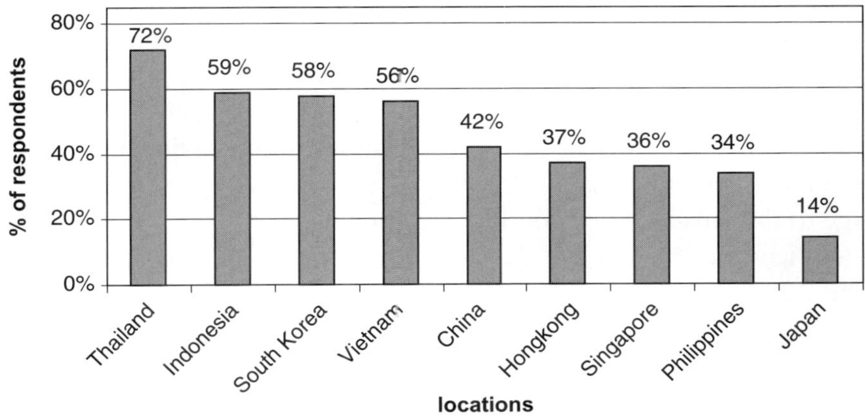

Figure 1:   Most important issues to be kept in mind when developing policy with the EU — economic issues

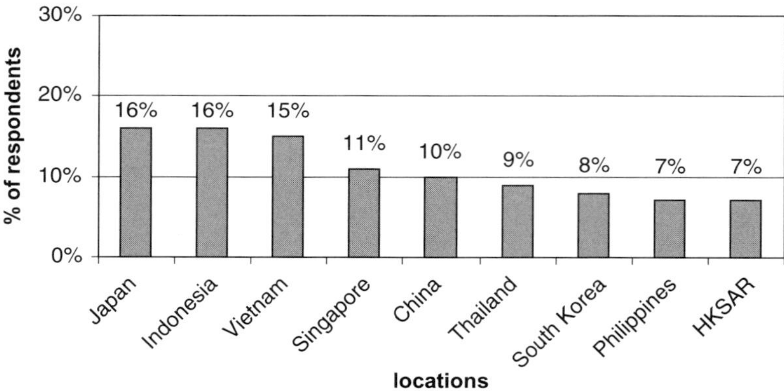

Figure 2:   Most important issues to be kept in mind when developing policy with the EU — political issues

Japan with just one-in-seven regarding trade as Japan's priority with the EU.

This exceptionalism, or at least the inverse finding, is further underlined in Figure 2: the Japanese respondents demonstrated comparatively more interest in political issues. In contrast, for all other locations, the EU relationship was clearly apolitical. Furthermore, culture and religious issues concerned many of the Japanese respondents, with more than 10% of respondents (the same in Singapore) mentioning 'culture/religion', while respondents elsewhere paid little or no attention to such issues when thinking about their country's relations with the EU. Interestingly, one in every four Japanese respondents brought up Japan-US relationship when talking about Japan-EU relations, often noting that Japan should be mindful when dealing with the EU so as to prevent any damage to the Japan-US relationship, for example.

Views on the EU as a developmental aid donor only appeared in the 2008 surveys. For these three developing Southeast Asia countries, the EU's development assistance did receive recognition from 10% of respondents. Issues that are given priority by the EU such as environmental protection and human rights promotion, received scant attention, registering score of only 3% and 4% respectively across the nine regions. Although skewed by a small response rate, human rights was the second most significant area in the mind of the Filipino when dealing with the EU (with 12% of respondents emphasized such importance).

Irrespective of this perceptions and reality mismatch, an average of 87% of all survey respondents thought that their country's relationship with the EU was positive (either "improving" or "steady"). Within this overall similarity there were some antagonistic trends displayed: in Japan (again) just 11% and in Hong Kong 14% described the relationship with the EU as "improving". In Vietnam, 77% of respondents chose "improving" while 15% said "steady". In the three of the Southeast Asian countries, the Philippines, Indonesia and Thailand, 14%, 8% and 7% respectively stated that bilateral ties were worsening reflecting the agricultural trade and aviation embargoes imposed by the EU. This negative view was less than 2% on average in the other six locations.

The measure of public perceptions that produced arguably the most interesting and distinctive comparative findings related to the mental images respondents had to the notion or concept "the European Union". In sum, four clear themes emerged (three positive towards the EU, one negative) when respondents were asked "When thinking about the European Union, what three images spring to mind..." As shown in Table 10, the common currency, the euro, has clearly stamped its identity on Asian citizens as the leading symbol representing the EU (only in the Philippines' case was it is not among the first four most frequently mentioned images). It is, in a sense, the "face" of a single Europe. While no doubt the architects of Economic and Monetary Union will rejoice in this now wide-spread recognition of the euro, as an accurate image of the EU27 it is both confusing as well as indicative of a powerful cognitive impact. At the time of the survey in 2006, the euro-zone consisted of just twelve of the then twenty-five Member States (although the Maastricht Treaty does make future participation obligatory for all members other than those with a 1992 negotiated "opt-out" clause). Thus the symbol of the collective EU27 in reality only represented around half of the Member States. The power of this image, though, was significant and it was the most commonly cited 'EU image' in China, Hong Kong

Table 10:   Spontaneous images of the EU

	1st	2nd	3rd	4th
China	Euro	Enlargement/internal	Union/integration	Trade
Hong Kong	Euro	Trade	Union/integration	Individual countries
Japan	Euro	Union/Integration	Individual countries	Disparities/unfairness
Singapore	Union/integration	Euro	Economic power	Individual countries
S. Korea	Union/integration	Euro	Individual countries	Exceptionalism/ problems
Thailand	Individual countries	Economic power	Trade	Euro
Indonesia	Monetary/Economic Union	Trade/Business	Euro	Democracy, good governance, rule of law
Philippines	Union/integration	Monetary Union	Development Aid donor	Employment
Vietnam	Union/integration	Monetary/Economic Union	Euro	Democracy, good governance, rule of law

and Japan, and the second most in South Korea and Singapore: only in Thailand was mention of the euro comparatively rare. The euro has undoubtedly helped to raise the profile of the EU and shape a benign international perception.

The second theme to emerge was also economic in nature: the role of the EU as a commercial power. This perspective was most evident in Thailand where "economic power" and "trade" were frequently used images, and even more so in Indonesia where "monetary/economic union" and "trade/business" were the first and the second most recognized images. However, it is interesting to note the weaker association with Europe's economic prowess compared with the dominance of the euro image and to underline that the old image of "Fortress Europe" was rarely in evidence.

A third image that emerged suggested a positive political perspective. Other than in Thailand and Indonesia, the values and virtues of the process of European integration — be that preventing war, creating multiculturalism or enhanced prosperity — were among the top three most cited EU images (and in the Philippines, Vietnam, Singapore and Korea this was the dominant image articulated). It is both insightful as well as sobering to reflect on this Asian perception of the contribution made by the integration process especially if one were to contrast this with the more stereo-type *Eurobarometre* Member State findings that too often emphasise the negative impact of the EU rather than extol its original ambitions and successes. It would appear that the EU looks much more successful and worthwhile from afar than it does from within. In addition in the 2008 data the EU's image as a "promoter of democracy, good governance, and the rule of law" or as a "development aid donor" surfaced. The EU's 'developmental face' was restricted to these three Southeast Asia countries, however.

The final theme draws us back to the split personality of the EU and the enduring impact of the nation state. In five locations (Hong Kong SAR, Japan, Singapore, South Korea and Thailand), respondents also conceptualised the image of the EU through individual countries with this mediating lens most pronounced in Thailand. If we combine Thailand's three other economic-based images to this perspective, it would appear that Bangkok has the more pragmatic view of the EU and the least idealistic one

Looking at all nine locations, however, perhaps, this combination of an awareness of "common" EU images as well as recognition of Europe as a conglomerate of individual countries is a realistic and balanced assessment of the current nature of European integration. Encouragingly, however, the positive common themes were more pronounced than those images that emphasised European diversity over unity.

The Elites

Generalisations are harder to delineate from the eight[16] different stakeholder studies partly because the information was collected through face-to-face interviews that leant themselves to discursive comments and a wider utilisation of open-ended responses in contrast to the more structured online public opinion surveys. In addition, the size (a total of 236 interviews) and the selected nature of the sample only permits broad conclusions to be suggested given the local diversity of the political/government, media, business and civil society elites questioned.[17] The findings from the public opinion surveys as well as the focus on economic and political issues in the media would suggest that it is these issues — rather than social or environmental concerns — that would dominate across all of the selected Asian elite representatives. To what extent was this the case?

Distinguishing between the EU as an international economic presence and its global political role produced some clear patterns

---

[16] At the time of writing, the data of Indonesian elite interviews was not available.

[17] Thirty-two interviews across the four elite sectors were conducted in each of three locations (Japan, Singapore and the mainland China); thirty-three interviews conducted in Vietnam; thirty-one interviews were done in both Hong Kong SAR and the Philippines; twenty-seven were completed in S. Korea but only eighteen in Thailand. The Thai figure was a consequence of the political turmoil created by the military coup during which period the interviews were to be conducted. Cumulatively, sixty-two political elite interviews were conducted, sixty-one media interviews while fifty-eight civil society and fifty-five business sector interviews were completed.

across our selected elites. In terms of Europe's trade and economic relations, an Asian elite consensus was clear. Significant majorities of the Singaporean, South Korean, Japanese, Vietnamese, mainland Chinese and Hong Kong elite samples referred to the EU as a great economic power. In terms of bilateral priorities China's business, civil, media and political elite were adamant that economic relations overshadowed all else: the topics cited were familiar — the ongoing arms ban, anti-dumping and the value of the Yuan. On average, over 70% of interviewees agreed with the view that the EU constituted an economic "great power".

In contrast to this common view, Asian stakeholder perspectives of Europe's international relations were more nuanced. In Hong Kong, the new political authority of the EU was embraced by under one-quarter of those sampled, while in Singapore it was only the interviewed political elite who were sympathetic to this emerging international EU role. The data on Japan gives the most sophisticated interpretation: three-quarters of their elite affirmed that the EU played an international leadership role while distinguishing between the EU as a strong normative power with some diplomatic influence, yet with constrained military capacity. The emphasis of the EU's normative power was uniquely found in Japan, with sixteen out of the thirty-two elites articulating this. This may be explained by the fact that Japan also sees itself as a normative actor, so places special emphasis on such aspects.

In general, however, when the issue of military capability and effective involvement in international relations was raised, the EU compared poorly, especially when matched against the USA. For the Hong Kong elite, "EU economic power is strongly endorsed while its political and military powers are questioned"; Singapore's elite insisted that the EU "lacks political power" and "is too diverse to be a military power" with the EU seen at best as a "broker" rather than a leader; for Koreans, the EU "is a great power in terms of economy, diplomacy, and norms but that is not the case in political and military terms"; and in China the EU was perceived "to be a significant source of power and influence, but not necessarily as a leader in the global political arena. In this regard, the EU might be considered just one great power among many in the multi-polar world".[18] According to one Filipino, the EU "is mainly an economic power, sometimes normative, whereas in political field, it lacks unity and the US is still up there"; while for a Vietnamese interviewee the EU "has an important voice un the world politics, but not yet a leader, one reason is its internal divergence".[19]

Following on from the consensus on the EU's economic profile within Asia, the elite findings on the EU's regional importance were all broadly similar and presented an overall perspective that saw the EU as one of many players impacting on their society (China, Russia, Japan and the USA were also mentioned), with South Korea evaluating the relationship with the EU the lowest comparatively (3.3 at present and 3.8 in future on a five-point scale). In assessments of the long-term relevance of the EU, encouragingly, the rating of the future importance is higher than of the present in all targeted locations. However, the degree of 'improvement' varied. In Hong Kong and Japan, the elites saw the EU modestly growing in importance (from 3.6 to 3.8 in the former and from 4.0 to 4.2 in the later) with the EU's future role most highly ranked by government and civil society in Hong Kong and by civil society elites in Japan. However, the perceived economic dominance in the EU relationship was also criticised by Hong Kong elites who wanted greater cooperation and exchanges in areas beside economics. Although the EU looks destined to remain an important player in Japan's vision of their future interests, there was a paradoxical elite belief that while the major future issues related to economic and environmental concerns, these concerns were generally couched within mutually ambivalent disinterest.

Conversely, Singapore's elite were primarily focused around prospects for an EU free trade agreement (FTA). As a result, the significance of the EU rose from 3.5 to 3.9. Vietnam shared the

---

[18] Quotations taken from the individual country chapters in the previous volume of this publication: Holland, Martin, Peter Ryan, Alojzy Nowak and Natalia Chaban (eds.), *The EU through the Eyes of Asia*. Singapore/Warsaw: ASEF/University of Warsaw, 2007.

[19] Quotations extracted from the 2008 data.

same figures with Singapore. Interestingly, while China's elites were less 'starry-eyed' about the future importance of the EU to China than the public survey, the EU was clearly identified as an important long-term relationship. Further, all Chinese elite sectors saw this importance increasing in the future to very high levels not found in any other elite survey (ranging between 4.2 and 4.6 on a five-point scale). The position of South Korean elites was towards the extreme end of the multi-polar perspective and reflected the peninsula's geo-strategic context, very low level of past engagement balanced against the on-going EU FTA discussions. The EU's potential as a mediator with North Korea was cited as a unique aspect of the importance of Europe among South Korea's elite. Like their counterparts, Korean elites also saw the EU relationship moderately strengthening in the future (from 3.3 to 3.8). The Thai figures were slightly higher than that of Korea, 3.4 at present and 3.9 in the future. The highest increase was found in the Philippines (3.5 to 4.1).

Turning from the level of generality to specificity, a common element across the elite interviews concerned Europe's public diplomacy and communication strategies. In a majority of locations, the role of the European Commission Delegation Office was assessed as widely unknown outside trade circles, a theme also found in other studies of the EU's external representation in the region.[20] Asian elites remain fixated on national European embassies or Chambers of Commerce as the better points of contact. The commentary on Japan best describe the general analysis within the region: no Japanese elites "could envision, or indeed currently had, beneficial contact with the EU body. The business elites were even less constructive in their responses, as many of them had never heard of the Delegation, and those that had could see little scope for constructive interaction between their organisations and the Delegation".[21]

---

[20] Chaban, Natalia, Serena Kelly, Jessica Bain, 'European Commission Delegations and EU Public Policy: Stakeholders' Perceptions from the Asia-Pacific', *European Foreign Affairs Review*, Vol. 14, No. 2, 2009, pp. 271–288.

[21] See Chapter 6 in this volume for a fuller discussion of this perspective.

The elites were also asked to comment on two specific EU topics: the Euro and the impact of EU enlargement. The Euro was generally viewed as a significant international currency, although a large proportion still regarded the US$ as the stronger and preferred international currency. This was especially the case in Hong Kong (48% of respondents agreed) as its currency, Hong Kong dollar, is pegged to the US dollar, and to a lesser degree in mainland China, South Korea and Singapore (39%, 36% and 29% respectively). While there was some diversity across the elite sectors in China, the overall view was again supportive of the euro's international role and prospects. Surprisingly, in the Philippines, a traditional ally of the US, all except two respondents viewed the euro more positively when comparing it with the US dollar. According to them, the euro was not only of higher value, it was more stable than the US dollar as the economy in the EU was healthy and huge. The Vietnamese case was the most extreme: while 42% of the respondents viewed the US dollar as the most popular and universal international currency in the world, 38% disagreed and argued that the euro was stronger and more stable than the dollar and hence better.

Remarkably, Chinese (both the mainland and Hong Kong) and Thai elites were virtual unanimous in their belief that EU enlargement did not present any significant risks to their economies, even if the consequences of Eastern enlargement were seen very much as a two-edged sword both in political and economic terms. Elites in Japan, South Korea, Singapore, the Philippines and Vietnam were perhaps more realistic in perceiving competitiveness risks as well as potential economic openings through enlargement. Interestingly, some elites from the Philippines and Vietnam mentioned concern over potentially losing developmental aid from the EU — an issue that was not found elsewhere. Given the major economic impact that both these issues potentially have — reforming the current international currency status quo and enhancing the EU's position as the leading global trader — the phlegmatic approach of Asia's elite was surprising. It will be interesting to revisit these perceptions after a decade when some of the longer-term ramifications may have become more apparent.

To conclude this comparative overview of elite perceptions, the elites were asked the same question as that given in the public survey: what images come to mind when you think of the EU? The Chinese and Hong Kong elites paralleled to a degree their public's perceptions by listing the euro and the example of positive integration as key mental reference points. In addition, there were also strong images related to the EU's economic prowess across all countries. In all locations except Thailand, the image of 'unity, integration or grouping up different countries' was another common answer. Moreover, Korea conformed to the dominance of the euro, while those in Singapore, the Philippines and Vietnam departed from this otherwise pervasive image of the euro found elsewhere (as well as differed from Singaporean and Vietnamese public opinions in this respect). Another similarity among these three ASEAN countries was the emphasis on the EU's cultural richness. Uniquely in Hong Kong, the EU flag was also mentioned (adding an interesting addendum to the controversial axing of this symbol from the revised Lisbon Reform Treaty).

The profile of elite opinion is in parts compatible with the public opinion findings, and in parts distinct. Broadly, the elites appear less enamoured with the EU's political persona and more focused on economic realities. As such their opinions are to some extent inconsistent with the news media projection of the EU as a balanced political and economic power. But as acknowledged earlier in this chapter, the qualitative nature of these elite perceptions while rich, are not quantitatively significant and should be treated as highlighted themes rather than empirical proofs. Taken in conjunction with the media and public opinion evidence, cumulatively the comparative analyses presented here paint a compelling portrait of how Asia perceives and interprets the European Union in economic and political terms. While these are the dominant frames in all nine studies, the broader analysis has also indicated that the EU is increasing being viewed as a more diverse and multi-faceted actor and it is this wider theme that the following chapter address in its analysis of Europe's image as a social, environmental and developmental actor.

Chapter 5

'Soft Power' and a 'Human Face': Images of the EU as a Social, Environmental and Developmental Actor in the Asian Media and Public Discourses

Natalia Chaban[1]

INTRODUCTION

In the eyes of the world, the phenomenon of European integration, marked by the existence of the European Union (EU) for more than 50 years, is frequently associated with economic might, financial virility and trading power. Increasingly though, the EU is presenting itself to the global community as an assertive and forceful international political actor.[2] For some scholars, such new appearances in the EU's

---

[1] The author would like to acknowledge the research assistance undertaken for this project by the following ESiA colleagues: Dr. Jessica Bain, Lai Suet Yi, Ma Shaohua, Chung Yoongu, Rachanirom Raveepaopong, Zhang Shuangquan, Yeo-Jung Seo and Eijiro Fukui.

[2] For examples, EU security and peace-keeping operations around the globe (the Balkans, Congo, Aceh (Indonesia), establishments of an anti-piracy agency to fight international pirates, and development of anti-terrorist strategies.

international profile indicate that "the EU is morphing from a regional *Zivilmacht* into a more fully fledged global superpower ... shift[ing] its identity from soft power to hard power".[3] This vision assumes that the EU's 'soft' power — i.e., "the ability to get what you want through attraction rather than coercion or payments"[4] — is already recognised around the globe. Testing that assumption, this chapter attempts to explore three facets of the EU's alleged 'soft' power profile — the EU as a vociferous social affairs advocate, an environmental 'champion' and a leading global developmental actor. In particular, the study explores how these three EU international roles are perceived outside the Union's borders.

Utilising a comparative approach, this chapter contrasts social, environmental and developmental images of the EU in Indonesia, Vietnam and the Philippines (researched in 2008) with the respective imagery in the six other Asian locations of Japan, South Korea, mainland China, Hong Kong SAR, Singapore and Thailand (all studied in 2006 using identical methodology). Given the tremendous diversity within Asia as a region, the number of Asian locations studied in this chapter is a relatively small sample size from which to make 'region-scale' conclusions. Nevertheless, these nine locations provide a significant number of unique results for comparison, justifying the size of the sample.

It was also assumed that the international media plays a key role in informing the international general public and foreign elites on the evolution of the EU. With the EU being a relatively new and complex polity to understand, representations of the Union as an actor in the social, environmental and developmental spheres (acting both inside and outside the EU) were hypothesised to have the potential to raise the EU's profile around the world due to the obvious appeal of 'human interest' topics.

---

[3] van Hamm, Peter, 'Place Branding: The State of the Art', *The ANNALS of the AAPSS* "Public Diplomacy in a Chaning World" (eds. Geoffrey Cowan and Nicholas Cull), Vol. 616, No. 1, 2008, pp. 126–149, p. 139.

[4] Nye, Joseph, *Soft Power: The Means to Success in World Politics*, New York: PublicAffairs, 2004, 256.

The chapter begins with an overview of the EU's links to the nine Asian locations in the social, environmental and developmental spheres, positioning this inquiry within an account of the EU's actions in the three policy areas. The study then analyses the depiction of the Union as a social, environmental and developmental actor in the Asian news media (in reputable press and primetime television news bulletins), comparing these portrayals with the leading perceptions of the EU amongst ordinary citizens in the selected North and South East Asian locations. The chapter concludes with a discussion on the visibility and content of the EU's 'soft power' imagery in Asian public and media discourses, positioning the findings within the debate on the EU's international identity.

EU–ASIA DIALOGUE: SOCIAL, ENVIRONMENTAL AND DEVELOPMENTAL ASPECTS

The EU's dialogue with Asia encompasses three principal geo-political directions — its relations with East, South East and South Asia. Four of the locations in the sample of this study belong to the East Asian sub-region: Japan, South Korea (hereafter referred to as Korea), mainland China (hereafter referred to as China) and Hong Kong SAR (hereafter referred to as Hong Kong); and five to South-East Asia (Singapore, Thailand, Vietnam, Indonesia and the Philippines).[5] It is suggested that past colonial links as well as current economic and political ties guide both the discourses of EU–Asia interactions and the modern-day imagery of the EU in Asian societies.

The legacy of European colonialism inevitably influences Asian visions of the EU (including its social, environmental and developmental practices). Japan and Korea were never colonised by Europeans and both featured prolonged periods of isolation from any foreign influence, including the European one. After World War II, both nations embarked on close and extensive relations with the USA, an interaction which has overshadowed the European

---

[5] The first South Asian country in the ESiA study — India — has entered the project only in 2009.

presence in terms of politics, the economy and even popular culture in both countries ever since. In contrast, China was extensively exposed to European influences from the Middle Ages through trading contacts. Since its coastal cities were once under European colonial rule (more specifically, British, German and French) while the mainland remained mostly unaffected by the European presence, China is sometimes called a former "semi-colony".[6] Two city-state economies in the group under study, Hong Kong and Singapore, were under British colonial rule, and thus the European influence pervaded everyday life in these two states. The three South East Asian nations of Vietnam, Indonesia and the Philippines have been extensively exposed to colonial European authority in the past with French, Portuguese/Dutch/British and Spanish colonisation respectively. In contrast, Thailand is a special case in the history of Europe's presence in South East Asia. It was never colonised, but was significantly influenced by two European powers ruling in neighbouring territories, namely, the British (who colonised Myanmar/Burma) and the French (who colonised Laos, Vietnam and Cambodia).

It is apparent that, throughout the Asian region, European colonial legacies can still be traced in "administrative and national boundaries, transport networks, parliamentary institutions, language and literature, science and technology and even sports and popular culture".[7] A consideration of European colonial legacies is regarded as crucial for any 'EU perception' studies in Asia. Insights into these legacies might explain the apparent contradictions in modern views on Europe. On the one hand, historic memories of Europe as an oppressor and antagonistic authority feed current anti-European, Euro-sceptic and nationalistic sentiments in Asia. On the other hand, Europe's influence in exposing Asian nations to different cultures,

---

[6] Bridges, Brian, *Europe and the Challenge of the Asia Pacific Change, Continuity and Crisis.* Cheltenham, UK, Northampton, MA, USA: Edward Elgar, 1999.

[7] Copland, Ian, *The Burden of Empire: Perspective on Imperialism and Colonialism*, Melbourne: Oxford University Press, 1990, pp. 196–198, as cited in Brian Bridges, *Europe and the Challenge of the Asia Pacific*, p. 17.

technologies, and styles of governance are still appreciated and valued. Undeniably, these ambiguous sentiments affect the social, environmental and developmental image of the EU; a Union which nowadays has become synonymous with 'Europe'.

While 'hard' politics is a relatively recent addition to the EU–Asia communication, it has entered the agenda on a variety of levels (multilateral, regional, bilateral, etc.) and is focused on diverse issues (peacekeeping missions, anti-terrorism strategies, anti-nuclear proliferation negotiations, etc.). However, economic rather than political themes typically dominate the ongoing interactions between Asia and Europe. Economically, while the EU27 is one of Asia's largest trading and investing partners and a major source of tourists in the region, Europe is increasingly aware of the importance of the Asian region's own economic powerhouses (especially in the context of the global financial crisis). The North East Asian locations in our sample include two of the EU's key trading partners, with Japan and South Korea being two OECD countries in the sample and China being the fastest growing economy in the world. The South East Asian economies in this study are, in contrast, relatively insignificant on the European trade 'radar' (Indonesia, the Philippines and Vietnam are among the least economically developed locations in our sample). Yet, despite some obvious disparities in their economic profiles, all nine Asian locations are sometimes seen to belong to a "conveyor belt of dynamic Asian economies",[8] representing several waves in Asia's economic boom.

The impressive economic progress in the selected locations has resulted in steadily increasing standards of living for their citizens. Arguably, there is growing interest among the Asian region's general public in European social and environmental practices and standards, which are sometimes considered only possible for the developed and wealthy. It is suggested that with the establishment of economic prosperity in Asia, 'rich' Europe and the EU will be transformed from a remote point of reference in Asian social and environmental

---

[8] Brian Bridges, *Europe and the Challenge of the Asia Pacific*, p. 49.

discourses to a reality that people in Asia can relate to. Growing wealth in the region also affects the popular vision of the effectiveness and rationales of the EU's developmental efforts in the region.

While political and economic interactions between the EU and Asia have always been the centre of practitioners' and scholars' attention, the social, environmental and developmental concerns in the dialogue have remained secondary and relatively peripheral. Yet, the three key areas where the EU exercises most of its influence in its interaction with Asia are human rights, developmental aid and environmental protection. The following sections highlight the peculiarities of the EU's dealings with the region in these three spheres, situating the inquiry within the broader EU context.

Social Contexts

The EU's achievements in the field of social affairs are among the major successes of the European integration project and are recognised globally. Indeed, EU citizens enjoy some of the world's highest living and social standards (including social and health benefits); the freedom to move freely within a borderless Europe; the realistic prospect of employment and economic stability due to the creation of a single market; and the guarantees of justice and security based on common values of democracy, the rule of law and respect for human rights, freedom and equality.[9] The European Commission (EC) and, specifically, the Directorate-General for Employment, Social Affairs and Equal Opportunities cites its mission in the social field as "the development of a modern, innovative and sustainable European Social Model with more and better jobs in an inclusive society based on equal opportunities"[10] in order "to make Europe the world's most competitive and dynamic knowledge-based economy, capable of

---

[9] Steponavičious, Gintaras, 'What the EU Must do to Silence its Human Rights Critics', *Europe's World* 5, 2007, pp. 139–141.

[10] European Commission, *Directorate General for Employment, Social Affairs and Equal Opportunities*, <http://ec.europa.eu/dgs/employment_social/index_en.htm>, accessed 12 September 2007.

sustainable economic growth, with more and better jobs and greater social cohesion."[11]

Predictably, the EU's internal social policies and practices have attracted intense international interest and its initiatives are considered either as successful examples to follow or provocative issues triggering national debates outside the EU's borders. Consider, for example, the EU's push to abolish the death penalty, the pan-European debate about the issue of *Invocatio Dei* in the much-debated Constitutional Treaty, the European stance on sexual rights and gender equality, the on-going modernisation of the EU's labour relations, the pending reform of immigration regulations and attempts to counter discrimination. In addition to its internal actions, the Union's external social roles, such as an international human rights advocate and a leading development aid conor, are also the subject of critical global attention.

In the EU's interface with Asia, one of the most sensitive 'social affairs' areas is human rights. Traditionally seen as an internal affair, the issue of human rights can become fraught when external interferences occur. In our sample, human rights issues are more prominent on the Sino–European political agenda, as well as in the EU's dialogue with ASEAN. According to Bridges,[12] a current dialogue on human rights between the EU and China, for example, is led by the so-called "quiet diplomacy" approach of encouraging China to respect human rights norms. The latter ASEAN case specifically relates to Myanmar (Burma) and the situation in East Timor. The EU's interactions with ASEAN (of which Vietnam, Thailand, Indonesia and the Philippines are members) on this issue are particularly sensitive, taking into account a conflict between the:

> so-called 'Asian' view, with its emphasis on the 'community' and socio-economic development and social cohesion as the first priorities, in conflict with the 'Western' view, advocated by both the United States and Western Europe, which focuses on individual rights and liberal democracy.[13]

---

[11] *Ibid.*

[12] Brian Bridges, *Europe and the Challenge of the Asia Pacific*, p. 108.

[13] *Ibid.*, 169

Environmental Contexts

The EU's strategic environmental vision for the future has been formulated using the assumption that "economic, social and environment policies are closely integrated":[14]

> Protecting the environment is essential for the quality of life of current and future generations. The challenge is to combine this with continuing economic growth in a way which is sustainable over the long term. European Union environment policy is based on the belief that high environmental standards stimulate innovation and business opportunities.[15]

Facing the grave threat that human activities pose to the global environment, the EU has developed a set of policies and legislations, implemented numerous measures, supported innovative research and raised awareness of environmental problems among its citizens. These diverse measures include, among others, protecting nature, wildlife and bio-diversity on the European peninsula; combating the effects of pollution and hazardous substances; controlling food safety and genetically-modified organisms; managing natural resources and tackling waste; supporting the efforts of industry and business in environmental protection; and funding environmental care.[16] The most recent scientific evidence of climate change with its numerous human, environmental and economic impacts is also seriously considered by the EU.

Unsurprisingly, this vast spectrum of EU activities serves as a collection of reference points and examples to follow for many international actors. In particular, the EU's approach towards tackling climate change and reducing greenhouse gas emissions is closely scrutinised around the world. The combined push of the EU27 for shared

---

[14] European Union, *Activities of the European Union: Environment*, <http://europa.eu/pol/env/index_en.htm>, accessed 12 September 2007.

[15] *Ibid.*

[16] European Commission, 'Choices for a Greener Future: The European Union and the Environment', *DG for Press and Communication*, 2002, <http://ec.europa.eu/publications/booklets/move/32/txt_en.pdf>, accessed 19 September 2007.

international actions to curb emissions and meet the targets of the Kyoto Protocol has reverberated globally, eliciting a wide range of reactions — from positive support to critical rejection. Arguably, these ambivalent attitudes towards the EU's environmental policies and measures illustrate the role of the Union as one of the most important and decisive actors in the current environmental debate.

In the case of the nine Asian locations in this study, their rapid economic progress in the second half of the 20th century has resulted not only in positive developments, such as an increase in the standards of living and national wealth growth, but also, regretfully, in numerous negative consequences for the environment, such as industrialisation, the extensive use of natural resources, urbanisation and an increase in population. These developments have not escaped the attention of European environmental activists, whose ecological advocacy in the late 1980s and early 1990s caused some tension and conflict between Europe and Asia.[17] Bridges suggests that a constructive modern-day dialogue between the EU and the nine Asian locations has been facilitated by an improved official dialogue (e.g., the EU's Joint Declarations with Japan in 1991), by re-visiting development aid packages (e.g., introducing support for related environment projects, such as saving the ASEAN region's rain forests or environmental protection programmes in the Philippines), and by joining efforts in a multinational treaty framework to deal with global warming and climate change.[18] All locations in the study are signatories of the Kyoto Protocol to the UN Framework Convention on Climate Change, as is the EU.

Even though each location in the study has its own unique set of environmental problems (e.g., air pollution in Hong Kong, aggressive urbanisation in Japan, and the deforestation of the rainforests in tropical ASEAN countries[19]), their signatures on the Kyoto Protocol mean that the nine locations are aligned and communicating with the EU

---

[17] *Ibid.*, p. 179.

[18] *Ibid.*, pp. 179–180.

[19] Food and Agriculture Organization of the U.N., 'The State of the World's Forests', 2003.

in an unprecedented network of international goodwill to save the planet.

Developmental Contexts

The emphasis on development is one of the strongest in the EU's self-defined international identity — the European Commission (EC) stated that "development is at the heart of the EU's external action, along with its foreign, security and trade policies".[20] The EU's interpretation of its role as a global leader in development includes its contribution to the eradication of poverty while promoting a set of ideals, namely, "respect for human rights, fundamental freedoms, peace, democracy, good governance, and gender equality, the rule of law, solidarity and justice".[21] The endorsement of these ideals by the EU's developing partners is recognised as a key condition for the EU's assistance in the developmental field. Unsurprisingly, a succession of EC aid agreements with developing countries — the Yaoundé Convention (1969–1975), the Lomé Convention (1975–1999) and the current Cotonou Agreement (2000–2020) — have increasingly stressed the conditionality principle. However, these agreements framed the EU's developmental engagement only with the African, Caribbean and Pacific regions. In contrast, Asian locations were excluded from those agreements and are dealt with on a individual basis, either coming in the form of the Generalized System of Preferences (GSPs) or in the form of EU Official Development Aid (ODA) to develop targeted sectors or programmes. In the developmental field, five out of our nine Asian locations are recipients of EU developmental aid — China and four ASEAN countries: Thailand, Indonesia, the Philippines and Vietnam. Significantly, the aid agenda carried out by the EU and its individual Members States is often politicised in the ASEAN cases,[22] and attempts to conditionally offer

---

[20] <http://ec.europa.eu/development/policiesgen_en.cfm>.

[21] *Ibid.*

[22] Brian Bridges, *Europe and the Challenge of the Asia Pacific*, p. 150.

aid have been "strongly resented and resisted by the Asian Pacific governments, especially by China and key ASEAN members".[23]

Developmental projects targeting China began in the mid-1980s and featured various projects of technical and financial assistance, while still emphasising economic cooperation — human resources, economic and social reform, business and industrial reform, and the environment.[24] In Thailand, Indonesia, Vietnam and the Philippines, a significant amount of the EU's development aid comes in the form of GSPs, a programme designed to promote economic growth in the developing world by providing preferential duty-free entry for targeted products. In addition, these ASEAN countries also get EU ODA packages which aim *to* "eradicate poverty and help enhance human development".[25] While the EU responds to the needs of partner countries in the region, according to the EC the general list of sectors targeted by EU ODA in the ASEAN countries includes education, health, population, water and sanitation, governance and civil society, programme assistance, economic infrastructure and services, and debt and emergency assistance.[26] Among the four, Vietnam is the largest recipient of the EU ODA — in 2007, "the total EU pledge was €719.9 million".[27] In Indonesia, ODA from all EU donors in 2006 was US$335.5 million. In the same year, Thailand received US$149.86 million and the Philippines US$93.64 million.[28] The largest of all EU donors in Indonesia is the EC, while France leads in Thailand and Vietnam, with Germany in the Philippines.[29]

In summary, the EU–Asia dialogue is increasingly inclusive of social, environmental and developmental themes. Arguably, it is a

---

[23] *Ibid.*, p. 170.

[24] An interview with a European Commission official, June 1996, as cited in Brian Bridges, *Europe and the Challenge of the Asia Pacific*, 100.

[25] ECD to Vietnam, <http://www.delvnm.ec.europa.eu/news/vn_news/vn_news10.htm>.

[26] EU Donor Atlas 2008, < http://development.donoratlas.eu/>.

[27] ECD to Vietnam.

[28] EU Donor Atlas 2008.

[29] EU Donor Atlas 2008.

reflection of the new international 'appeal' of the EU in the three areas. Relevant research claims that EU external efforts in the areas of social justice, human rights, developmental aid and environment protection have sought an international reputation as a 'soft', 'normative' power, able to exert global influence without 'hard' political means.[30] Yet, the question remains as to whether these official and scholarly visions of the EU correspond to the popular external images of the Union among the general public and in reputable mass media in Asia. Addressing the lack of comprehensive accounts of the EU's external image, the next section systematically surveys images of the EU created and disseminated by the Asian news media discourses and compares them to the public perception of the EU (assumed to be partially influenced by the mass media).

FINDINGS: MEDIA ANALYSIS

This project studied news media in Japan, Korea, Thailand, China, Hong Kong and Singapore in 2006; and Vietnam, Indonesia and the Philippines in 2008. Both years were marked by a prominent event in the EU–Asia dialogue — the biannual ASEM meeting.[31] It was assumed that Asian media and public attention to the EU would be heightened due to this major summit occurring. To enter the sample, a news story had to reference the 'European Union/EU', its institutions (European Commission, European Parliament, European Central Bank or European Court of Justice), and/or 'ASEM' at least once, even briefly. As discussed in the Introduction to this volume, in each location, the study monitored three types of daily papers (a reputable paper with the highest circulation, a business paper and an English-language newspaper) and one prime-time television news bulletin.[32]

---

[30] Parag Khanna, "The Metrosexual Superpower", *Foreign Policy*, July/August, (2004), 67.

[31] The ASEM6 was held in Helsinki in 2006 and ASEM7 was held in Beijing in 2008.

[32] Press outlets in Korea, China, Hong Kong SAR, Thailand and Singapore were monitored for 12 months in 2006. Television news bulletins in these locations were

The overall project sample constituted 10,436 news items referencing the EU, its institutions and/or ASEM[33] (out of those, 10,153 articles were located in the leading newspapers and 283 items were found on the prime-time television news). Despite predictable differences in the presentation of EU news content, the 27 reputable newspapers and eight national television broadcasts monitored in this study presented a common specific vision of the EU in the field of social, environmental and developmental affairs. The analysis of this shared imagery of the EU produces some rather disconcerting results, discussed in detail in the following sections.

Low Profile in the News Media

Across the nine locations, the EU's actions in social affairs were reported in 1,358 news items (or 13% of the total sample), EU environmental matters were profiled in 399 articles (almost 4% of the total sample), and EU developmental issues were represented in 166 items (1.6% of the total sample) (Figure 1). In contrast, reportage of the EU's economic actions was found in 4,790 news items (46% of the sample) followed by the coverage of EU political affairs in 3,723 articles (35.6% of the sample).[34] Evidently and somewhat predictably, the portrayal of the EU in Asian media extensively featured familiar images of the EU as an economic 'giant'. It is interesting too, that the media also presented an increasingly prominent profile of the EU as a political actor. Arguably, this depiction could indicate a reflection of the shifting external perception of the EU, namely from an inward-oriented civil authority to an internationally visible 'powerhouse'.

---

monitored between February–December 2006. The Japanese sample included six months of press monitoring (July–January 2006) and no television data. News outlets from Vietnam, Indonesia and the Philippines were monitored for six months in 2008 (January–June).

[33] Sample of 10,325 news items mentioned by Martin Holland in Chapter 4 referred only to the news items that referenced the European Union/EU (and its institutions and officials), and did not include the ASEM-focused articles.

[34] The imagery of the EU as a political and economic actor are studied in a greater detail in the Chapter by Martin Holland in this volume

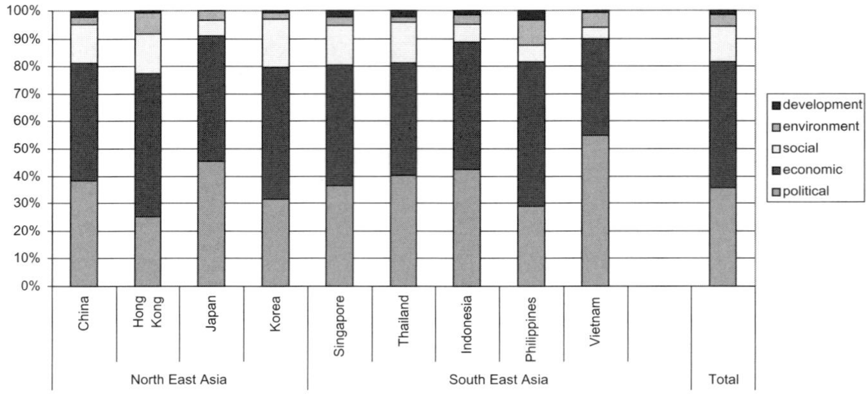

Figure 1:   Distribution of the frames in the total EU/ASEM coverage across nine locations

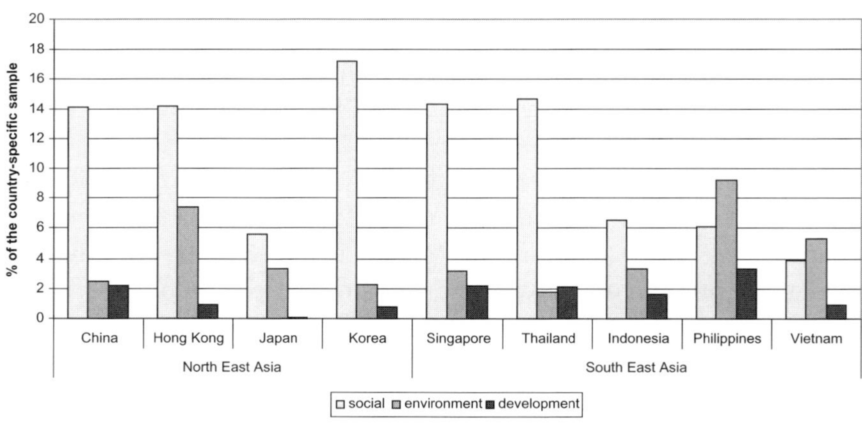

Figure 2:   Proportional distribution of social, environment and developmental themes

Comparing the proportional distribution of social, environment and developmental themes in the EU coverage for each location (Figure 2), EU *social affairs* led the reportage in all but two locations (in the Philippines and Vietnam more attention was given to the EU's environmental matters) (Figure 2). In Korea, Thailand, Singapore,

Hong Kong and China, the *social affairs* themes surfaced in more than 10% of the media sample (17.2%, 14.7%, 14.3%, 14.2% and 14.1% respectively). In the other locations (including the three South East Asian locations which are the focus of this volume), the proportional coverage of EU social affairs was under 10% (7.1% in the Japanese sample, 6.6% in the Indonesian, 6.1% in the Philippines and 3.9% in the Vietnamese). The EU *environmental* coverage constituted more than 5% of the total EU/ASEM sample in three localities — the Philippines (9.2% of all collected news), Hong Kong (7.4%) and Vietnam (5.3%). In the other six locations, media attention to the EU's environmental actions was minimal with a meagre 3.3% in Japan and Indonesia, 3.2% in Singapore, 2.5% in China, 2.3% in Korea, and 1.8% in Thailand. The average coverage of *developmental* issues across the nine locations was a tiny 1.5%. The Philippines was the only example in which the share of EU developmental news was slightly higher than 3%. The Thai, Singaporean and Chinese media each devoted 2.2% of their coverage to the EU's developmental actions. Only 1.6% of the Indonesian sample profiled developmental actions while the Hong Kong, Vietnamese and Korean samples each dedicated a only 0.9% to EU developmental news. Japan's media attention to EU developmental actions was miniscule (0.1% of the country-specific sample).

When analysing an actor's visibility in news media, it is important to assess both the proportional distribution of its frames and the actual volume of news production. In absolute numbers, the print media was found to be more detailed and consistent in presenting the Union as an actor in social, environmental and developmental spheres. In contrast, these themes were practically invisible in the prime-time television news coverage — out of 1,923 news items referencing the three themes across the nine locations, only 67 appeared on television prime-time bulletins and almost half of those came from China's *CCTV* channel (33 articles). Most of the television news on China's leading channel (20 items) presented the EU as a social affairs actor, focusing on various aspects of EU initiatives in healthcare and social legislation. All development-themed news on *CCTV* (7 items over 12 months) presented the EU as a developmental actor assisting third countries (e.g., Palestine or Indonesia) but not China itself. The Chinese TV environmental news (6 items over one year of monitoring) focused on reporting EU policies targeting the reduction of green gas emissions. Korea's *KBS TV* had the second largest coverage with 12 news items over 12 months, 11 of which represented the EU as a social affairs actor and one which reported the EU's aid to Palestine. The Indonesian *TVRI* produced 10 items over six months — six of them profiled the EU's social affairs actions (more specifically when addressing anti-Islamic sentiment in Europe and dealing with migration to the EU), two covered EU aid to Palestine, and two reported the EU's policies on climate change and carbon emission reductions.

The other locations had a very small number of EU social, developmental and environmental news stories. Over 12 months of monitoring, there were only five items on Hong Kong's *TVB*, four on Singapore's *Channel 8*, and two on Thailand's *ITV*; over six months of observation, there was only one news item on Vietnam's *VTV1*. The Philippines' TV channel did not produce a single item covering any of the three themes over six months. As with the 'leaders' in EU television coverage described above, the most prominent profile of the EU was again in *social affairs*, reporting the already familiar themes of the EU's healthcare initiatives, social legislation and European attitudes towards Islam (all discussed in greater detail in the next section). In contrast, the developmental and environmental angles were neglected. The Singaporean, Thai and Korean prime-time news bulletins had no coverage of the EU's *environmental* actions, and Hong Kong's *TVB* and Vietnam's *VTV1* had only one such item each (both focusing on the EU's general environmental policy direction). The EU's *developmental* actions did not enter the television prime-time news agenda in Hong Kong, Vietnam or Thailand while Korea's *KBS* and Singapore's *Channel 8* produced only one piece of such news each (focusing on the EU's aid to Palestine and Indonesia, respectively).

The fact that the EU's actions in the social, environmental and developmental fields were virtually invisible on television prime news is significant As described in the 'Methodology' chapter, all of the television channels chosen for this study have nation-wide reach and boast the highest viewership numbers in each location, thus serving as one of the main providers of current political information for citizens. Moreover, as discussed in previous chapters, television news remains the public's main source of international information, in general, and EU news in particular.

While the number of EU news items in the press was higher than those on television, the study revealed a very low press coverage of the three fields in question. Comparing the volume of news production in the press, this study contrasted a monthly average per print outlet in the nine locations (Table 1). Assessing a larger regional picture across the three frames and three chosen papers in each location, the Hong Kong press produced the highest monthly average of stories about the EU's social, environmental and developmental news. The Singaporean and Chinese press followed. In contrast, the three countries which are the focus of this volume — Indonesia, the Philippines and Vietnam — profiled an extremely low volume of the news in question.

Somewhat predictably, the 'popular' and 'English-language' dailies (papers which most often prioritise 'human interest' stories) had a tendency to publish more EU *social affairs* news on average than their 'business' counterparts. This was observed in China, Singapore, Thailand, Indonesia, the Philippines and Vietnam, Yet, breaking from this trend, Japan's business paper *Nihon Keizai Shimbun* had the greatest coverage of the EU's social news in that location, and Hong Kong's *Economic Journal*, Korea's *Maeil Business* and Thailand's *The Manager* had the second greatest coverage of the social developments of the EU after their country's 'popular' papers.

In the *environmental* frame, Hong Kong's three papers were the obvious leaders among the nine locations. Two Singaporean papers and one Philippine daily also had a relatively high monthly average in comparison to other locations. In Japan, the 'business' daily was the leader. This positioning of the news was expected from the onset of the study — the EU's environmental projects and policies could be seen as having an immediate financial impact on the localities in

Table 1:   Monthly average of news items in the three print outlets in each location

	Social Affairs Frame			Environment Frame			Development Frame			
	Popular	Business	English	Popular	Business	English	Popular	Business	English	Total
China	8.6*	4.9	8.6	1.8	0.4	1.4	1.3	0.6	0.9	28.5
Hong Kong	9.8	8.2	7.6	4.5	4.6	4.3	0.8	0.2	0.8	40.8
Japan	2.8	4.3	0.8	1.2	3.3	0.2	0.2	0	0.2	13
Korea	6.2	4.7	1.8	0.7	1.1	0.1	0.4	0.2	0.2	15.4
Singapore	9.8	3.3	7.2	2.3	1.6	2.6	3	0.2	3.2	33.2
Thailand	1.5	1.8	7.4	0.3	0	1.1	0.3	0	2	14.4
Indonesia	4.2	0.5	1.8	0.8	0.3	1.8	1.2	0	0.3	10.9
The Philippines	1	0.2	1.5	0.3	1	2.5	0.3	0	0.8	7.6
Vietnam	0	0	1.3	0	0.3	1.5	0	0	0.3	3.4

* Darker background marks outlets with higher monthly volume of news.

question. Yet, contrary to our expectations, the 'English-language' papers in all six South East Asian locations led the coverage of the EU's environmental actions. Considering that their audience is comprised of local elites and educated youths proficient in English as well as expatriates (with the exception of Singapore and the Philippines where English is one of the official national languages), the appeal of the EU's environmental news appears to remain very limited to the general audiences of this sub-region.

Coverage of the EU's *developmental affairs* was concentrated mainly in 'popular' and 'English-language' papers (presumably due to the 'human interest' angle stressed by these types of media outlets). 'Business' papers in Japan, Thailand, Indonesia, the Philippines and Vietnam did not devote a single item to this topic in EU reportage. While Japan is not an EU ODA recipient, the four other locations are and the absence of this type of coverage in their 'business' papers is significant — the newsmakers in these outlets did not communicate the immediate connection between the economic development of their locations and the EU's ODA. The Singaporean press was the only media in the study that paid a more pronounced degree of attention to the EU as a developmental actor.

In addition to the low levels of coverage, the representation of the EU as a social, environmental and developmental actor, both in the press and on television, was minor (see Figures 3, 4 and 5). The EU's relevant actions in the nine Asian locations were predominantly reported from a *minor* perspective, meaning that the EU was referenced in a news item only briefly.

In the *social affairs* frame (Figure 3), the news media in China and the Philippines assigned the EU's representation a slightly higher intensity than did the media outlets in the other locations (the share of the news that profiled the EU as a main focus was proportionally higher in these two instances). Also, the two locations with the highest volume of EU social affairs coverage — Hong Kong and Singapore — featured a very high share of news that reported these EU actions from a minor perspective. This peculiar pattern is believed to be counterproductive to the visibility of the EU as a social actor. It is also worth noting that the Indonesian media had the fewest minor

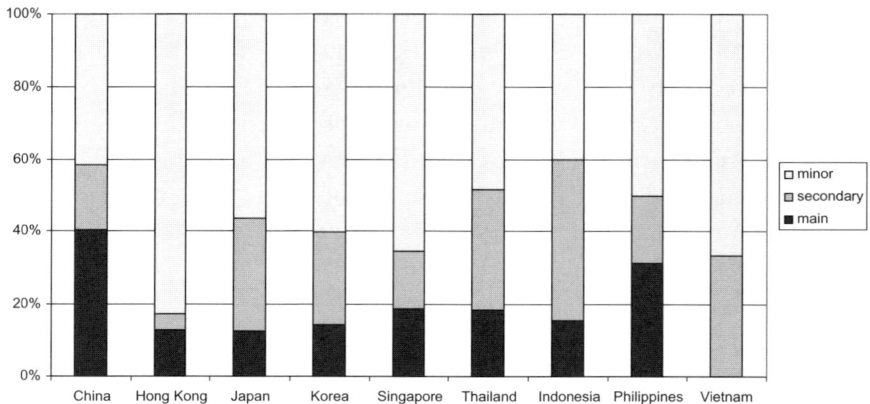

Figure 3:   Distribution of degree of centrality in the social affairs frame

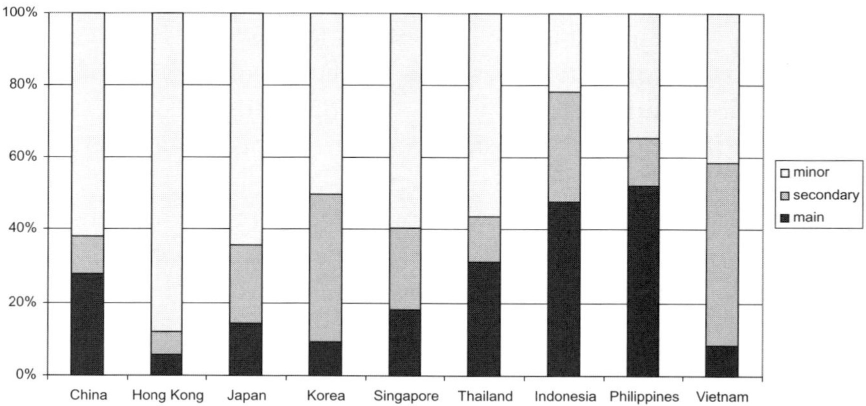

Figure 4:   Distribution of degree of centrality in the environmental frame

representations of the EU, possibly indicating that local newsmakers saw the EU as a major actor in the social field. Indeed, in the Indonesian media's framing of the EU's social affairs, the Union was more prominently positioned as a secondary actor (acting on a par with other national or international actors). In contrast, the Vietnamese print and television coverage of the EU as a social actor

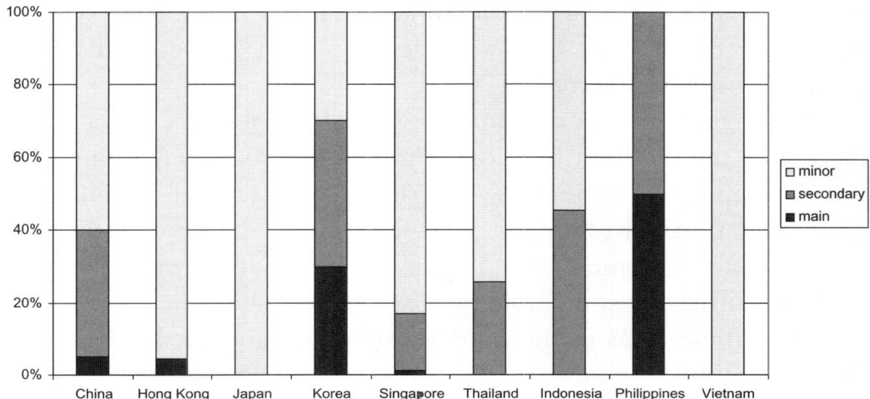

Figure 5: **Distribution of degree of centrality in the developmental frame**

ignored the EU as a major actor in the field and the Union was framed only as a secondary or minor actor.

In the *environmental* frame (Figure 4), the EU's role as a major and secondary actor was more visible on average, even though the actual number of news items was low. Only the Hong Kong media assigned less than 20% of its coverage to presenting the EU as a main or secondary actor. Indonesian and Philippines' media had the highest share of coverage representing the EU as a major actor; Vietnam had the highest share representing the EU as a secondary actor.

In the *developmental* frame (Figure 5), while the actual number of news items was extremely low, the coverage in terms of EU centrality was diverse. In seven out of the nine locations the intensity of the EU's representation was low. For example, in Japan and Vietnam, the monitored media only framed the EU's developmental actions from a minor perspective. In Thailand and Indonesia, there was no EU news where the Union was framed as a major actor; and in China, Hong Kong and Singapore the share of news representing the EU as a main actor was miniscule. In contrast, a relatively high share of Korean and Philippines' news coverage framed the EU as a major and secondary actor. In addition, the Philippines' coverage of the EU did not have a single news item where the EU was featured as a minor actor.

It is suggested that, despite subtle differences in the coverage of the EU in the different locations, the Union's social, environmental and developmental actions have a particular pattern of 'visibility' in Asian media; namely, limited coverage (very low in the environmental case and extremely low in the developmental frame) and a predominantly almost invisible view of the EU. Thus, the EU's media profile in these areas in the nine locations is marginal. Evidently, in 2006 and 2008, the news media in the nine Asian locations devoted more attention to the EU as a significant economic power and political actor. At the same time, the media's spotlight left images of the EU as a social, environmental and developmental authority in the shade. In pragmatic terms, exposure conveys a subject's importance to the audience. If it is important enough to be mentioned in the media, it is important for the public. The more frequently a subject is mentioned, the more importance it is accorded by the viewing public. Therefore, it can be argued that the EU's social, environmental and developmental activities were not considered significant either internally or internationally. The virtual absence of the EU's environmental and developmental profiles in reputable national newspapers and on television (the most popular news medium) arguably contributes to the formation of a very peculiar vision of the EU in the region. This is a vision where the EU's 'human face' and 'soft power' interactions with the region remain unacknowledged.

The External Grounding of the EU Actions

Assessing whether the coverage of the EU's actions in social, environmental and developmental fields was presented as relevant to and producing a direct impact on the location, the study evaluated the positioning of the EU in various geo-political contexts. More specifically, the study identified if the EU's actions were reported as locally grounded or if those actions were presented as being 'anchored' in external contexts. In the distribution of the foci of domesticity in the

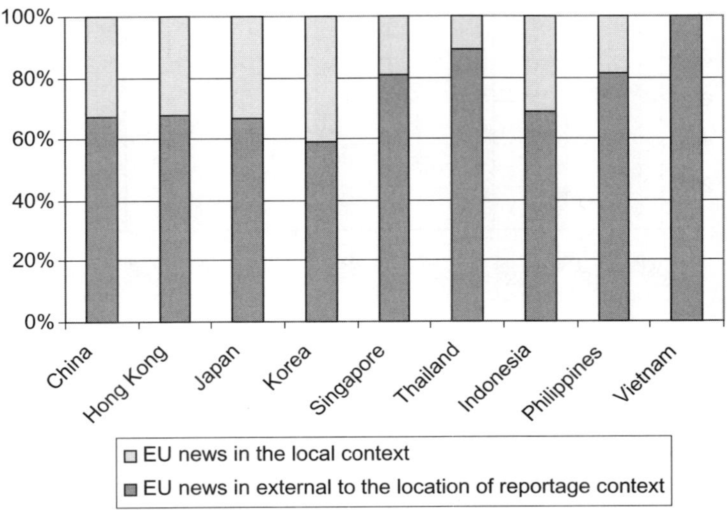

Figure 6: **Distribution of the foci of domesticity in *social* news**

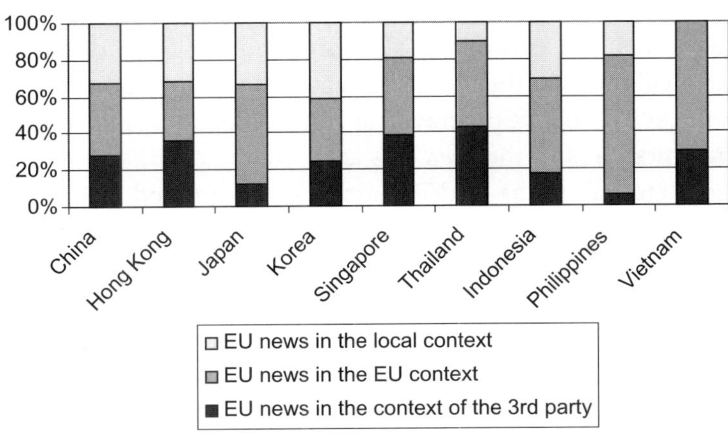

Figure 7: **Distribution of the foci of domesticity in *social* news (refined analysis)**

three frames, the angle external to the country of reportage prevailed (Figures 6, 7 and 8).

More than 60% of news in each of the nine locations reported EU *social* actions from an 'external' angle, i.e., reports of the EU's actions

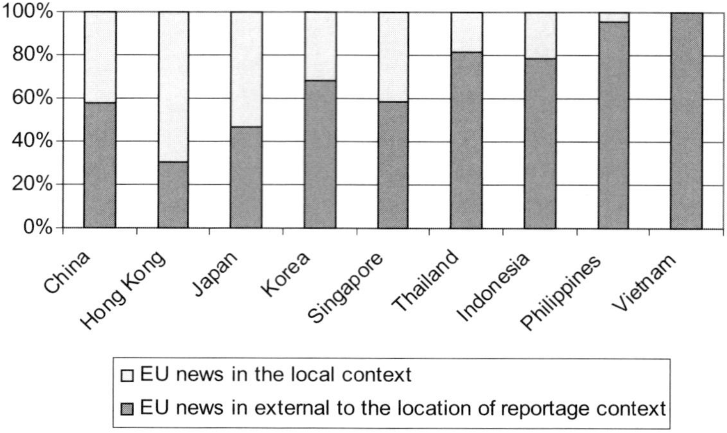

Figure 8:   Distribution of the foci of domesticity in *Environmental* news

were predominantly reported as international news rather than news of local importance (Figure 6). Remarkably, the 'local' grounding of such news was non-existent in Vietnam. Arguably, the dominance of the 'external' focus in this frame indicates the lack of local 'hooks' and results in the EU being portrayed as not immediately relevant to local audience members in the area of social affairs.

The 'external' focus of domesticity was compiled from two categories in this analysis — news reported in the EU context and EU news reported in the context of a third party (neither the EU, nor the country of reportage). Within this refined analysis of the 'external' focus of domesticity, three different patterns were observed across six locations in the *social affairs* frame (Figure 7). Media in China, Japan and all five South East Asian countries prioritised visions of the EU as a social actor in the EU context. This particular framing usually presents a rather detailed Europe-focused reportage, intended, in a way, to educate the audiences about a foreign counterpart (the EU in our case). Yet, it can overlook possible local links and neglect visions of the EU as a truly international actor whose social actions matter to other international actors. This 'international' vision was dominant in Hong Kong where the third-party angle in anchoring EU social actions was the most visible. Uniquely, the Korean media gave priority to a local context for EU social news. This localised perspective is known to raise the importance of the *Others* to the local audiences by bringing the 'foreign' closer to 'home'. However, if this strategy dominates, it risks overlooking international developments that have no direct grounding in domestic discourses.

A peculiar dichotomy was observed in the analysis of EU *environmental* news, namely a higher share of locally-grounded EU environmental news in the North-East Asian locations and Singapore (Figure 8). In contrast, the media in the three countries which were the focus of this volume plus Thailand explicated a very low share of locally-anchored news presenting the EU as an environmental actor (in Vietnam, the localization of such news was again wholly absent). Arguably, this dichotomy could signify that the newsmakers in the more industrially developed nations in this study framed the EU's policies and actions in the environmental field as being of greater direct relevance to local happenings. In contrast, the national media in the four South East Asian nations of Thailand, Indonesia, the Philippines and Vietnam did not frame the EU as a locally-significant environmental actor. This finding was unexpected — as discussed above, the EU generously subsidizes various environmental programmes (e.g., reforesterization of the rain forests) in these countries.

A more detailed look at the 'external' angle of domestication in EU *environmental* coverage — reporting the EU's action inside the Union or reporting those actions in the context of a third party — revealed that the North East Asian and Singaporean media under analysis profiled a relatively balanced coverage of the two angles (Figure 9). In contrast, the Thai, Indonesian, Philippines and Vietnamese media preferred to frame the EU's actions mainly *within* the Union. This particular framing can result in a certain image of the EU — an environmental actor whose actions are significant mainly on its own turf, while the external validation of such actions remains obscure.

Another dichotomy was observed in the distribution of the foci of domesticity in the *developmental* frame (Figure 10). The analysed

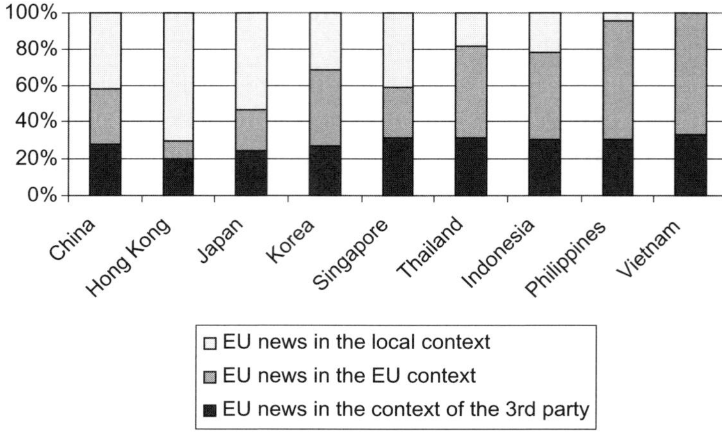

Figure 9:   Distribution of the foci of domesticity in *environmental* news (refined analysis)

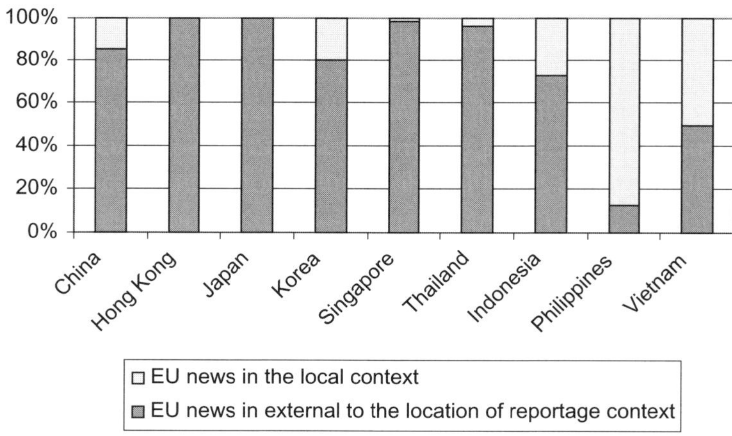

Figure 10:   Distribution of the foci of domesticity in *developmental* news

media in all North East Asian locations and two South East Asian ones (Singapore and Thailand) featured a very low share of locally grounded news (with the Hong Kong and Japanese samples lacking 'domesticated' news entirely). In contrast, media in Indonesia, the

Philippines and Vietnam profiled a higher share of locally-grounded news, with the Philippines' media reporting the EU's developmental actions in predominantly local contexts. This local positioning of the EU was predictable — the Union and its members are important developmental actors in the three locations and their actions carry an immediate impact for the societies in question. However, it should be remembered that the actual volume of news in the three locations remained very low (over 6 months of monitoring, there were 11 developmental news items in Indonesia, 8 in the Philippines and 2 in Vietnam).

A more detailed insight into the 'external' focus of domestication showed a heavy grounding of the EU's *developmental* actions in the third party context, namely offering or withdrawing aid to Palestine as a reaction to Hamas elections (Figure 11). This particular framing may arguably indicate a vision of the EU as an active international performer in the field of developmental affairs, yet this angle does not intimately connect the EU to the respective interests of the country of reportage.

The prevalence of the external framing in the EU's social, environmental and developmental actions may arguably be related to the

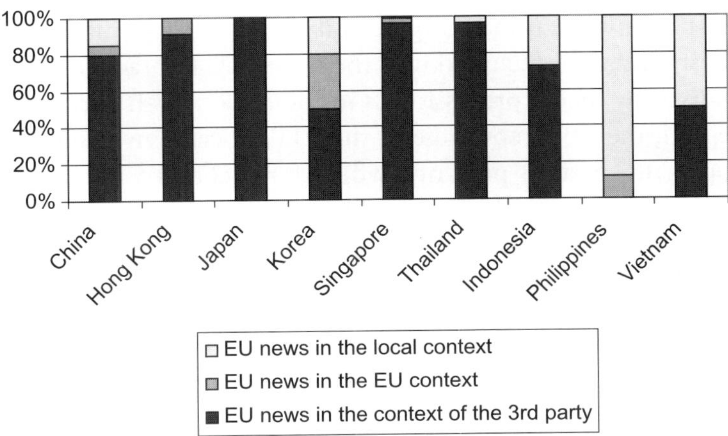

Figure 11:   Distribution of the foci of domesticity in *developmental* news (refined analysis)

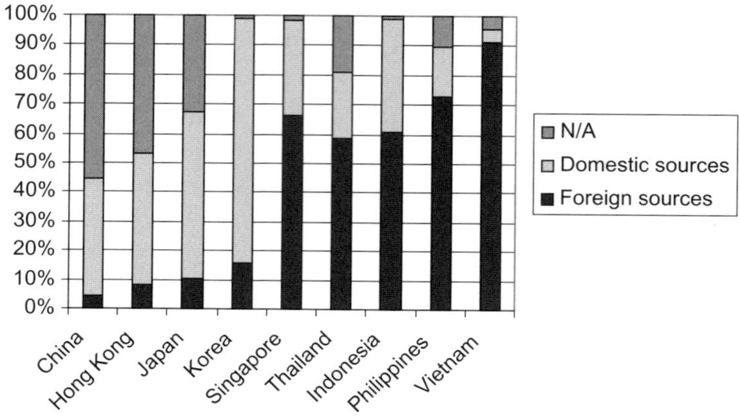

Figure 12:   Distribution of news sources

profile of the news sources. Sources-wise, the sample was divided between attributed international sources (agencies and correspondents), news originating from local sources (agencies and correspondents) and non-attributed news (Figure 12).

If we consider that local media outlets usually acknowledged local authors to strengthen the impression of their own expertise and excellence, then it is fair to suggest that non-attributed news items could be news of international origin, translated and modified by local journalists and then included into the newscasts (a practice admittedly widely used by media professionals in the region).[35] If this suggestion is accepted, then the reportage of the EU's social, environmental and developmental actions presents two patterns (Figure 13). In the first case, the four North East Asian locations had a higher share of domestic sources. In the second case, coverage of the EU in the five South East Asian locations was led by international sources (Indonesia had a proportionally higher share of locally-authored news among this five and Vietnam had the lowest share).

The large-scale use of news agencies by media in developing countries is often attributed to the lack of resources needed to sustain

------

[35] From an interview with a Thai newsmaker who preferred to remain anonymous.

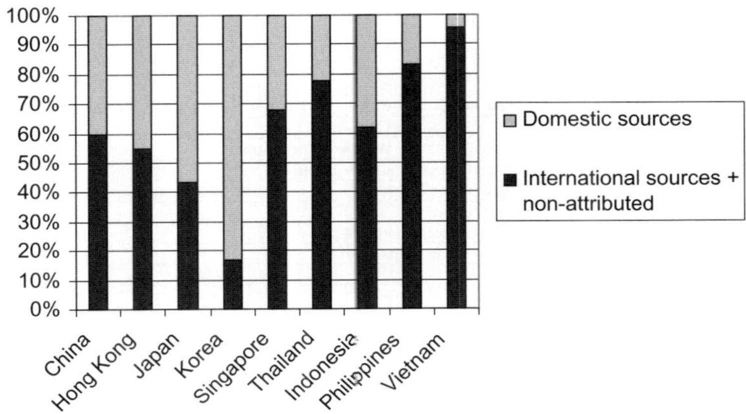

Figure 13:   Distribution of news sources (revisited)

larger numbers of foreign-based correspondents. Most foreign news comes from the international wires, which tend to report actions of the foreign actors in an external (more generic), not local (more specific), discourse in order to sell such news to a wider global audience. In contrast, richer media organisations have more resources to support their own foreign bureaus and externally-based journalistic staff (both its own correspondents and 'stringers', or freelancers, working from abroad). The existence of such correspondents generally leads to far more accurate and voluminous reporting, with more obvious local links.

To conclude, the majority of the representations of EU actions in the area of social, environmental and developmental affairs were grounded in contexts external to the country of reportage. In such framing, the EU's actions were not portrayed as directly relevant to the citizens of the nine Asian locations. Yet, as the analysis below shows, it was those 'domestically-grounded' topics which got the most media attention in the individual localities.

Diverse Themes

Even though the frames presenting the EU's social, environmental and developmental affairs were the least visible subjects in the investigated

Table 2:   Distribution of the news topics representing the EU in the field of social affairs

<table>
<tr><th colspan="6">2006</th><th colspan="3">2008</th></tr>
<tr><th>Japan</th><th>Singapore</th><th>China</th><th>Hong Kong</th><th>Korea</th><th>Thailand</th><th>Indonesia</th><th>Philippines</th><th>Vietnam</th></tr>
<tr><td colspan="9">Immigration</td></tr>
<tr><td colspan="9">Social Legislation, Welfare, Human Rights</td></tr>
<tr><td colspan="8">Multicultural Diversity and Islamic Issues</td><td></td></tr>
<tr><td colspan="7">Education</td><td></td><td></td></tr>
<tr><td colspan="6">Research, Science and Technology</td><td></td><td></td><td></td></tr>
<tr><td></td><td colspan="6">Health care</td><td></td><td>Health care</td></tr>
<tr><td></td><td colspan="6">Art/Entertainment</td><td></td><td></td></tr>
<tr><td></td><td colspan="6">Sports</td><td></td><td></td></tr>
<tr><td></td><td colspan="5">Demographic developments</td><td></td><td></td><td></td></tr>
<tr><td></td><td colspan="5">Safety</td><td></td><td>Safety</td><td></td></tr>
<tr><td></td><td colspan="5">Crime</td><td></td><td></td><td></td></tr>
<tr><td></td><td colspan="4">Intellectual property rights</td><td></td><td></td><td></td><td></td></tr>
<tr><td>Cultural habits and lifestyle</td><td></td><td></td><td colspan="2">Cultural habits and lifestyle</td><td></td><td></td><td></td><td></td></tr>
</table>

Asian news media, the EU representation of these three frames was extremely diverse in terms of the topics reported.

Social Affairs Frame

Thirteen topics were featured in more than one locality (Table 2). Two topics were profiled by news media in all nine locations — migration and the EU, and EU actions in the field of social legislation, welfare and human rights. The Singaporean media was found to present great diversity in the *social* topics (primarily because Singapore was the leader in the overall volume of social news).

Migration and the EU

The challenge of how to guarantee a safe and secure society has been growing in importance over the past decade. A key component of societal security, defined by Buzan as "the threats and vulnerabilities that effect patterns of communal identity and culture",[36] is immigration. There is a perceptible concern that inward migration (both legal and illegal) can become a fundamental threat to states' social and

---

[36] As cited in Brian Bridges, *Europe and the Challenge of the Asia Pacific*, pp. 173–174.

political stability. Two countries in the study — Japan and Singapore — have experienced an influx of migrants from less economically developed countries in the region, thus justifying their interest in relevant practices around the world. In particular, there has been an increase in the mobility of illegal labour from poorer Asian countries to more prosperous ones (observed mostly in Japan), as well as refugees from war-affected neighbouring regions and areas devastated by the Asian tsunami (observed mostly in Singapore). Other countries have sizable diasporas in Europe and their media reported the conditions of entry into the EU for Asian migrants and their treatment by Europeans.

The representations of the EU in migration matters were predominantly neutral, yet they featured a larger share of negative compared with positive assessments. Notably, positive modalities in this particular sub-frame were very rare. The *neutrally* coloured news reported various dynamics of immigration to the EU in a factual manner. In news which registered *positive* evaluations, the EU's internal migration was seen as an instrument for turning the EU into a 'seamless economic dynamo' that can compete with the United States and emerging Asian powers. The more numerous *negative* reports presented migration in the Union as a challenge to the EU and its people, mainly due to a growing anti-immigrant backlash among many EU citizens. EU citizens' fears were represented by the Asian news media as a fear of the social impact of globalisation and enlargement in general, and of massive Turkish immigration in particular. Illegal migrants to the EU from Africa were also mentioned. The lack of a continent-wide policy regarding migration was depicted as leading to social tensions which fuelled the rise of xenophobia in the EU, potentially affecting its Asian migrant communities.

EU social legislation, welfare and human rights practices

The EU's actions in the areas of social legislation, welfare and human rights are numerous and often treated as a useful reference to consider around the world. The news media in the nine Asian locations reported a wide array of related events in the Union that dealt with gender equality, employment conditions, the abolishment of the death penalty, prisoners' rights, the treatment of ethnic and sexual minorities, freedom of expression, antismoking measures, etc. Most of these reports presented the EU's actions towards its own citizens as aiming to improve Europeans' lives and protect their rights. Occasionally, the EU was reported as an 'exporter' of human rights values to the world in general (and to the region in particular) — EU actions towards Zimbabwe, China, Mayanmar (Burma) and Guantanamo were mentioned, but very rarely.

A *neutral* tone dominated the coverage of EU regulations concerning working hours in EU countries, the EU's policies on equal job opportunities and the EU's regulations establishing the minimum level of poverty. *Positive* evaluations surfaced when journalists described the EU's protection of the rights of various groups (e.g., sexual minorities or journalists) while *negative* assessments were observed in media reports of the EU's efforts to liberalise its state employment sector (efforts which met with public resistance), with trade unions described as 'fuming' at the EU.

EU Multicultural diversity and anti-Islamic sentiments

All locations (with the exception of Vietnam) devoted a significant portion of their EU social affairs coverage to discussing the EU's cultural and religious diversity and multicultural practices. In this context, reports of racial discrimination and the treatment of the Muslim minority in Europe were the most frequent. The first perspective illuminated problems encountered by various Asian diasporas while living in Europe. The second perspective was initially dominated by the news on the scandal around the offensive cartoons of Prophet Mohammad published by a Danish newspaper. Later, the reportage became more diverse, portraying various examples of anti-Islamic sentiment in Europe. The media in the five South East Asian countries were, unsurprisingly, the most prolific in discussing this topic as these countries have large Islamic communities.

While neutral evaluations prevailed in descriptions of the EU's actions on Islamic matters, in each location the share of negative assessments was higher than the share of positive ones. A *neutral* tone was detected in daily updates reporting the development of events regarding the cartoon publication scandal (including global protest demonstrations by Muslims) in a factual, rather than evaluative, tone. News items with *positive* assessments were relatively rare. Most such items reported the actions and statements of EU officials as attempting to 'bridge the gulf' between Muslims and Christians in the EU. Those actions and statements were classified as the EU's struggling attempts to mend relations. *Negatively* coloured news presented the EU in two major ways. Firstly, the EU's citizens were reported as failing to distinguish between extremist and moderate Islam. As a consequence, EU citizens of Islamic descent were seen as the victims of unfair attitudes and prejudices. Secondly, the EU's relations with the wider Muslim world were considered to be deteriorating. Finally, racial discrimination was also reported, specifically describing the treatment of migrants from Asia to Europe. Notably, the controversial theory of the 'clash of civilizations'[37] was frequently cited in Asian media.

EU and education, science, research and technology

Europe as an educational hub and a centre for science, research and technology was yet another theme that surfaced in the majority of the observed media outlets. The reason for this particular focus of media attention is self-explanatory. Most of the locations in this study could be described, using the words of Bridges, as "densely populated and poorly endowed with natural resources",[38] thus there is a strong push towards "the best use of their human resources".[39] Bridges argues that in these locations education is seen as an "important tool in creating efficient and well-equipped labour-force".[40] In addition, growing standards of living in Asia allow many ordinary citizens to

---

[37] Huntington, Samuel, 'The Clash of Civilizations"' *Foreign Affairs*, Vol. 72, No. 3, <www.AllanNoble.net/articles_by_samuel_huntington.htm>
[38] Brian Bridges, *Europe and the Challenge of the Asia Pacific*, p. 51.
[39] *Ibid.*
[40] *Ibid.*

educate their children overseas. Thus, European universities are not only attractive but increasingly affordable, and the EU's exchange programmes facilitate this interaction. Asian locations are also increasingly competitive in the technological and industrial fields, and a vigilant interest in the EU's activities was predictable.

Despite the prevalence of a neutral tone in the reporting of this topic, the share of positive representations (compared with negative ones) was higher in each country's case (except South Korea). Most of the *neutral* news items represented (or even advertised) the studies at universities located in the EU, as well as reported on various joint research projects between the home location and the EU. *Positive* news items depicted the EU as a place that encourages scientific curiosity and facilitates the unforeseeable outcomes that are characteristic of cutting-edge research. In this context, well-known universities in the EU were presented as a desirable destination for Asian students. *Negative* assessments were rare in this coverage, with the exception of South Korea. In the Korean media, the EU was mentioned as losing the battle to retain the world's finest minds. With prestige and money at stake, many leading scholars and researchers were described as looking towards the US as their research 'hub', and the EU was reported as lagging behind in its efforts. The general level of education was commented on too — it was reported that more than a third of adults in the EU cannot perform basic computer tasks. It was also noted that the cost of education in Europe — and the UK in particular — is prohibitive for international students. European universities were depicted as being in a 'race', competing with each other to attract talented students from abroad. Given the value attached to international education in South Korean society, the negative assessment in this case is evident.

Healthcare

Healthcare in the EU was another topic that attracted Asian newsmakers' attention. According to Keukelerie and MacNaughtan,[41]

---

[41] Keukelerie, Stephan & Jennifer MacNaughtan, *The Foreign Policy of the European Union*, New York: Palgrave Macmillan, 2008, pp. 249–250.

health in the global context is of increased importance to the EU for two primary reasons: firstly, "health threats to the domestic populations",[42] and secondly, the "promot[ion of] global public health".[43] The authors noted that the first issue, while bordering wider security concerns, includes EU vulnerability to the spread of infectious diseases on a transnational level, bio-terrorist attacks, and the scarcity of highly-needed vaccines.[44] The latter issue is part of the EU's agenda on development and international trade.

With the Union's heightened attention to health issues then, it is unsurprising that this topic was also visible in the external media's coverage of EU social affairs. The monitored reportage combined several major news themes but coverage of the EU's reactions to the avian flu pandemic (in terms of social consequences both in Asia and in the EU) was the most visible in 2006. In Thailand, the coverage of the EU's reactions to the avian flu was the most prominent topic for two reasons. Firstly, Thai poultry exports to Europe are important for the country's economic well-being. The EU's economic restrictions on potentially infected imports were seen as negatively influencing the well-being of the Thai people. Secondly, Thailand had a significant number of people affected with the disease, thus, the EU's practices in coping with the disease in Europe were scrutinised. Unsurprisingly, the assessments of the EU's actions in these scenarios ranged from neutral-positive (in the latter reportage) to strongly negative (in the former case).

The majority of news on the avian flu topic presented the EU in a *neutral* manner — the EU was reported as a participant in various international and internal meetings discussing a range of measures to prevent the escalation of the pandemic. The *positive* evaluations surfaced when the EU was portrayed as a provider of substantial global technical and financial support — particularly to developing countries — to stop the spread of the virus. The EU's *negative* portrayals (more common than positive ones, but less frequent than

---

[42] *Ibid.*, p. 249.

[43] *Ibid.*

[44] *Ibid.*, pp. 250–251.

neutral) depicted the EU's citizens as seized by fear and panic, and, as a result, pressing the EU administration to stop trading poultry with Asia.

However, this theme was not the only one in the coverage of the EU's practices in healthcare — Asian newsmakers were also interested in reporting various EU initiatives to protect and improve the health of its citizens. Among those reports, there were items on better standards for vaccines, strict tests for new medicines and cosmetics, safety standards for toys and drinking water, the fight against obesity, measures against genetically modified organisms and food, etc. In these reports, the EU's actions were often evaluated from neutral and positive angles.

Art, entertainment, sports, cultural habits and lifestyle

A smaller part of the EU social news reportage presented the Union's more 'cultural' side (a category which combined such themes as art, popular culture, sports and everyday customs and lifestyle choices). Arguably, in these representations, the EU was often mentioned as a synonym for the wider concept of 'Europe' as a cultural entity. Part of this reportage presented the EU's cultural activities in the Asian localities (e.g., music, art and film festivals, concerts, photo exhibitions, fashion shows, etc.) or Asian explorations of modern Europe (e.g., a local band's tour or tourism/travelling story, etc.). Another part of this reportage focused on 'Europe in Europe', discussing various cultural happenings, major sporting events, celebrities, as well as European family values or work habits.

With neutral assessments again leading the depictions, there were more positive images of the EU in this category across the nine localities. *Neutrally* toned items reported on the 16th EU Film Festival across South Korea, Hong Kong, Singapore and Thailand. Such coverage also covered European computer game habits or commented on EU-funded broadcasts. *Positively*-coloured news presented the EU as a desirable travel destination with unique cultures, traditions and history. *Negatively*-coloured items presented the bizarre story of an EU commissioner who was literally caught with his pants down, sunbathing nude with a female companion.

Crime, intellectually property rights and safety

Categories of "crime" and "safety" included EU social news that reported various criminal incidents in Europe (such as prostitution, people-trafficking, murders, illegal employment of migrants, illegal exports of caviar, counterfeiting of the euro, an increasing crime rate, illegal websites, computer hackers, etc.) and the Union's responses to those law violations. These stories were portrayed as internal matters for the EU. It was noted that the EU attempted to defend its intellectual property rights internationally. This 'external' rubric also included EU anti-terrorist activities (e.g., the introduction of biometric passports and the agreement to share data on airline passengers), and the Union's measures to secure the safe existence of its citizens (e.g., introducing strict standards for airlines flying into Europe, protecting people from forest fires, reducing work-place mortality, facilitating safer driving, etc.).

The majority of news items in these categories were found to be neutral in tone. More positive news stories were found than negative — the EU was presented as openly facing and fighting illegal activities and being proactive in protecting its citizens.

Demographic situation in the EU

The final identified category of EU social news was reports of the Union's demographic patterns, namely the ageing population and declining birth rates. According to Keukelerie & MacNaughtan,[45] "the change in Europe's demographics ranks alongside climate change and energy security as a major preoccupation for Europe in the decades to come". The media in several locations in this study paid some attention to this EU development with two Asian countries in the sample (Korea and Singapore) drawing parallels with their own population trends. Most of the news in this category evaluated the EU from a *neutral* position, reporting the dynamics of population growth and decline in a purely factual manner.

---

[45] Keukelerie & MacNaughtan, *The Foreign Policy of the European Union*, p. 252.

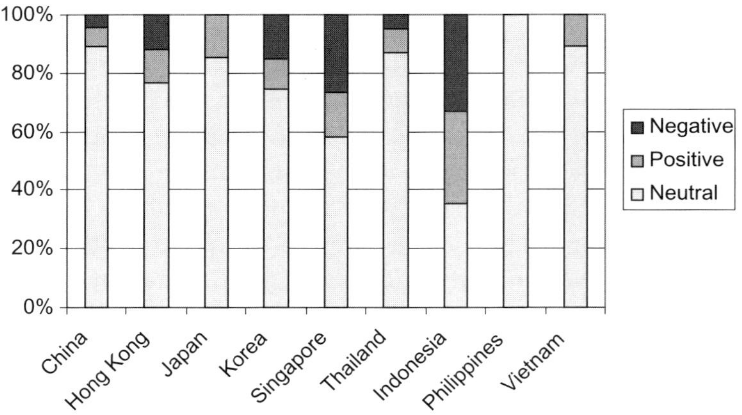

Figure 14:   Distribution of evaluations in social affairs coverage

To conclude, the diverse yet minimal reportage of the EU's social affairs by newsmakers in nine Asian locations were all united by a predominantly neutral evaluation of the Union's actions in this field (Figure 14). The three countries that are the focus of this volume displayed three very different assessment patterns. Across the nine locations, the Indonesian media featured the highest share of both negatively- and positively-charged social news leading to the conclusion that media opinion on the EU's social activities in this country was more polarised than in any other in the sample. In the other locations, a neutral tone prevailed. Notably, in the Philippines, neutrality was the only tone detected. Against a background of neutrality, the Singaporean and Korean media had higher shares of negative news than positive news and in contrast, Japan, Vietnam and the Philippines did not feature any negatively-coloured news reporting EU social activities.

Environmental frame

Approaches to tackling climate change and reducing greenhouse gases have triggered heated global discussions, of which the EU is a leading participant. Three topics — the EU's role in the Kyoto Protocol, the EU's attitudes to climate change and the EU's actions

Table 3:   Distribution of the most visible topics representing the EU in the field of environmental affairs

Aspect	2006						2008		
	Singapore	China	Hong Kong	Thailand	South Korea	Japan	Indonesia	Philippines	Vietnam
Industry	Car emissions, engines standards, eco-friendly cars, Word Car Free Day cars								Cars
	Airlines emissions							Airlines emissions	
	Energy production				Energy production				Energy production
	Ship emissions			Fishing					
						Eco-friendly agriculture		Agriculture	
Policy	Air pollution		Air pollution						
		Emissions trading scheme			Emissions trading scheme			Emissions trading scheme	
	climate change, global warming								
	E-waste treatment					Waste treatment			
	Kyoto protocol								
		Animal protection							
		EU-China Biodiversity Programme		Replanting forests project	EU Organic farming regulations	REACH regulations		Bio-fuels	
	Recycling							Recycling	

to reduce CO_2 emissions — appeared in the environmental frame across the nine locations in our study (Table 3).

However, the EU has also been active in many other environmental areas, claiming, according to Vogler, "leadership in global environmental actions".[46] These include the "dissemination of the environmental practices and standards",[47] specifically in the context of the EU's enlargement; the incorporation of environmental clauses in EU agreements with third countries, particularly its neighbours to the east and to the south; and its leading role in other multilateral agreements.[48] This array of roles was somewhat reflected in the

---

[46] Vogler, John 'The European Contribution to Global Environmental Governance', *International Affairs*, Vol. 81, No. 4, 2005, pp. 835–850, pp. 835–837, as cited in Keukelerie, Stephan & Jennier MacNaughtan, *The Foreign Policy of the European Union*, p. 246.

[47] Keukelerie, Stephan & Jennier MacNaughtan, *The Foreign Policy of the European Union*, p. 246.

[48] Bretherton and Vogler cited the Montreal Protocol on Substances the Deplete the Ozone Layer, the cross-border movement of hazardous chemicals and the attempt to provide a regulatory framework for GMOs (see Bretherton, Charlotte and John Vogler *The European Union a Global Actor*, London: Routledge, 2006, p. 105, as cited in Keukelerie, Stephan & Jennier MacNaughtan, *The Foreign Policy of the European Union*, p. 246.

nine Asian locations' coverage of the EU's environmental activities. The frame featured two sub-frames, namely, reportage of the EU's industry-related actions and the EU's policy-related actions and statements.

The Hong Kong coverage of the environmental frame (the leader in terms of volume) was the most diverse. It prioritised reporting the EU actions in conjunction with air pollution issues — a major problem for this highly urbanised location where the government is attempting to achieve better air quality using EU policies as reference points. The Singaporean environmental news (the second largest in volume) focused its attention on the issues of CO_2 emissions (for cars, planes and ships, as well as the Emission Trading Scheme). With Singapore being a major transport hub in Asia, this media attention is arguably expected. A similar, and perhaps predictable CO_2 emissions focus in EU reportage was traced in Korea, a heavily industrialised economy facing the growing challenge of tackling carbon emissions. The Japanese media extensively reported on talks in Nairobi and the future of the Kyoto Protocol. In China, the topics of climate change and the 'greenhouse effect' received a substantial share of media attention. The Thai coverage, which was exceptionally low, did not feature any visibly recurring theme. Focusing on the three South East Asian countries which are investigated in-depth in this volume, their media centred its low-volume reportage on the relevant EU actions and policies in tackling global climate change and reducing international CO_2 emissions.

Overall, a neutral assessment of the EU's actions dominated reporting on these three topics, yet, identifiably positive assessments were more visible than negative ones (Figure 15). *Positive* evaluations were evident in reports on the EU's practices to improve air quality (Hong Kong); the EU's search for alternative energy sources as well as energy saving measures (Singapore, Hong Kong); the EU's standards in monitoring CO_2 emissions for various means of transportation (Singapore); the EU's example in curbing greenhouse gases (China); the EU's practices in eco-friendly agriculture (Japan); and the EU's preference for organic farming (Korea). The

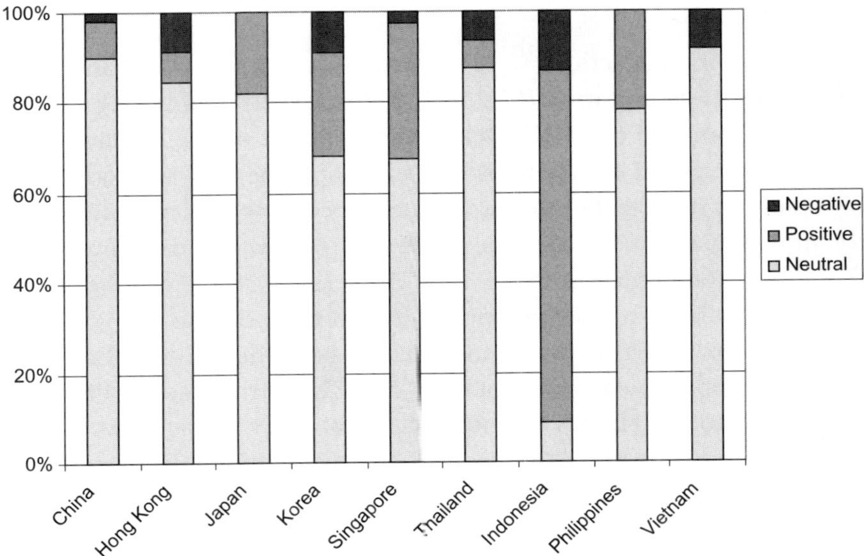

Figure 15:   Distribution of evaluations in environmental coverage

Indonesian media had the highest proportion of positive evaluations of the EU's environmental actions, assigning this assessment to the coverage of the EU's attitudes to climate change and its actions to reduce CO_2 emissions. The less frequent *negative* evaluations were found in the coverage of the EU's actions to endorse a directive on the restriction of the use of certain hazardous substances in electrical and electronic equipment[49] (RoHS) and the effects of these actions on local electronic manufacturers (Hong Kong). Media representations of the EU's commitments to the Kyoto protocol, the EU Emission Trading Scheme, and the Union's contribution to developing an efficient global carbon market received predominantly *neutral* evaluations.

---

[49] European Parliament and Council, *Directive 2002/95/EC of the European Parliament and of the Council of 27 January 2003*, http://europa.eu.int/eur-lex/ pri/en/oj/dat/2003/l_037/l_03720030213en00190023.pdf, accessed 31 May 2005.

Developmental frame

EU developmental actions were presented from three major angles — EU assistance to countries outside Asia, the Union's aid to neighbours in the region, and the EU's help to the locality of the media source (Table 4). Several news items talked about the EU rendering aid internally to its Member States and neighbours on the continent, but the numbers across the nine locations were so low that a separate sub-frame was not singled out.

The Chinese media prioritised the theme of the EU's aid to countries around the world in general, and the Middle East and Palestine in particular. The topic of the EU cutting aid to Palestine in reaction to the Hamas election victory was one of the most prominent topics in 2006 in the region. In terms of the EU's regional actions, Chinese outlets reported on EU aid to Indonesia after a devastating tsunami. This topic also received a lot of attention in Hong Kong where media preferred to cover the EU's relevant activities in the regional context (rather than in unrelated countries). More specifically, the Hong Kong media featured news on how the EU helps poorer Asian countries, such as North Korea in the North East and East Timor and other developing ASEAN countries in the South East. Notably, the South Korean media did not pay any attention to the EU's developmental efforts towards North Korea, mentioning instead the EU's assistance to relieve the consequences of the tsunami in Sri Lanka and Indonesia. Aid to the Philippines for border control as a part of anti-terrorist actions and EU peace-keeping actions in Aceh were reported in Singapore, yet again the vast number of local articles dealt with the EU's aid to Palestine. The only exception in the frame was the Philippines' coverage, which focused on the EU's assistance to the locality in terms of supplying ODA, supporting various developmental projects (e.g. the development of the Philippines' justice system and aiding the Philippines' Bureau of Customs) and facilitating the peace process (in particular, helping Muslims in Mindanao). The coverage of EU developmental actions was miniscule in Japanese and Vietnamese media (2 news items over 6 months in each location).

Table 4: Distribution of the most visible topics representing the EU in the field of developmental affairs

	2006						2008		
	Singapore	China	Hong Kong	Thailand	Korea	Japan	Indonesia	Philippines	Vietnam
3rd party	Aid to Middle East (in general) and to Palestine (in particular)								
		Aid to Africa, Chad					Aid to Tanzania		
Region			Aid to North Korea						
	•	Aid to Indonesia				Aid to Indonesia			
	Aid to the Philippines					Aid to Sri Lanka	Aid to Myanmar		
	Peacekeeping in Aceh		Aid to China				Aid to China		
Locality		EU aid to China for management training					Aid for construction		
		Food aid					Aid to fight bird flu		
		Helping the poor			Helping the poor		ODA		
				GSP on shrimps					

Similar to the distribution of evaluations in the *environmental* frame, the dominant assessment of EU *developmental* news was *neutral*, with a higher share of positive representations than negative ones (Figure 16). The Indonesian media presented the highest share of both positive and negative news, suggesting that the attitudes expressed by the local newsmakers were more pronounced and polarised. The Philippine and Thai media, while featuring positive tones, did not include any negative assessments. Finally, the Japanese and Vietnamese samples (both with 2 articles each) featured only neutral assessments. Taking into account that aid and assistance are highly appreciated and valued, neutral to positive assessments are predictable. Most of the negative assessments discovered in the analysis referred to the EU's decision to cut aid to Palestine after the Hamas election.

The predominantly neutral perspective in the reportage of the EU's diverse social, environmental and developmental actions could

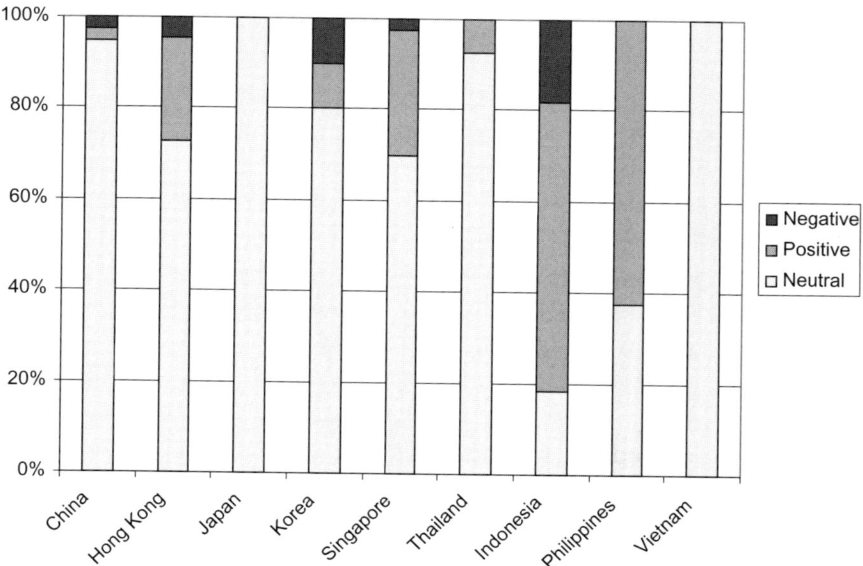

Figure 16:   Distribution of evaluations in developmental coverage

be dictated by specific cultural norms in Asian societies, which prioritise the notion of 'harmony' and 'politeness' (such as those inherent in the concepts of *honne* and *tatemae* in Japanese society).[50] In this light, any expression of negativity is considered to be rude and antagonistic. Asian journalistic attitudes and practices are assumed to follow these cultural norms to a certain degree. The priorities of foreign policy could also be a contributing factor to the dominant neutral vision. For example, the priority of Chinese foreign policy on sustaining its fast economic growth could contribute to leading media assuming a politely neutral or positive tone on seemingly 'marginal' issues, like the EU's social, environmental or developmental affairs, and expressing more pronounced attitudes in assessments of the EU's economic activities. The prevailing neutrality could also indicate a certain level of indifference on behalf of the Asian newsmakers and news consumers when it comes to the EU's social, environmental and developmental affairs.

In summary, the reportage in Vietnam, Indonesia and the Philippines, which are the focus of this publication, was found to be among the lowest in volume (although, Indonesian television was among the three regional 'leaders'). Moreover, external sources dominated the coverage of the three areas in the three locations, and all three prioritised an external grounding of the EU actions in social and environmental frames. However, if compared to other locations, the three South East Asian countries in question profiled a much higher share of locally-grounded EU news in the *developmental* frame. Moreover, the major and/or secondary degree of intensity in EU representations was on average higher than in other locations' media. These findings possibly indicate that even though the volume of news in these three locations was extremely low, there is a tendency to highlight the Union's presence and involvement with the locality. The Indonesia media also featured the highest share of polarised opinions, possibly revealing a higher degree of local interest in and more pronounced attitudes towards the EU's actions in the social,

---

[50] See also Hendry, Joy, 'To Wrap or Not to Wrap: Politeness and Penetration in EthnoFigureic Inquiry'. *Man*, Vol. 24, No. 4, 1989, pp. 620–635.

environmental and developmental spheres. In contrast, the Philippine and Vietnamese reportage featured very high shares of neutrally coloured news.

FINDINGS: PUBLIC OPINION SURVEY

The survey respondents in each location were asked to give three associations they have when they hear the words 'the European Union'. The top four most frequently mentioned spontaneous images of the EU are presented in Table 5.[51]

These findings indicate that the (stereo)typical image of the EU in the public in the nine Asian locations does not associate the EU with such characteristics as a 'social affairs champion', an 'environmental champion' or a 'developmental trendsetter'. Instead the immediate interpretations of the EU by the general public seemed to correlate to the most visible media portrayals of the Union, which stressed economic and political representations of the EU and de-emphasised its social, environmental and developmental roles. Such images as the euro; the Union's integration into a bigger geopolitical unity; the EU as a global economic power with greater bargaining abilities because of its size; the EU's trading capacities; and the EU comprising of individual Members States, instead dominated public opinion in the region.

Notably, the image of the EU as linked to the administration of developmental aid did enter the top four immediate associations in one case — the Philippines. It is suggested that the Philippine peoples' personal experiences of the EU's actions on the ground might be the leading factor in the priority of this particular perception. However, our media analysis also showed that in the Philippines' news discourse the share of developmental news was slightly higher in comparison to the media in the other two locations investigated in this volume. Moreover, the Philippine news profiled the highest share of locally-grounded EU developmental

---

[51] These images are also discussed in the chapter by Martin Holland in this volume.

Table 5:   Dominant images of the EU (spontaneous responses)

	1st	2nd	3rd	4th
China	€	Enlargement	Union/Integration	Trade
Hong Kong	€	Trade	Union/Integration	Individual countries
Japan	Union/Integration	Union/Integration	Individual countries	Disparities/Unfairness
Singapore	Union/Integration	€	Economic power	Individual countries
Korea		€	Individual countries	Exceptionalism/Problems
Thailand	Individual countries	Economic power	Trade	€
Indonesia	Monetary/Economic union	Trade/Business	€	Democracy, good governance, rule of law
Philippines	Union/Integration	Monetary union	Developmental aid donor	Employment
Vietnam	Union/Integration	Monetary/Economic union	€	Democracy, good governance, rule of law

news and did not feature any negative evaluations of such news. In addition, the EU as a developmental actor was always presented with either a major or secondary degree of intensity, while minor representations in this frame were totally absent from the media sample. The combination of personal and media-related factors could arguably have contributed to the public's higher ranking for this particular image.

Arguably, the variables of personal experience and exposure should be taken into consideration when trying to understand why the issues of democracy, good governance and rule of law entered the list of top four spontaneous associations in Indonesia and Vietnam. The volume of news coverage of these issues was very low in these two locations and the news media in both countries did not report the EU in the developmental field as a major actor. Yet, while the Vietnamese news in particular did not feature any local 'hooks' in the social or environmental frames, this angle did surface in the developmental frame. It is also worth mentioning that the Indonesian media delivered the most polarised representations of the EU among the nine locations when evaluating the Union's developmental actions. These factors could be tangentially related to the elevated status of these particular images among the public in those two locations.

The respondents were also asked what issues should be kept in mind when their governments were developing diplomatic ties with the EU. The top eight most frequently mentioned recommendations on how to improve local governments' agendas when dealing with the EU are listed in Table 6.

Trade and more general economic issues were once again among the most frequent responses. Respondents also prioritised the importance of securing each location's interests (economic and political) in the dialogue with the EU. Arguably, these findings are further evidence of the media's influence on public opinion when it comes to foreign policy coverage. Encouragingly, social, environmental and developmental aspects entered this list too. For example, the need to stress cultural exchanges with the EU and to recognise Europe's cultural differences and its current cultural

Table 6:   Issues to keep in mind when local governments develop diplomatic ties with the EU

Japan	South Korea	Mainland China	Hong Kong	Singapore	Thailand	Indonesia	The Philippines	Vietnam
Politics/US	Trade	Trade/Anti-dumping	Trade	Trade	Trade	Economy	**Employment**	Program/Campaign/Policy
Respect/Equality/Fairness	Economy	Economy	Economy/Monetary	Mutual benefits/Good politics/Closer relations	Economy	Cooperation/Relation with EU	Issues/Concerns	Economic Support
Culture/Ethnicities/Religion	*Cultural exchanges*	Politics	HK interests	Economy	Politics	Trade	Privilege/Rights	Reduce trade taxes
Japan's interests	Closer relations with the EU	Arms embargo	China	*Cultural issues*	*Environment*	*Education*	Improvement	Trade/Business
Trade	*Environment/Standards*	Technology	*Environment/Standards*	*Democracy/Human rights*	EU–Thailand relations	Defence/War/Military Conflict/Stability	Business	Improvement

(*Continued*)

Table 6:   (*Continued*)

Japan	South Korea	Mainland China	Hong Kong	Singapore	Thailand	Indonesia	The Philippines	Vietnam
Economy/ Monetary	Politics/US	*Environment/ Energy*	Closer relationship with the EU	Singapore's interest	Thailand's interests	*Development aid*	Relationship	Issues/ Concerns
EU internal developments	Korea's interests	*Human rights*	*Human Rights/ Democracy/ Social affairs*	Politics	*Human Rights*	*Employment*	Economic Support	*Democracy, human rights, good governance, rule of law*
Environment/ Standards			Taxes	Dealings with different EU MSs	Dealings with different EU MSs	Investment	*Democracy, human rights, good governance, rule of law*	*Education*

challenges was voiced by respondents in Japan, South Korea and Singapore. The need for dialogue with the EU on human rights and democracy was stressed in the Chinese, Hong Kong, Singaporean, Thai, Philippines and Vietnamese surveys. The public in the three South East Asian locations studied in this volume did not rate environmental issues on the agenda of governmental interactions with the Union. In contrast, the need to interact with the EU on environmental matters (and environmental standards in particular) was noted in the public responses in all other locations (with the exception of Singapore). The need to continue dialogue with the EU in the area of developmental aid was highlighted by the Indonesian public. A request to continue the dialogue on education was highlighted in the Philippines and Vietnamese surveys. Finally, both the Philippines and Indonesian responses indicated that the social affairs issue of employment needs to stay on the bilateral agendas (specifically, in the case of the Asian migration to the EU). Evidently, public opinion in the nine Asian locations considers the EU an important social, environmental and developmental actor worth being considered by officials formulating foreign policy agendas.

DISCUSSION AND CONCLUSIONS

At a time when new global actors are vying to be world superpowers and when the priorities in international interactions are expected to shift, systematic research into the EU's external imagery in the Asian media and public discourses has presented some thought-provoking results. The EU's intense and increasing economic contacts with Asia, its combined economic importance for the nine locations in question, and its growing and diversifying international presence are features of the early 21st century. Yet, despite these, the EU's self-proclaimed reputation as an internationally visible human rights advocate, a development actor and an environmental 'champion' was found to be largely invisible for the public in the nine Asian locations. While a broader study discovered that in the eyes of the Asian public the EU was not ranked as the leading present-day partner,[52] this research revealed a fundamental imbalance between the emphasis put by the Union on its social, environmental and developmental messages in the dialogue with the world on the one hand, and the minimal response of the Asian public and media to these messages on the other.

When it comes to the media coverage outside the Union's borders, the EU's global influence on social and environmental issues was initially expected to translate in media terms into the news values of "importance", "significance" and "human interest",[53] and thus to be popular topics in international media representations of the EU. Indeed, many of the EU's policies and measures in these areas have an immediate economic and political impact on the nine locations in this study, often triggering controversial responses and critical self-re-evaluations. Additionally, it was presumed that news audiences can more easily relate to social, environmental and developmental topics. While the EU's political and economic existence is complicated and permanently in flux, human interest matters are easily communicated to global news audiences. However, it was observed that both newspapers and television news in the nine locations did not prioritise the 'human face' of the EU.

Across the nine news media discourses, the media portrayals of the EU as an actor in the social, environmental and developmental fields were among the least visible features, possibly communicating that these actions are rather insignificant in the hierarchy of the EU's activities. Moreover, coverage of the EU was random (confusing?); disconnected from domestic concerns (irrelevant for local public?); and, finally, not eliciting distinct emotions or attitudes from the local audiences (politely-indifferent?). Undoubtedly, the EU's political novelty, operational complexity and constantly evolving nature add to the growing concern that the EU is still profoundly misunderstood

---

[52] Holland, Martin, Peter Ryan, Alojzy Nowak and Natalia Chaban (eds), *The EU through the Eyes of Asia*. Singapore/Warsaw: ASEF/University of Warsaw, 2007.

[53] Shoemaker, Pamela and Stephen Reese, 'Mediating the Message, in *Theories of Influences on Mass Media Content*, 2nd ed., White Plains, NY: Longman, 1996.

outside its borders.[54] Such invisible, unrelated and haphazard news coverage of the EU's social, environmental and developmental actions adds to cognitive confusion when Asian audiences attempt to understand and categorise the EU and it is argued to contribute to the formation of the most frequent stereotypical mental images of the EU, which exclude information on the EU's social, environmental and developmental features. Indeed, the views of the general public in the region were found to de-emphasise and consistently overlook the images of the EU as an 'adopter' and 'influencer' of one of the world's most progressive and sophisticated social, environmental and developmental agendas.

Geographical and cultural distances are partially to 'blame' for the peculiar media and public profiling of the EU in the three spheres in the nine Asian locations. The EU's peaceful and integrationist presence is another reason why the international news media, which is often characterised by its "willingness to dig out scandals, falsehoods, and problems",[55] may overlook the EU. The external under-representation of these three key features of the EU is also the responsibility of EU institutions that have arguably failed to communicate both the social, environmental and developmental achievements of the EU's integration process and the EU's impacts on international community in these areas. Arguably, this failure deprives the EU of an additional mechanism for legitimating its international influence. Indeed, according to Bridges, economics have been the leading gateway for post-colonial Europe to re-enter Asia.[56] Such issues as business, trade, investment and technology have overshadowed budding political interactions, leaving social, environmental and developmental affairs out in the cold. As a result, "the cultural, educational, and other links are still comparatively insubstantial".[57]

---

[54] Gouveia, Philip Fiske de and Hester Plumridge, *European Infopolitik: Developing EU Pubic Strategy*, London: The Foreign Policy Centre, 2005.

[55] Rubin, Bury, *How Others Report Us: America In The Foreign Press*, 'The Washington Papers'. Vol. VII, The Centre for Strategic and International Studies Georgetown University, Washington, D.C., Beverly Hills/London: Sage Publications, 1979, p. 13.

[56] Brian Bridges, *Europe and the Challenge of the Asia Pacific*, p. 200.

[57] *Ibid.*, 201.

Intriguingly, most of the coverage of the EU's social, environmental and developmental activities positioned the Union outside the locations, even if the EU's actions had a direct impact (positive or negative) on these areas. For example, the news on EU's social affairs prioritised what the Union does for its own citizens, and overlooked the EU's regional efforts in this regard. Locations that benefit from the EU's developmental aid efforts choose to prioritise reporting the Union's assistance to third parties, and overlook the impact of such aid locally — as seen, for example, in the issue of the cessation of EU aid to Palestine which was the most visible across the region, despite five out of nine locations in this study receiving substantial packages of EU developmental aid themselves. Similarly, the Union's environmental initiatives were most visible as global policies and internal-to-Europe actions. In addition, the resulting images sometimes differed, or even directly clashed with the EU's self-vision (for example, the negative evaluations visible in the coverage of the RoHS scheme by Hong Kong news).

Encouragingly, this study discovered a general tendency to assign more positive than negative evaluations to the EU's social, environmental and developmental actions (with a neutral evaluation still dominating). Initially, a reverse trend — namely, a heavier share of negativity — was expected. Two factors shaped this expectation: first, anti-European and nationalistic sentiments as a possible response to an imperialist and colonial European presence in Asia in the past and the complex and controversial multicultural landscape in Europe nowadays; and second, the tendency of the news to "distort, sensationalize, and focus on 'negative' aspects of the foreign counterparts."[58] It is suggested that a more perceptibly positive representation of the EU by Asian newsmakers in these fields would be both promising and useful for raising the EU's profile in Asia. Such evaluative preferences may indicate that the EU's social, environmental and developmental activities add to the EU's international image as a 'soft' and 'normative' power' and may also indicate that the core issues in the EU-Asia dialogue, primarily focusing first on economics

---

[58] Rubin, Bury, *How Others Report Us: America in the Foreign Press*, p. 14.

and then on politics, are seen as being increasingly intertwined with social, environmental and developmental topics. This positive profiling of the EU in reputable news media is argued to contribute to the formation of public opinion on what issues should be prioritised in official dialogue with the EU. A need for social, environmental and developmental interactions entered this list, yet did not occupy leading positions.

While this study accepts that news audiences do not passively consume and accept the meanings proposed by news discourses, certain forms of media discourse do have a stronger persuasive power than others and foreign news is one of those forms. As foreign policymaking is the prerogative of a select group of national elites, and with foreign affairs being out of the immediate reach of the majority of the population, foreign news is often an uncontested source of information for the general public.[59] Foreign news representations in domestic discourses may therefore influence what people see as the most important information about foreign affairs and policy making, and thus influence people's images of distant and close international partners. While Mainland China and Vietnam were different in this special case study (their media are controlled by the government), the seven other locations are societies which claim that their media are free. In such societies, there is a need for a well-informed public able to execute control over and vocalise feedback to powerful elites (both in domestic and international affairs). Respectively, governments in such societies will draw heavily on the view of the EU available in their own reputable press and broadcasts. But even in those societies where the media is under stricter government supervision, the media images of the EU could be what Rubin calls a "prime indication"[60] and even the "best source of evidence"[61] of current official attitudes towards the EU. Rubin argues that in such societies "the press is used by such foreign governments both for

---

[59] Cohen, Bernard, *The Press and Foreign Policy*, Princeton, NJ: Princeton University Press, 1963, pp. 12–13.

[60] Rubin, Bury, *How Others Report Us: America In The Foreign Press*, p. 7.

[61] *Ibid.*

diplomatic signalling and for shaping the ideas of their people. Even so, leaders may be more affected by the clichés of their own coverage that one might expect."[62]

In an increasingly globalising and interdependent world, the EU and its Asian counterparts need to critically re-evaluate the course and strength of their relationship. In promoting candid dialogue between Asia and Europe, it is crucial to identify points of mutual understanding and acknowledge divergent views. As Siamak Movahedi argued, "images and perceptions of other nations provide the basic framework within which the conduct of international relations and conflict resolution takes place."[63] It is with this framework in mind that this chapter offers a systematic and detailed account of the imagery of the EU in Asian public discourses. This study suggests that the findings may in fact turn out to contradict the EU's initial expectations and self-assessment, and this is where such research is of a great value to both the EU and the Asian locations studied.

For the EU, ignorance or partial awareness of how Asian societies recognise (or do not) the Union may potentially affect the quality of its foreign policy-making regarding the region. There is the risk that the development of the EU's foreign policy goals and actions, as well as its assessment of its capabilities and expectations in Asia, may be inappropriate, unrealistic, irrelevant or inefficient. As a result, this hindered global understanding threatens to de-prioritise the Union in the eyes of its important Asian partners in favour of other powerful world players. Importantly, such an impaired understanding and reaction to external perceptions has serious internal consequences. Indeed, a perception of Europe as 'failing' internationally in social, environmental and developmental affairs — be it in promoting international human rights, endorsing the Kyoto

---

[62] *Ibid.*

[63] Movahedi, Siamak, 'The Social Psychology of Foreign Policy and the Politics of International Images", *Human Affairs*, Vol. 8, No. 19, 1985, <http://www.faculty.umb.edu/siamak_movahedi/Library/social_psychology_of_foreign_policy.pdf>, accessed 11 August 2006.

protocol targets, or supporting various developmental programmes around the world — puts at risk the notion of integration and its legitimacy for EU citizens.[64]

Equally, a low awareness of the EU jeopardises the Asian position in its dialogues with global powers. Mutual challenges shape Asia and Europe, such as better understanding of the diversity of cultures and civilisations, the impacts of global warming and climate change, gender equality issues, better education for children, good heath for all and a safer, more prosperous existence. Fed vague and unclear imagery of Europe and its social, environmental and developmental activities, Asian societies may not fully engage with the EU in new ways, overlook the need to initiate contact, or miss out on a range of activities in established areas of interaction. This study argued that an honest, sober and consistent account of such imagery is crucial for a reassessment of the dynamics of EU-Asia relations. This re-evaluation is necessary to boost a more effective dialogue between the two regions in order to meet regional and global challenges.

---

[64] Martin Holland, "The Common Foreign and Security Policy", in *Developments in the European Union*, edited by Laura Cram, Desmond Dinan and Neill Nugent, London: Macmillan (1999), 243.

Chapter 6

ASEM under the Radar: Media Portrayals of Asia-Europe Meeting in Asia

Suet Yi Lai and Natalia Chaban

INTRODUCTION

In mid-October 2008, forty-three state leaders from Asia and Europe, the European Commission (EC) and Secretariat of Association of Southeast Asian Nations (ASEAN) finished their inter-regional meeting in Beijing under the Asia-Europe Meeting (ASEM) framework[1] with a historically high attendance and increased attention from the international community. The Beijing Summit marked the twelfth anniversary of ASEM as well as its largest membership after

---

[1] The Asia-Europe Meeting (ASEM) framework officially began in March 1996, the inaugural Bangkok Summit. The inter-regional dialogue was established to complete the triangular relations among North America, Europe and Asia. More information is available at <www.aseminfoboard.org>

enlargements in both the EU and ASEAN.[2] Unsurprisingly, ASEM's growing size and its global exposure have resulted in mounting academic reflections on its role and impact on the dialogue between Europe and Asia.[3] However, any systematic scholarly accounts of the images and perceptions of ASEM among the wider European and Asian public have been absent. Consequently, this chapter aims to identify the images of ASEM as portrayed in leading Asian newspapers. The leading research questions are *How does Asia's reputable press frame ASEM for its readers?* and *How can ASEM's image be improved?* The prestigious national newspapers analysed in this study were considered to be reliable sources of current political information,

---

[2] In the inaugural 1996 Bangkok meeting there were twenty six parties represented in ASEM, seven member states of Association of Southeast Asian Nations (ASEAN7 were Brunei, Indonesia, Malaysia, the Philippines, Singapore, Thailand and Vietnam), three Northeast Asian countries (China, Japan and South Korea), fifteen EU member states and European Commission. The first enlargement of ASEM took place in 2004 to admit three new ASEAN members (Burma, Cambodia and Laos) and ten new EU members. The third ASEM enlargement came into effect in ASEM7 to include also India, Mongolia, Pakistan and ASEAN Secretariat on the Asian side, Bulgaria and Romania on the European side. Today ASEM is a framework of 45 parties.

[3] See Reiterer, Michael, 'Asia-Europe Meeting (ASEM): Fostering a Multilpolar World Order through Inter-Regional Cooperation', *Asia-Europe Journal*, Vol. 7, No. 1, 2009, pp. 179–196; Pereira, Rui, 'The Helsinki Summit and the Future Course of Asia-Europe Meeting', *Asia-Europe Journal*, Vol. 5, No. 1, 2007, pp. 17–21; Yepes, César de Prado, 'The Effect of ASEM on European Foreign Policies', *Asia-Europe Journal*, Vol. 3, No. 1, 2005, pp. 25–35; Dent, Christopher, 'The Asia-Europe Meeting and Inter-Regionalism: Toward a Theory of Multilateral Utility', *Asian Survey*, Vol. 44, No. 2, 2004, pp. 213–236; Reiterer, Michael, *The New Regionalism and Regional Identity Building: a Lesson from the Asia-Europe Meeting (ASEM)*, paper at the CHIR Conference on Regional Integration and Cooperation, Tokyo University of Foreign Studies, 17 September 2004; Rüland, Jürgen, *The European Union as an Inter- and Trans-regional Actor: Lessons for Global Governance from Europe's Relations with Asia*, paper presented in a conference "The EU in International Affairs", National Europe Centre, Australian National University, 3–4 July 2002; Stokhof, Wim and Paul van der Velde (eds.), *Asian European Perspective: Developing the ASEM Process*, London, Curzon Press, 2001; Rüland, Jürgen, *Transregional Relations: The Asia-Europe Meeting — A Functional Analysis*, paper at the International Conference "Asia and Europe on the Eve of 21st Century", Chulalongkorn University, Bangkok, 19–20 August 1999.

trusted by both the general public and national decision-makers[4] and serving as news leaders and agenda-setters for other sections of the mass media.[5]

Since its inception in 1996,[6] ASEM has biennially brought together leaders from Asia and Europe for informal dialogues. As stated in the European Commission publication *"ASEM7 in Beijing"*,[7] the inter-regional dialogue was created to "fill the missing link among the Triads",[8] (East Asia, Europe and North America), and strengthen the relationship between Asia and Europe.[9] As a result, ASEM provides a unique opportunity for the leaders of Asia and Europe to regularly meet each other on an informal and equal footing.[10] Due to this informality and multi-dimensionality, the leaders from the two regions are free to adjust the agenda of the summit. Hence, topics ranging from the political interaction to environmental protection have the opportunity to be highlighted. This allows ASEM to be more reactive to the changing contemporary situation in the world than most other bilateral or multilateral arrangements which focus on a single area and thus, the heads of

---

[4] Schulz, Winfried, *Foreign News in Leading Newspapers of Western and Post-Communist Countries*, paper presented at the 51st Annual Conference of the International Communication Association, 24–28 May 2001, Washington, D.C.

[5] Larson, James, 'International Affairs Coverage on U.S. Network Television', *Journal of Communication*, Vol. 29, No. 2, 1979, pp. 136–147.

[6] The ASEM1 was held in Bangkok (1–2 March 1996); ASEM2 was held in London (3–4 April 1998); ASEM3 was held in Seoul (20–21 October 2000); ASEM4 was held in Copenhagen (22–24 September 2002); ASEM5 was held in Hanoi (8–9 October 2004); ASEM6 was held in Helsinki (10–11 September 2006); ASEM7 was held in Beijing (24–25 October 2008).

[7] Hwee, Yeo Lay, *ASEM7 in Beijing*, 2008, European Commission, p. 6.

[8] See also Chen, Zhimin, 'NATO, APEC, ASEM: Triadic Inter-regionalism and Global Order', *Asia-Europe Journal*, Vol. 3, No. 3, 2005, pp. 361–378; Hänggi, Heiner, 'ASEM and the Construction of the New Triad', *Journal of the Asia Pacific Economy*, Vol. 4, No. 1, 1999, pp. 56–80.

[9] <http://www.aseminfoboard.org/page.phtml?code=About>.

[10] Informality and equal partnership are two of the four key characteristics of ASEM. The other two are multi-dimensionality and dual focus on high-level and people-to-people. For more information: <http://www.aseminfoboard.org/page.phtml?code=About>.

state/government can almost immediately address issues where common concern and interest lie. However, conversely, this informality, as well as the absence of a permanent coordinating body, has created the impression in some people's eyes that ASEM is merely a "talking-shop".[11]

Like any respected international organisation, ASEM needs to consider its projected imagery and how it is understood. Such images and perceptions of ASEM can be regarded as "intangibles"[12] — immaterial but essential assets building the substantial foundation of the institution. Impaired or overlooked intangibles may lead to flawed policies, mismanaged resources and imprecise ideas of how an organisation functions. Subsequently, this chapter argues that a systematic study of ASEM's external imagery (media imagery in our case) will be instrumental in understanding this atypical inter-regional forum as it enters its second decade. Moreover, it is believed that a comparative account of such imagery will assist ASEM to undertake a sober self-evaluation and make improvements accordingly.

METHODOLOGY

This chapter focuses its attention on the ASEM imagery in reputable national newspapers across eight Asian locations, namely four North East Asian localities of Japan, South Korea, mainland China and SAR Hong Kong; and four South-East Asian countries of Singapore, Thailand, Indonesia and the Philippines. In order to warrant comparability in the analysis of the media content in this multilingual analysis, this chapter focused on the media portrayals of ASEM in the English-language press in the region (Table 1).

---

[11] "Time for new rules to guide world economy", *Strait Times*, 26 October 2008; "Opportunity to unite or a talking shop?", *South China Morning Post*, 24 October 2008; "Crisis upgrades Asia-Europe Meeting", *Bangkok Post*, 23 October 2008; Overview Report on ASEM Initiatives, <http://www.asem6.fi/news_and_documents/en_GB/1146137012358/>

[12] Zambon, Stefano, *Visualizing Intangibles as Company Drovers of Innovation and Growth Some Recent European Developments*, presentation given at National Centre for Research on Europe, University of Canterbury, New Zealand, 22 July 2005.

Table 1:   Monitored English-Language dailies

Locations	English-Language Dailies Chosen	Ownership	Circulation
North East Asia			
Mainland China	*China Daily*	Communist Party of China	300,000[13]
Hong Kong SAR	*South China Morning Post*	SCMP Group[14]	107,080[15]
Japan	*Japan Times*	Japan Times Ltd	70,000[16]
South Korea	*Korea Herald*	Herald Media	50% market share[17]
South East Asia			
Indonesia	*Jakarta Post*	PT Bina Media Tenggara	35,000[18]
The Philippines	*Manila Bulletin*	Manila Bulletin Publishing Corporation[19]	47% market share[20]
Singapore	*Strait Times*	Singapore Press Holdings	388,500[21]
Thailand	*Bangkok Post*	Post Publishing Public Co. Ltd[22]	63,000[23]

[13] <http://www.chinadaily.com.cn/cd/introduction.html>.

[14] 34.9% of stake of SCMP Group is owned by the Kuok's family who owns Kerry Group since 1993.

[15] Average net circulation of per issue from January to June 2008 according to Audit Report of Hong Kong Audit Bureau of Circulation, <http://www.hkabc.com.hk/en/index.htm>.

[16] Source: *Asia Media Project-Japan*, Michelle Wong and Vivian Mak, Journalism and Media Studies Centre of Hong Kong University, <http://jmsc.hku.hk/students/jmscjournal/critical/michellevivian_03.htm>.

[17] Thr *Korea Herald* dominates more than 50% of market share of English-language newspaper market in Korea, <http://www.heraldm.com/english/sub-business_e01.htm>.

[18] *Jakarta Post* Media Kit 2006, <http://old.thejakartapost.com/adsspecial/medkit06/fast_facts.html>.

[19] *Manila Bulletin* Publishing Corporation is owned by a Filipino-Chinese business mogul Emilio Yap.

Every location in this study has a reputable English-language daily which is typically read by local leaders, educated elites (including students) and foreigners (either residing in an Asian location, or following local events from abroad).[24] The local English-language press is also read by media professionals from outside the locality as a guide for external newsmakers in reporting domestic current events. Such newspapers tend to employ both local and foreign journalists and editors with proficiency in English and extensive international experiences. These outlets also tend to cooperate closely with international news wires. Due to the profile of their readership and staff, the English-language dailies in the Asian locations examined in this study create a unique and highly respected forum for the exchange of ideas on regional and international developments. Arguably, such newspapers should feature a high interest in the major international summits and their impact, ASEM included.

This comparative analysis concentrated on the 'peak' periods in ASEM's media coverage — one month before the ASEM summit to one week after the two-day meeting both in 2006 and 2008. The monitoring period for ASEM6 (Helsinki) was from August 10 to September 18 in 2006, and for ASEM7 (Beijing) from September 24 to November 1 in 2008. The news outputs of the English-language

---

[20] On 22nd December 2007, survey results by Nielsen Media Research "Nielsen Media Index Study (Enhanced Wave 2)", covering the whole year of 2007, indicated that the *Manila Bulletin* had 47% of readership in the Philippines, <http://newsinfo. inquirer.net/breakingnews/nation/view_article.php?article_id=108388>.

[21] Press release of Singapore Press Holdings, <http://www.asiamediajournal.com/ pressrelease.php?id=530>.

[22] Its major shareholders include the Chirathivat family (owners of Central Group), the *South China Morning Post* of Hong Kong and GMM Grammy Pcl., a local media and entertainment firm.

[23] Press release from Koenig and Bauer AG, May 23, 2007, <kba-print.de/ Filestore.aspx/...&lang=en&filetype=rtf&index=true>.

[24] In this project, three sampled newspapers in the Philippines and two in Singapore were in English.

newspapers for these two periods were searched using the key phrases of 'Asia Europe Meeting', 'ASEM' or 'Asia Europe Summit'.[25] A total of 190 news items were collected and analysed (averaging 17.3 news items per week per outlet).

RESULTS

Is ASEM Visible in Asian News Media?

Figure 1 illustrates a peculiar, 'peaking' pattern in the distribution of the 190 identified news items which referenced the ASEM process in the English-language newspapers. References to the ASEM summit 'skyrocketed' during the week of the meeting, with 52 articles in 2006,[26] (70% of the total coverage for that period), and 80 articles in 2008,[27] (representing 69% of the coverage that period).

Comparing the number of articles in the two respective years, a significant growth in volume was observed — from 6.5 news stories per week on average in 2006 to 10 news items per week in 2008. Among the 190 news articles collected, 74 covered ASEM6 in 2006 and 116 referenced ASEM7 in 2008 — a remarkable 57% increase in volume of news mentioning ASEM. The growth in attention of the news media towards ASEM was found in almost all newspapers that were monitored. One exception was the *Manila Bulletin* in the Philippines, which was found to halve its ASEM coverage from eighteen to nine news stories. Also, both the *Strait Times* of Singapore and the *Japan Times* were found to produce one item less in 2008, compared with 2006. In contrast, the volume of news referencing 'ASEM'

---

[25] For Indonesia and Philippines, on-line database FACTIVA was used. Data from other locations was located on various e-search engines by local researchers employed in the project. Vietnam's English-Language newspapers were not available either through FACTIVA, or other e-search engines, thus it was excluded from this analysis.

[26] from 7th to 13th September 2006.

[27] from 21st to 27th October 2008.

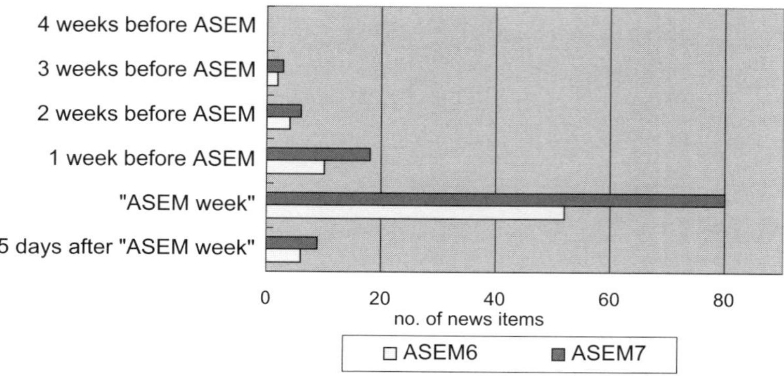

Figure 1:   Distribution of news items referencing 'ASEM' by week

increased dramatically in the remaining five monitored newspapers. The *China Daily, Bangkok Post* and *Korea Herald* more than doubled their coverage of ASEM, the *Jakarta Post* nearly tripled it and Hong Kong's *South China Morning Post* more than tripled its news output on ASEM, as demonstrated in Figure 2.

Arguably, several factors influenced the Asian media's heightened attention on ASEM7 in 2008. Among those, the major one was the global financial crisis of 2008 which dominated not only the front pages of the regional press in the region, but also the agenda of ASEM7. Unsurprisingly, local media followed the summit which was anticipated to find some viable solutions to the financial disaster. Indeed, 62 out of 116 'ASEM'-referenced news items in 2008 (54%), focused on ASEM7 in the context of the global financial crisis. For example, the influential Thai newspaper *Bangkok Post* acidly noted that

> the unfolding global effort to address the international financial crisis has become a blessing in disguise for the Asia-Europe Meeting (Asem), normally a bland talkshop, which opens tomorrow in Beijing.[28]

Singapore's *Strait Times* noted that ASEM was "a biennial summit of leaders which has taken on greater significance this year because of the

---

[28] "Crisis upgrades Asia-Europe Meeting", *Bangkok Post*, 23 October 2008.

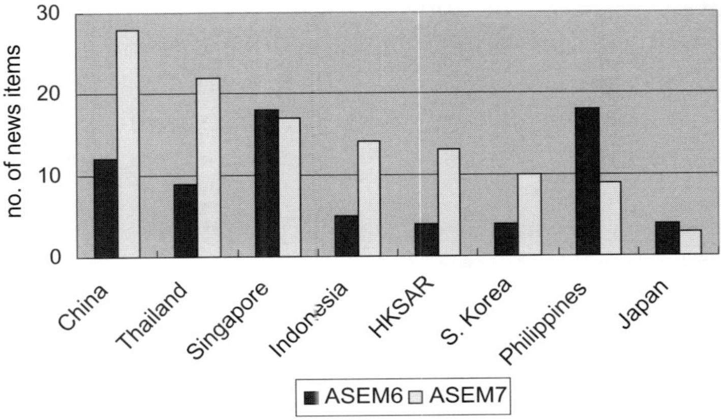

Figure 2:   **Number of news items referencing 'ASEM' across eight Asian locations**

global financial crisis".[29] The *Korean Herald* echoed their sentiments predicting that ASEM7 summit would "be dominated by the global financial crisis".[30] According to Hong Kong's *South China Morning Post,* "There are rising hopes for the summit, the first large-scale international meeting since the global financial crisis kicked in."[31] The French ambassador to Thailand, Laurent Bili, told the *Bangkok Post* that "the forum [ASEM] would be a good opportunity for Asian and European leaders to discuss the crisis that has devastated financial markets across the world".[32] All of the examined newspapers agreed that the US-triggered global financial turmoil topped the agenda of ASEM7, even though the US was not a part of the ASEM process.

The second possible reason for the Asian media's increased attention to the 2008 meeting was the venue of the summit. ASEM7 was held in Beijing, China, 'close to home', whereas ASEM6 was held in Helsinki, Finland, and perceived to be distant and thus perhaps less

---

[29] "FTA to be inked when PM Lee visits China'", *Strait Times,* 22 October 2008.

[30] "East Asian leaders agree on $80b war chest", *Korea Herald,* 25 October 2008.

[31] "Opportunity to unite or a talking shop? Leaders at Asem meeting will have a chance to prove the bloc can make a difference", *South China Morning Post,* 24 October 2008.

[32] "Asem to examine crisis", *Bangkok Post,* 9 October 2008.

relevant. Predictably, in 2008 the volume of 'ASEM' news grew sharply in the *China Daily* (from 12 in 2006 to 28 in 2008), and in the *South China Morning Post* of Hong Kong (from 4 to 13). At least for several weeks in the two year-period between the summits, for these two locations, ASEM moved 'closer to home' and became a leading item of local news.

The larger volume of Thailand coverage of ASEM may be explained somewhat differently. Obviously, the two factors discussed above were instrumental, however, two events with a local 'flavour' also contributed to the higher profile for ASEM in the local press. Firstly, in the sidelines of ASEM7 there emerged a chance to conduct talks between Thai Prime Minister Somchai Wongsawat and his Cambodian counterpart Hun Sen about their border conflict (almost 40% of the Thai ASEM news reflected this topic).[33] Importantly, the Cambodia-Thai border conflict also attracted attention from the *Strait Times* and *Jakarta Post*, who devoted some space to report the talks between the two leaders during ASEM7 summit.[34]

Secondly, there was a fear of yet another military coup in Thailand while its Prime Minister Somchai was overseas attending ASEM7 (almost 20% of the 'ASEM' coverage in the *Bangkok Post* mentioned this topic).[35] The 2006 military coup, which forced former Thai Prime Minister Thaksin to resign coincided with his trip to ASEM6 in Helsinki and a UN meeting in London. Several Thai publications linked ASEM7 with the protests in Bangkok predicting the coup.

Paradoxically, the sharp drop in visibility for ASEM7 in the *Manila Bulletin* could be attributed to the comparatively high visibility of ASEM6. The 2006 meeting featured the Japan–Philippines Economic Partnership Agreement (JPEPA), signed by Japan and

---

[33] Examples: "Somchai seeks talks with Hun Sen, says external mediation not necessary", *Bangkok Post*, 19 October 2008; "Border dispute — Cambodia reports temple damage to UN, says external mediation not necessary", *Bangkok Post*, 27 October 2008.

[34] Examples: "Tensions cool — for now", *Strait Times*, 17 October 2008; "SBY backs new Southeast Asian funding program", *Jakarta Post*, 17 October 2008.

[35] Examples: "PM tries to calm global concern", *Bangkok Post*, 9 October 2008; "With fears of another coup rife, PM heads to Beijing", *Bangkok Post*, 24 October 2008; "Thaksin verdict brings no relief", *Strait Times*, 24 October 2008.

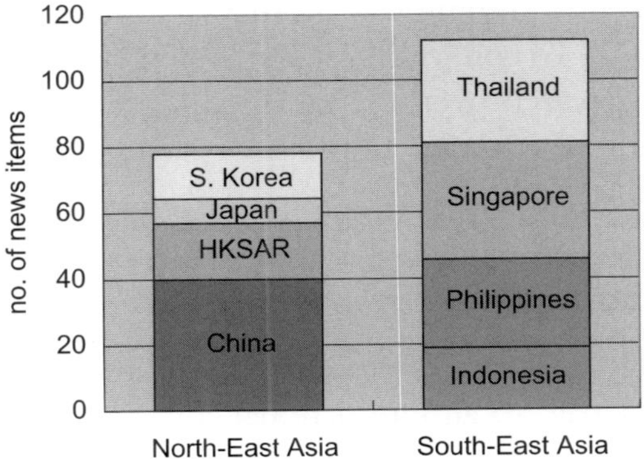

Figure 3:   **Number of news items referencing 'ASEM' in North-East and South-East Asia**

the Philippines in Helsinki by the countries' leaders attending the meeting. Unsurprisingly, the Philippines' media prioritised that ASEM6 outcome — half of the ASEM articles in 2006 mentioned ASEM simply because it represented the time and venue of signing the JPEPA.[36]

Figure 3 describes the volume of the news referencing ASEM geographically, illustrating the dichotomy of ASEM's visibility between North-East *vs.* South-East Asia. ASEM proved to be significantly more visible in the South-East Asian press. Moreover, more than a half of the ASEM articles in North-East Asia came from the one source, the *China Daily*, revealing a relatively low visibility of ASEM on the pages of the other three North-East Asian English-language dailies from Hong Kong, Japan and South Korea.

In general, there has been a growth in the volume of ASEM-news in the Asian press. As shown, the relevance of the official agenda as well as that of the sideline events are proportional to the space which newsmakers in the related countries are willing to devote. Further, the

---

[36] Examples: "Under RP-Japan Economic Partnership Agreement", *Manila Bulletin*, 31 August 2006; "Japan, RP to sign bilateral EPA in Helsinki next week", *Manila Bulletin*, 5 September 2006.

venue for the ASEM summit was another factor that affected the news media's coverage. To confirm these initial observations, it is necessary to repeat this research over a longer period of ASEM summits: the mirror reflection of coverage in the European papers would also add to our sparse knowledge.

Is ASEM a Stranger?

While visibility in terms of volume is an important indicator of media attention paid to an international counterpart or meeting, this analysis also employs the qualitative tool of content analysis to measure the appearances of ASEM in the Asian English-speaking press to identify the intensity and degree of local relevance. The methodology used to operationalise local relevance employed the *focus of domesticity* (see Introduction to this volume). Depending on the local or external grounding of ASEM in a news item, each item was analysed according to a four-set model — *pure ASEM news* (a story solely devoted to and occurring at the ASEM summit); *local ASEM news* (a story with domestic storyline in the context of ASEM, e.g., report of China's actions in ASEM found in the *China Daily*); *regional ASEM news* (a story about a regional partner in the context of ASEM, e.g. coverage of Malaysia's actions in ASEM in the Singaporean *Strait Times*); and, finally, *international ASEM news* (a story reporting a non-ASEM country in the context of ASEM). Since this study has originated from a larger project "The EU in the Eyes of Asia", it also paid special attention to the *EU ASEM* news (a story focusing on the EU in the context of ASEM). The distribution of the *foci of domesticity* in ASEM coverage (combining data from 2006 and 2008) is illustrated in Figure 4.

To answer the question of whether ASEM was framed by the local press as a relevant event for the home locality three foci were used — *local, regional* and *pure ASEM*. It was found that ASEM was reported most frequently in *local* news (almost half of the sample — 48% of news articles — fell into this category). For instance, in 2006, the *Japan Times'* report entitled "No talks at ASEM with Wen, Roh"[37]

---

[37] 26 August, 2006.

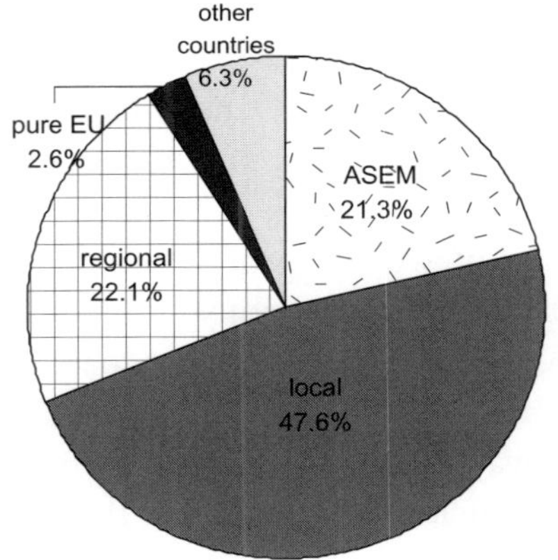

Figure 4:   Focus of domesticity (average of ASEM6 and ASEM7 coverage)

actually focused on Japan's relations with China and South Korea. The *Strait Times'* report "Singapore beefs up anti-terror controls at ports"[38] concentrated on the ASEM discussion of Singapore's port control on strategic goods to fight against terrorism. The *Bangkok Post's* article "Democracy out of whack?"[39] reported talks between former Thai Prime Minister Thaksin visiting the ASEM summit and the Thai media. Examples in 2008 included the *China Daily's* "Public gets a glimpse of envoys"[40] reporting the press conference which also gave information about the Beijing ASEM after the accreditation ceremony for new Chinese ambassadors. The *Korea Herald's* "Seoul plans anti-crisis measures"[41] described South Korea's follow-up of the bilateral and multilateral agreements reached during ASEM7 against the financial crisis. The *Jakarta Post's* "Indonesia ratifies ASEAN Charter"[42] stated Indonesia's ratification of ASEAN's new Charter before the ASEAN leaders meeting which was to be held in the sidelines of ASEM7.

---

[38] 11 September, 2006.

[39] 17 September, 2006.

[40] 20 October, 2008.

[41] 27 October, 2008.

[42] 22 October, 2008.

Pure ASEM news was less frequent, yet still accounted for a fifth of the sample (21%). Some examples included the *China Daily*'s "Yantai to host ASEM tourism forum"[43] and "Pakistan, India, Mongolia invited to join ASEM";[44] the *Manila Bulletin's* "Asia, EU leaders to focus on trade at Helsinki summit";[45] the *Jakarta Post*'s "ASEM summit vows better migrant worker protection";[46] and the *South China Morning Post*'s "Summit big on promises but short on solutions".[47]

The *regional* focus represented a similar share of media attention — 22%. For example, the *South China Morning Post*'s "Wen reaffirms commitment to six-way talks on N Korea"[48] focused on China's role in the North Korean nuclear issue entering the ASEM agenda. Or the *Manila Bulletin*'s "De Venecia proposes Asian financial stimulus package"[49] discussed cooperation in Asia against the global financial crisis and ASEM's role in this. Table 2 reports the distribution of the foci of domesticity in the coverage of ASEM for 2006 and for 2008.

Comparing over time, while *pure ASEM* news received a similar share of attention in 2006 and 2008, the *locally*-angled news decreased in its visibility, while *regionally*-grounded ASEM news became more voluminous. Arguably, a heightened *regional* perspective

Table 2:   The focus of domesticity during ASEM6 and ASEM7

	Focus of Domesticity				
	Pure ASEM (%)	Local (%)	Regional (%)	Pure EU (%)	International (%)
2006 ASEM6	20.9	53.4	17.6	2.7	5.4
2008 ASEM7	21.6	44.0	25.0	2.6	6.9

---

[43] 29 August 2006.

[44] 11 September 2006.

[45] 8 September 2006.

[46] 16 October 2008.

[47] 26 October 2008.

[48] 12 September 2006.

[49] 17 October 2008.

is due to the fact that ASEM7 was held in the region, in Beijing, 'closer to home'. With ASEM8 taking place in Brussels in 2010, a follow-up study would be helpful to further trace the dynamics in the grounding of ASEM in Asian press (with the regional focus possibly decreasing again with the summit taking place in Europe if this tentative hypothesis holds).

To sum up, the prevalent *local* anchoring of ASEM when combined with the *regionally*-focused stories accounted for 71% of the total coverage of ASEM in 2006 and 69% in 2008. These indicators suggest that the ASEM process is not something foreign or irrelevant to Asian media and audiences but rather is considered both familiar and important.

Is ASEM a Main or a Minor Actor?

While *focus of domesticity* informed us of the imaginary distance a reported event is from the locality, the next indicator — *degree of centrality* — specified the intensity of ASEM's representation. The intensity was coded in this study in tri-partite terms — ASEM as a *major, secondary* or *minor* actor in a news story. ASEM was a *major* actor when the story focused on the summit itself and when ASEM's actions dominated the storyline. ASEM was a *minor* actor when the summit was mentioned in the article only once, in a brief or fleeting manner. ASEM was classified as a *secondary* actor when it was reported acting *on par* with other international/regional actors and the story's attention was equally split between those actors.

As shown in Figure 5, the coverage of ASEM6 and ASEM7 was substantially dominated by a *minor* degree of centrality, despite the process's growing reputation and membership numbers.

There was virtually no change in the *degree of centrality* over time. However, the volume of news featuring ASEM as a *major* actor did increase slightly — from 15% in 2006 to 21% in 2008 with this gain paralleled by a decrease in the numbers of articles presenting ASEM as *minor* actor. Nevertheless, news which profiled ASEM as merely a *minor* actor still clearly dominated. Moreover, in many reports, ASEM was not seen as an *actor* at all. Many of the *minor* centrality

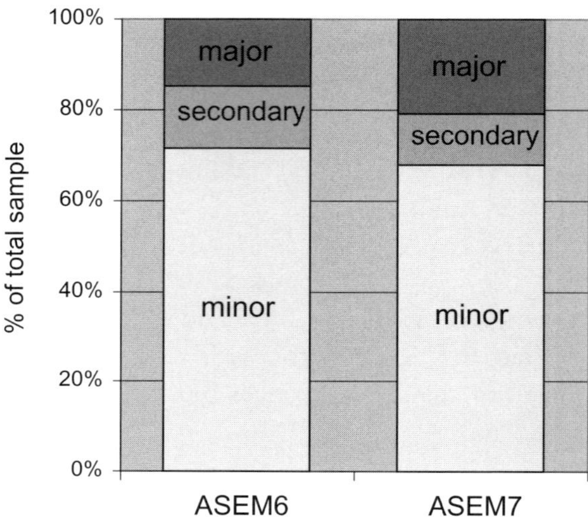

Figure 5:   Degree of centrality in the coverage of ASEM6 and ASEM7

news stories treated ASEM as a *venue* where one head of state/ government was meeting with other heads of state/government rather than as an important political process!

Revealingly, actions and views of leaders on their local home-issues attracted more media attention than coverage of communal actions and decisions. Asian editors and journalists often appeared more interested in covering the 'sidelines' surrounding the ASEM summits than reporting actual ASEM happenings. In one of the most obvious examples, ASEM only appeared in Thai and Singaporean newspapers in 2006 when former Thai Prime Minister Thaksin spoke about the political instability in Thailand during the 'sideline' of ASEM6. In another example, journalists from mainland China, Hong Kong SAR, Japan and South Korea were more concerned whether former Japanese Prime Minister Koizumi would greet or talk to his Chinese and Korean counterparts than about ASEM6 outcomes. The EU arms embargo against China discussed in ASEM's sidelines received greater attention from the Chinese press than the overall content of ASEM6. Interestingly — and perhaps revealingly — journalists often asked questions on issues which were irrelevant to the agenda of the actual summit.

ASEM is famous for meetings which 'mushroom' around major ASEM events, bilaterally, trilaterally and multilaterally. The bilateral ones are the most numerous, predictably attracting major media attention due to proximity and the importance of issues discussed. Yet, notably, regional meetings (such as among ASEAN members or ASEAN + 3 participants) also occur and are frequently mentioned by local reporters. Arguably, a growing number of reported 'sideline' events in 2008 solidified an image of ASEM as merely serving as a big 'shell' or 'umbrella' for numerous other meetings among the participants. For instance, a *China Daily* article about Sino-Japanese relations referenced ASEM as: "...the two-day sixth Asia-Europe Meeting (ASEM) where leaders of 13 Asian countries mingled on the sidelines of the summit."[50]

Table 3 displays the programme of 'sideline' meetings in ASEM 6 with 21 state-to-state bilateral meetings, one trilateral meeting,[51] three regional organisation-state inter-regional meetings (with the EU as a single actor), one region-to-region inter-regional meeting (EU and ASEAN) and one regional meeting (ASEAN + 3).

Table 4 illustrates 'sideline' events two years later at ASEM7 — the agenda was even busier with a total of thirty-four such meetings: twenty-seven state-to-state bilateral meetings, one trilateral, four regional organisation-state inter-regional meetings and two regional meetings.

To summarise, two-thirds of the ASEM sample profiled the 2006 and 2008 meetings from a *minor*-centrality perspective. 'Non-ASEM stories' in the margins appeared to be much more appealing to the Asian media and their readers. Even though the number of ASEM news stories seems to be substantial, local readers would learn hardly anything about the ASEM process itself from such reportage. Clearly, the minor intensity of ASEM framing is counterproductive to raising awareness of ASEM in the region.

---

[50] "Wen: Yasukuni Shrine visits must end", *China Daily*, 13 September 2006.

[51] The expected trilateral meeting among China, Japan and South Korea did not take place at the end.

Table 3:   'Sideline' meetings reported in the press in 2006

ASEM 6							
Korea Herald	**SCMP**	**China Daily**	**Straits Times**	**Manila Bulletin**	**Bangkok Post**	**Jakarta Post**	**Japan Times**
			ASEAN+3				
		Sino-EU	EU-ASEAN			EC-Indonesia	
		NO Japan-China-S.Korea talk		EU-Korea			
			Japan-Philippines		Thai-Cambodia		
			Singapore-Malaysia		Thai-Malaysia		
				Philippines-Singapore	Thai-Singapore		
	Sino-Vietnam				Thai-Vietnam		
Korea-Romania	Sino-Latvia				Thai-France	Indonesia-France	
	Sino-Holland	Sino-Denmark		Philippines-Finland	Thai-UK	Indonesia-Germany	
	Sino-Poland	Sino-Slovakia				Indonesia-Italy	
						Indonesia-Spain	

Table 4:   'Sideline' meetings reported in the press in 2008

ASEM7							
Korea Herald	SCMP	China Daily	Straits Times	Manila Bulletin	Bangkok Post	Jakarta Post	Japan Times
ASEAN+3			ASEAN+3				
			ASEAN				
		Sino-EU			EU-Indonesia		
					EU-Thai		
		Sino-Singapore			EU-Singapore		
Korea-Japan	Sino-Japan				Sino-Thai	Sino-Indonesia	
Japan-China-South Korea talk	Sino-India						Japan-India
	Sino-Cambodia	Thai-Cambodia			Thai-Cambodia		
Korea-Vietnam	Sino-Belgium	Singapore-Vietnam					
Korea-Denmark	Sino-Denmark	Indonesia-Singapore			Indonesia-Singapore		
	Sino-Finland	Thai-Singapore			Indonesia-Thai		
Korea-France	Sino-France						
Korea-Poland	Sino-Ireland	Singapore-Poland					
	Sino-Holland	Singapore-Holland		Thai-Malaysia	Indonesia-Cambodia		
Sino-Germany	Sino-Slovenia	Singapore-Philippines		Thai-Philippines			

How Does the Press Frame ASEM?

While the *degree of centrality* and *focus of domesticity* helped to identify some features in the media portrayals of ASEM, it is also important to inquire about what the leading thematic representations of ASEM were. The methodology used to analyse this dynamic employed a five-fold typology to code themes in ASEM reportage — ASEM as a *political* actor, as an *economic* actor, as a *social* actor, as an *environmental* actor and as a *developmental* actor (see Figure 6).

Political Framings

Asian newsmakers saw ASEM as a *prima facie* political event. 59% of the sampled news portrayed ASEM in this frame. Yet, as discussed above, a large portion of the coverage clustered around the 'sideline' meetings rather than ASEM itself. During the ASEM6 and ASEM7 monitoring periods, the share of politically themed news reporting the 'sideline' meetings was 54% (2006) and 55% (2008). Importantly though, these news items did not carry in-depth consideration of either the ASEM agenda, or topics discussed during the summits.

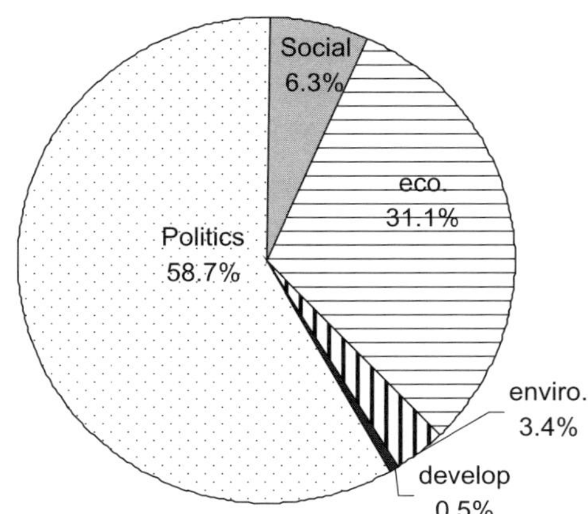

Figure 6:   Thematic framing of ASEM (average of ASEM6 and ASEM7)

As a result, in its totality, the news portrayed ASEM as a high-level gathering of political leaders with no concrete agenda — but rather a place where country leaders are "hobnobbing with other heads of state".[52]

The remaining 46% of ASEM news framing the 2006 summit as a political event focused on several topics on its agenda, among those regional security, climate change and energy security, human rights issues in Myanmar, ASEM's contributions to strengthening multilateral arrangements, as well as an evaluation and enlargement of ASEM process. As the *Jakarta Post* commented, the agenda was typically wide-ranging:

> …The summit issued a special declaration on climate change to strengthen efforts to reach agreement in international climate negotiations….The leaders also underlined that the Doha Development Agenda (DDA) must be complemented and supported to allow negotiations to resume. A healthy and stable multilateral trading system is critical to ensure the economic prosperity of all countries.[53]

ASEM6 was featured as a pure political event by three of the eight news outlets under monitoring — the *Bangkok Post,* the *Japan Times* and the *Korea Herald* (see Figure 7). Conversely, ASEM 7 coverage featured generally a much lower share of news profiling the summit from a political vantage point. Only 44% of ASEM7 news was 'political', compared with 82% at ASEM6. The share of political-framing news in 2008 was replaced by economic news reflecting the global financial crisis and this is shown in Figure 8. As mentioned above, many news articles of ASEM7 only concerned the sidelines meeting between certain heads of states/governments instead of the summit itself. In 2008, the feasibility of a China-Japan-South Korea meeting,

---

[52] *Associated Press* news quoted by *Japan Times* and *Strait Times*: "Hobnobbing marred by China, South Korea, Koizumi completes last trip with laughs at ASEM", *Japan Times,* 13 September 2006; "Chinese and Korean leaders snub Koizumi", *Strait Times,* 13 September 2006.
[53] "Enlarged Asia-Europe forum", *Jakarta Post,* 13 September 2006.

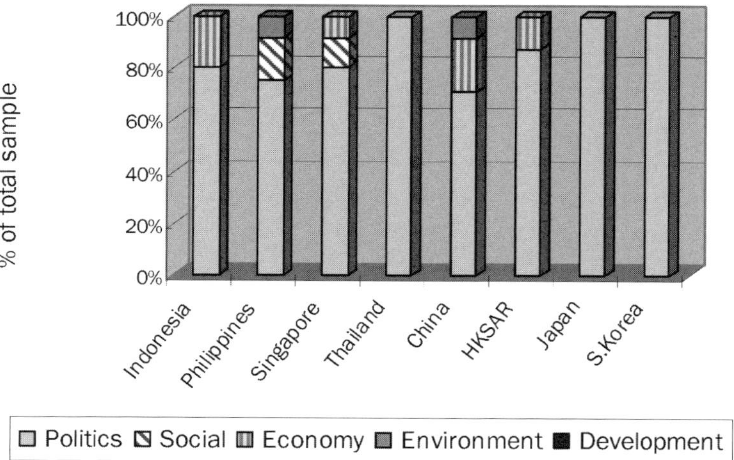

Figure 7:   Framing of ASEM6 agenda in news

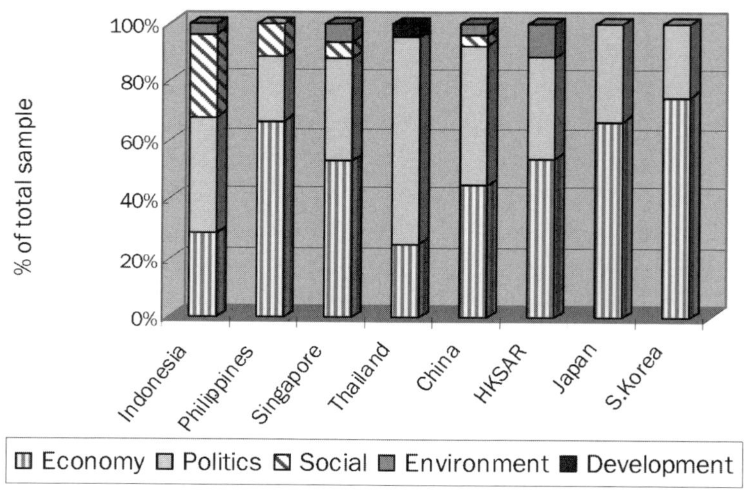

Figure 8:   Framing of ASEM7 agenda in news

talks between the Thai Prime Minister and Cambodian Prime Minister on their border dispute as well as a meeting among ASEAN+3 leaders on the financial crisis were under the spotlight. The remaining politically-framed news items either simply reported the attendance of individual head of states/governments at ASEM7[54] or briefly listed the issues addressed during the two-day meeting.[55]

Other Media Framings of ASEM

Scrutinizing the *economic* framing of ASEM news, such representations accounted for one-third of the news sample in general, but were more frequent in the coverage of ASEM7. Indeed, the share of economic-framed reportage rose nearly seven-fold — from 7% in ASEM6 to 46% in ASEM 7. Five out of the eight newspapers based more than half of their ASEM news in 2008 on economic themes (see Figure 8). Comparisons of the press coverage of the agendas of ASEM6 and ASEM7 revealed that in the eyes of the newsmakers, the summits tended to be dominated by a single issue — the global financial crisis. Strikingly, "discussion among ASEM leaders on the financial crisis" appeared in 60 out of 116 news stories in 2008. As a result, ASEM7 was depicted more as an economic event than ASEM6. During ASEM7, the second most visible topic, climate change, was reported only in four news items.

In contrast, reports on *environmental* actions at ASEM were more evenly spread across time and location. In 2006, the *China Daily* recorded ASEM6's commitment on climate change, sustainable development and energy security;[56] the *Manila Bulletin* wrote about ASEM's efforts at ocean protection.[57] In 2008, newspapers in mainland China, Hong Kong SAR, Singapore and Indonesia outlined climate change as one of the top items on ASEM7 agenda.[58]

---

[54] Examples: "Much to discuss when Japan's new PM visits", *South China Morning Post*, 6 October 2008; "Japanese PM'S wife Halls Hospital's role in Friendship", *China Daily*, 25 October 2008.

[55] Examples: "Asia-Europe Summit to see record attendance", *China Daily*, 15 October 2008; "SBY leaves for Beijing to attend ASEM meeting", *Jakarta Post*, 22 October 2008.

[56] "Finland offers experience in clean energy", *China Daily*, 12 September 2006.

[57] "National Day of Indonesia", *Manila Bulletin*, 17 August 2006.

[58] "Going green in tough times", *China Daily*, 22 October 2008; "Rich nations lack climate commitment: RI", *Jakarta Post*, 22 October 2008; "Energy issues: Think outside the box", *Strait Times*, 24 October 2008; "Leaders reaffirm pledges to tackle climate change", *South China Morning Post*, 26 October 2008.

Social framing in ASEM coverage occupied 6% of the sample. Curiously, all of the news stories in this thematic angle came from just three Southeast Asia countries of Indonesia, the Philippines and Singapore. Four out of the five 'social' articles of ASEM6 concerned the first ASEM Labour and Employment Ministers' Meeting in Potsdam, Germany. Four out of seven social-framed ASEM7 articles were devoted to the second ASEM Labour and Employment Ministers' Meeting in Bali. Not surprisingly, all of them were found in the *Jakarta Post*. It would seem that social activities of ASEM appear to be invisible in the press outside these three Southeast Asian states.

Finally, and importantly, ASEM was virtually never seen as a *developmental* actor by the Asian press. Only one news item out of a total of 190 was dedicated to developmental issues. Found in the *Bangkok Post*, it reported on cooperation between Thailand and the EU as ASEM members on establishing an emergency food crisis fund.[59]

Overall, ASEM was depicted predominantly as either a political or economic high-level summit. While ASEM6 was put conspicuously into the political frame, ASEM7, whose agenda was pre-occupied by the financial tsunami, was reported more as an economic-oriented summit. As a consequence the themes of environmental protection, promotion of development and human rights have been largely ignored.

Credits or Criticism?

This study also measured the assessments assigned to the ASEM summit by the Asian newsmakers. This methodology used, *positive*, *neutral* and *negative* evaluations, to code the tone of the articles (Figure 9).

Our analysis showed that actions of ASEM in economic, social, environmental and development fields failed to elicit an emotive response from Asian newsmakers — the coverage was dominated by

---

[59] "Thailand pledges better European cooperation", *Bangkok Post*, 26 October 2008.

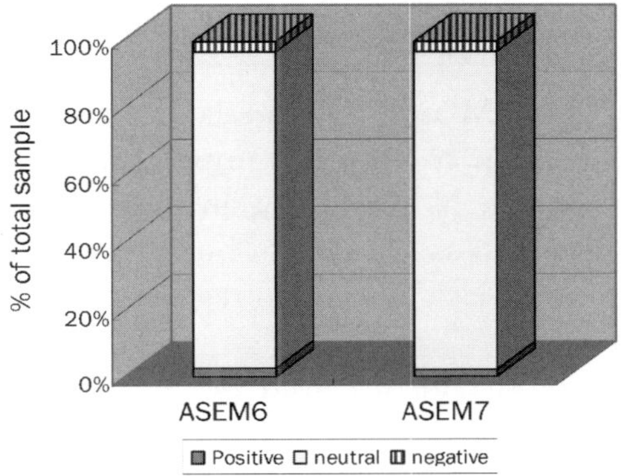

Figure 9:   Distribution of evaluations of ASEM-news

neutral assessments. Infrequent *positive* and *negative* evaluations were found only in politically-framed news. Arguably, three factors could explain this particular distribution of assessments: journalistic practices; Asian cultural norms; and general lack of interest. Firstly, neutrality and objectivity are claimed to be the two professional values leading modern-day media practices. Secondly, cultural norms in Asian societies often view criticism to be impolite and thus attempt to avoid it. With newsmakers being a part of the cultural fabric of society, this cultural resistance to criticism may find its reflection in news production in Asia. Thirdly, a predominantly neutral evaluation could also reveal an indifference towards the subject of ASEM (an obser-vation which is supported by some other findings, such as a predominantly minor degree of ASEM representation in news). These two findings seem to go hand-in-hand — hardly any evaluation of tone can be ascribed to just one or two sentences referencing ASEM from a minor degree of centrality. In addition, news on the global economic crisis were where critical evaluations were found for many news outlets, and consequently and unsurprisingly, ASEM stayed in the shade of the global financial turmoil.

Coverage of ASEM6 attracted positive attention for its achieve-ments in the growth of inter-regional trade; for widening the political dialogue, raising mutual awareness and understanding between Asia and Europe; for facilitating various multilateral fora; and for the promotion of regional cooperation, especially in East Asia. Critical reports pointed at ASEM as "long on talk but short on substance"[60], specifically when it came to the commitment on climate change and human rights abuses in North Korea and Myanmar. On the other hand, some saw ASEM6 as a failure in building consensus among its participants, due to the lack of unity in regional blocs, namely the EU and ASEAN.

The ASEM7 reportage featured positive assessment for promoting a wide-ranging and high-quality Asia-Europe partnership and being a prolific forum — according to the *China Daily*, ASEM7 yielded fruitful results, including three formal statements and a record of 17 proposals.[61] ASEM7 was also seen to help shape future solutions for international problems and facilitate international multilateral cooperation despite the severe financial crisis by narrowing down the differences between Asia and Europe. Negative reports mentioned ASEM's "lack of concrete action", "broad[ness] but not deep dialogue" and "fail[ure] to reach consensus".

Paradoxically, while ASEM is an inter-regional summit that seeks to promote multilateralism, it earned credit in media reports for facilitating bilateral ties between individual participating states. The European Union Ambassador to Korea, Brian McDonald, told the *Korea Herald* "ASEM makes it possible for neighbouring nations to speak to each other and exchange information for the purpose of tackling some of the biggest issues facing those nations today".[62] Singaporean Prime Minister Lee thanked ASEM for providing him and his Malaysian counterpart with a good opportunity to catch up.[63] Feng Zhongping, European studies director at the China Institute of Contemporary International Relations, told the *South China Morning Post* that the major added value of ASEM was that it allowed leaders

---

60 "Asia, EU leaders to focus on trade at Helsinki summit", *Manila Bulletin*, 8 September 2006.

61 "Wen calls for restructuring of global system", *China Daily*, 27 October 2008.

62 "Tough challenges at ASEM", *Korea Herald*, 20 October 2008.

63 "PM Lee and Abdullah discuss Johor in talks", *Strait Times*, 12 September 2006.

to meet and chat with each other in an informal style.[64] Arguably, through these meetings, mutual trust and understanding are built up.

The data presented here indicates that ASEM has rarely elicited any strong sentiment among the Asian newsmakers. This was partly caused by the limited space and attention devoted to the process, and partly understood as a cultural practice in the monitored locations.

CONCLUSIONS

Studies of the media framing of ASEM are interesting not only from a purely scholarly perspective — indeed, only recently have ASEM's media portrayals been systemically addressed in Asian scholarship — but also from a pragmatic, policy-making perspective. The analysis of 190 media reports has been instrumental in putting forward a set of recommendations on how to improve the outcomes and impacts of ASEM, specifically when it comes to its public outreach in the region.

Firstly, it seems that ASEM could benefit if its agenda included several permanent entries — the forum would then have a chance to be associated with these issues and would benefit from improved recognition of its profile. Substantial changes in the agenda at consecutive summits seems to be counterproductive, especially when membership numbers are expanding. According to the *Strait Times*[65] and *Jakarta Post*[66] candidate areas could include strengthening multilateralism to address security threats; promoting human-centred and sustainable development; managing globalization; and enhancing dialogue among cultures and civilizations. Obviously, for many of these issues, ASEM will not be the sole actor — for instance, when it addresses strengthening multilateralism, ASEM can tie its work on anti-terrorism with ongoing counter-terrorism efforts in the ASEAN Regional Forum (ARF) and the UN framework.

---

[64] "Opportunity to unite or a talking shop? Leaders at ASEM meeting will have a chance to prove the bloc can make a difference", *South China Morning Post*, 24 October 2008.

[65] "Working towards greater cohesion", *Strait Times*, 7 September 2006.

[66] "Enlarged Asia-Europe forum", *Jakarta Post*, 13 September 2006.

Secondly, follow-up mechanisms should be discussed and implemented by the ASEM participants. Discussions occurring during the meeting are important, but without subsequent continuation they enhance the summits' reputation as a 'talk-shop'. One possible way of overcoming this problem is the facilitation of joint initiatives and programmes with well-designed follow-up procedures. For example, a declaration of commitment to energy security and efficiency could be translated into a programme of concrete actions, such as development of renewable and alternative energy sources conducted in several ASEM countries simultaneously. A *Jakarta Post* publication also suggested that "ASEM economic ministers should follow up the trade facilitation action plan and the investment promotion action plan adopted at the fifth ASEM summit in Hanoi in 2004 with a clearer set of measures".[67]

Thirdly, ASEM needs to increase its transparency and the sense of ownership for its citizens. The successes of the Asia-Europe Foundation (ASEF) in establishing and maintaining people-to-people contacts, educational and intellectual exchanges are impressive and they deserve wider publicity in the region.[68] Increased visibility for ASEF activities will be key to increasing ASEM's overall visibility.

Finally, ASEM should develop an effective and centralised strategy for disseminating information about itself and gauging feedback through the mass media. Studies such as this are among the first to attract attention to the key role played by media in the region when communicating ASEM's messages. Importantly, the media could facilitate reporting on the implementation of ASEM agreements at home and on the successes and challenges of ASEM-initiated processes. Yet, as this analysis showed, most of the media coverage is devoted only to short-term ASEM events or solely the sideline events,

---

[67] *Ibid.*

[68] The Asia-Europe Foundation (ASEF) was established in February 1997 under the framework of the Asia-Europe Meeting (ASEM) process. ASEF seeks to promote mutual understanding, deeper engagement and continuing collaboration among the people of Asia and Europe through greater intellectual, cultural, and people-to-people exchanges between the two regions, <www.asef.org>.

rather than to long-term implementations of ASEM decisions in-between the biennial meetings. Moreover, occasionally the Asian media, (notably in Korea, Indonesia and the Philippines), even mis-represent ASEM. For instance, the *Korea Herald* thought that "ASEM meetings take place every year".[69] The *Manila Bulletin* wrongly stated that ASEM began at the 1998 London summit.[70] To avoid basic mistakes and to increase ties with the public in the region, ASEM should consider further targeted programmes working with the Asian newsmakers in order to raise its profile and ensure a better understanding of this particular mechanism for dialogue between Europe and Asia.

This study has examined a total of 190 news items which refer-enced ASEM in 2006 and 2008 from eight prestigious English-language dailies in Asia. It was found that although ASEM is present in the Asian media, its visibility is relatively low and its por-trait is rather vague. ASEM rarely basked in the media spotlight in Asia and was easily overshadowed by its 'sideline' events and issues. In general, ASEM6 was framed by the Asian press as a rather abstract political event which triggered no distinct emotions; ASEM7, on the other hand, was portrayed as a half-political and half-economic event. The coverage rarely provided any detailed information or the agenda being discussed or implemented. If ASEM is serious about connecting with decision-makers and the general public both in Europe and in Asia, this forum should concentrate and add value to a limited number of important areas, as well as transform its vague declarations into concrete actions. Such measures could result in higher attention and a sincere appreciation given to ASEM's efforts in the future.

---

[69] "Roh counts on ASEM support for N.K. policy", *Korea Herald*, 8 September 2006.

[70] "President Gloria Macapagal Arroyo to attend the Seventh Asia-Europe Meeting in Beijing", *Manila Bulletin*, 23 October 2008.

Chapter 7

Policy Recommendations and ESiA

Peter Ryan

INTRODUCTION

The Asia-Europe Meeting process (ASEM) constituency now stands at 45 partners[1] in a unique, informal structure which has the following key characteristics:

- Informality (complementing rather than duplicating the work already being carried out in bilateral and multilateral fora);
- multidimensionality (devoting equal weight to political, economic and cultural dimensions);
- emphasis on equal partnership, eschewing any "aid-based" relationship in favour of a more general process of dialogue and co-operation; and,
- high-level focus, stemming from the ASEM Summits themselves.

The ASEM Intergovernmental Dialogue is marked by its ever-growing list of subjects covered and a political response to urgent issues as they

---

[1] Partners include the twenty seven EU member states, the ten ASEAN member states plus China, India, Japan, Korea, Mongolia, Pakistan, the EC Commission and the ASEAN Secretariat.

arise on the global scene. The relevance of this bi-regional dialogue was reiterated by the ASEM Foreign Ministers at the 9th ASEM Foreign Ministers' Meeting in Hanoi in May 2009.[2] In the context of ASEM, the Asia-Europe Foundation (ASEF) has been mandated to respond to significant international trends and emerging policies. The mandate of ASEF is intentionally wide, so that it can be responsive to change and able to adjust its functions in a flexible way.

To this end, ASEF draws on a set of certain guidelines which are both very specific and yet broad. The guiding principles behind ASEF were adopted by ASEM leaders during Ireland's 1996 EU Presidency and are referred to as the *"Dublin Principles"*. Amended during the ASEM5 Summit in Hanoi, Vietnam, in 2004, the Dublin Principles regulate the mission and legal capacity of ASEF as well as its administrative structure and funding and have been effective in seeking a deepened understanding and an improved cross-cultural awareness between the Asian partners in ASEM and the integrating and enlarging EU.

Translating these guidelines into practice was the challenge for the founding Executive Director of ASEF, Ambassador Tommy Koh, who took it as a mandate "to interpret important developments taking place in one region to the people of the other region and to increase the points of convergence and reduce the points of divergence between the thinkers of the two regions".[3]

This is the background to ASEF's interest in the building of a broad Asia-Europe alliance to deliver on the 'EU through the Eyes of Asia' project, and in making the outcomes and analysis available to inform policy makers and civil society — including the media, academic, business & NGO stakeholders — in both regions.

The results are of particular benefit to policy-makers who can draw beneficial lessons for a number of sectors, ranging from academic cooperation to environmental and development issues to cultural issues. The findings not only help to provide a reference point

---

[2] Chairman's Statement from 9th ASEM Foreign Ministers' Meeting in Hanoi, Vietnam, May 2009.

[3] Koh, Tommy, 'Asia and Europe', Yeo Lay Hwee & Asad Latif (eds.) *Essays and Speeches by Tommy Koh*, Singapore: World Scientific, 2000, p. 143.

for the views of the EU as an economic, political, social, developmental and environmental actor, they also provide further insights into the nature of relations among Asian countries with the EU. This information is critical to ensuring ASEM collaboration delivers "a common purpose for sustainable economic development, social responsibility, a rule based society, energy security, environmental excellence, food safety and public health".[4]

As far as ASEF is concerned, there are few of our areas of work that do not directly benefit from the increased understanding we can glean from the analysis of the outputs from the "EU through the Eyes of Asia" project. This holds true for the thematic areas of work on which ASEF will focus in the lead-up to the 8th ASEM Summit which is scheduled for October 2010. These themes have been identified by the ASEM leaders and ministers and ASEF's plans can be summarised as follows:

1. Economy and Society
    In response to the ongoing global financial crisis, ASEF works to facilitate dialogue on the role of regional integration processes and the potential for common action between Asian and European partners.
2. Environment and Sustainable Development
    In the lead-up to the international negotiations on climate change in Copenhagen in December 2009, ASEF has redoubled its efforts to help facilitate an Asia-Europe response on global challenges such as climate change, drawing on the Asia-Europe Environment Forum.
3. Pandemics and Public Health
    ASEF has initiated a platform for enhanced collaboration on health-related issues between Asia and Europe.[5]

---

[4] Speech by H. E. Mr. Dirk Achten, Secretary-General of the Ministry of Foreign Affairs of the Kingdom of Belgium, at the 9th ASEM Foreign Ministers meeting in Hanoi, May 2009.

[5] The stockpile phase of the ASEM Initiative for the Rapid Containment of Pandemic Influenza financed by the Government of Japan was launched at the 9th ASEM Foreign Ministers meeting in Hanoi, May 2009.

In addition, ASEF will continue to build on its unique and substantial contribution to date in the areas of Interfaith Dialogue, Cultural Exchange as well as activities to promote educational links and understanding between institutions and civil societies in the two regions. ASEF has also been actively working to bring journalists from the two regions together through events such as the ASEF Journalists Colloquium. All of these activities are important for building understanding amongst key opinion leaders and are the richer when better informed by the outcomes of the "EU through the Eyes of Asia" project.

This can be illustrated by two specific examples — the thematic areas of 'Economy and Society' and 'Environment and Sustainable Development'. A closer look at these two themes provides us with an interesting insight into how the EU packages itself in the Asian region and offers useful examples on how the data collected can help to inform policy and help to assist the efforts to raise the visibility of the European Union. On the one hand, the EU's economic power resonates well in Asia and the EU remains an important trading partner to Asian economies. Whereas on the other hand, the EU's environmental policy, though progressive and extremely committed, does not resonate too highly in Asia — which is disappointing, given the importance of the EU as a global actor and the leadership role it has assumed in the environment sector.

ECONOMY AND SOCIETY

ASEF has initiated a pillar of activities under the heading of 'Economy and Society', commencing with a conference on the sidelines of the ASEM7 summit in Beijing — the Connecting Civil Society III — An Asia Europe Dialogue on Economy and Society.[6] In addition to

---

[6] The co-organisers of the Connecting Civil Societies III Conference were the Asia-Europe Foundation, the Centre for Comparative Regional Integration Studies of the United Nations University, the Research Centre for Sustainable Development of the Chinese Academy of Social Sciences, and the Irish Institute of Chinese Studies of University College Cork. The Asia-Europe Business Forum and the Asia-Europe People's Forum were partners for the conference.

facilitating dialogue, the meeting produced a comprehensive set of policy recommendations for presentation to the ASEM leaders during the Summit meeting. The multi-stakeholder discussions acknowledged the interrelation and interdependence of the three major issues of the day: Financial Market Instability, Energy Security, and Food Security with one another. On top of the key recommendations of these three key economic areas, the conference outcomes also included suggested actions for business groups, media and NGOs.

Our work with the National Centre for Research on Europe (NCRE) and other partners in the ESiA project has also enabled the bringing forward of specific policy recommendations — in this publication, one such recommendation on managing the global financial crises presents a special insight into how data such as the predominance of the euro symbol in Asia might be drawn upon as a reference for policy makers. The recommendation states:

- ASEM should promote greater cooperation in monetary and financial affairs within Asia and Europe and between the two regions. Such cooperation should be built on existing regional arrangements and initiatives such as the Chiang Mai Initiative.

Policy makers and stakeholders alike can use the seemingly high interest in the EU firstly as a single economic area and secondly the positive perception of the euro, as leverage for producing more informed and effective policy. This last statement rings especially true when examining the policies of the two regions of the EU and ASEAN and how they interrelate with one another. With the ambitious proposals of ASEAN to implement a single economic area by 2015, it is important and timely to gauge how the EU's experience is perceived by and communicated to the people on the ground across ASEAN, both at grass roots and at elite level.

Taking the media recommendation as the link into the findings of the ESiA research, the document outlines that:

- ASEM should promote greater exchange between media outlets and professionals to strengthen the relationship between existing institutes and media organisations, for example Asia Pacific Broadcasting Union (ABU) and the European Broadcasting Union (EBU).

- ASEM should expand existing media research initiatives to promote greater understanding of the two regions.[7]

The data provided by "The EU through the Eyes of Asia" project challenges policy-makers to examine the data and to consider some of the discrepancies between media representations in Asia and Europe. If European policy makers are to influence a cross-section of opinion in Asia, it is important that they address the gaps drawing on the information which the ESiA data provides. The implications of tackling this divergence of media relations can filter down to areas such as trade, tourism and an equitable recognition of the importance of individual Member States within the EU.

The importance of the euro, as a wide reaching symbol of European unity, displays the power of the Asian perceptions of the EU as an economic actor but more importantly it shows the tangible impact that the single currency has had by capturing the attention of Asians. In the words of Jacques Rueff, writing in the 1950s, "Europe shall be made through the currency, or it shall not be made".[8] This rings true today as the euro is perceived in Asia as displaying in concrete terms the unity and global power of the EU. Furthermore, the euro is perceived to provide a functional example to other regional organisations that monetary integration can fasten regional integration as a whole and portray a sense of unity abroad. So the European experience in implementing the euro can help ASEAN policy-makers in their work to achieve closer economic integration. This symbol of unity is not in line with the reality,

---

[7] ASEF Connecting Civil Societies III report, <http://www.asef.org/index.php?option=com_ project&task=view&id=467>.

[8] The Economist, *A Tortuous Path: From Breton Woods to Euro,* <http://www.economist.com/displaystory.cfm?story_id=13767451>, accessed June 11, 2009.

however, given that only sixteen of the twenty seven EU Member States use the euro as their currency.

ENVIRONMENT AND SUSTAINABLE DEVELOPMENT

ASEF has been working in the area of 'Environment and Sustainable Development' for the past six years since the inception of the Asia Europe Environment Forum in 2003 and a number of other initiatives focusing on the links with Cultural, Media, and Education networks and Youth programmes.

The Asia-Europe Environment Forum (EnvForum) is a platform for dialogue and debate on sustainable development and environment issues in Asia and Europe, with a strong organisational base through partnerships with the Hanns Seidel Foundation, the Swedish International Development Cooperation Agency — Swedish Environmental Secretariat for Asia, the Institute for Global Environmental Strategies and the United Nations Environment Programme, the Asia Development Bank, the ASEAN Secretariat, the Earth Council and Kehati, the Indonesian Biodiversity Foundation. The EnvForum serves as "an interface between government and civil society for policy recommendations", and the programme provides a platform to convey the findings of the "EU through the Eyes of Asia" on perceptions of the EU as an environmental actor, to policy-makers.

In the area of environment and sustainable development the data collected throughout this research project represents some unexpected findings. For the past decade the EU has seen itself as a global leader on climate change and other environmental issues. In terms of the EU's external communications of its work, the EU promotes the ideal that it is taking a strong stance on the issue and promoting its lofty ambition to tackle climate change.

The comments below, from European Commission President Barosso, illustrate the EU position:

> 2009, culminating in the Copenhagen conference, is a crucial year for the battle against climate change, but in fact climate change has been the

defining issue for this Commission, and I fully expect it to be the defining issue for the next Commission. Why is that? Because environment policy in general, and climate policy in particular, are natural European issues. Carbon emissions don't stop for checks at national borders. Actions we take — or don't take — inside the European Union have a direct impact on the rainforests of Brazil and Borneo, and on the thickness of the Greenland ice sheet.[9]

Statements of ambition such as this convey the EU as a global power both politically and morally on environmental issues. Yet a rather large misnomer exists; in Asia the image of the EU as an environmental powerhouse is almost non-existent. This might be attributed to a shortcoming in the way in which the EU is promoted to Asian partners. The ESiA research project identifies that the two key images of the EU that resonate in Asia are economic and politically based. This shortcoming might be addressed in a variety of ways including not only public policy but also through grass roots exercises to ensure that the image of the EU as an environmental actor is raised with Asian partners.

The same might be said of the EU as a development actor — once again the EU is a world leader in terms of development aid; it is the world's largest donor, providing more than half of global development aid, together with its members. In addition, "it also tackles universal issues, promotes good governance, human and social development, security and migration and natural resources".[10] Despite this fact, the EU's lack of visibility in this area in Asia is a cause for concern. The EU's external image should be benefiting from the enormous sums given to assist developing countries and the worthwhile programmes that many of the countries who have taken part in this research project have benefited and continue to benefit from.

---

[9] Barroso, José Manuel Durão, 'The Road to Copenhagen', *Green week closing session*, Brussels, 26 June 2009.

[10] Europe-Aid is the implementation body for the European Commission's external aid instruments, both those funded by the Union's budget and the European Development Fund. <http://ec.europa.eu/europeaid>.

It is evident from the lack of visibility of the EU as an environmental power that the external packaging of the EU is failing to deliver the message of the EU as a major global environmental actor. The data collected throughout the course of the research project can provide leverage for the EU to look at its external relations policies and examine how the packaging of the EU in Asia could fail to highlight the ongoing commitments of the EU to the environment and climate change in particular. While at the same time, the data will give EU environmental policy-makers the scope to examine the Union's dealings with its Asian partners and examine their relationships. Not only is the lack of visibility an issue for communications policy and strategy, it is a reflection of the environmental policies laid down and their own ability to generate attention with Asian partners.

Clearly, environmental issues are key to the public, perhaps ranking second only to the economic and financial issues, so the absence of any visibility of the EU as a dominant global actor in this area should be a matter of some concern to EU stakeholders. It is to be hoped that the presentation of this information will help encourage policy-makers to ensure their activities are more effectively communicated.

In terms of the impact that "The EU through the Eyes in Asia" research project can have on the other ASEF work areas, it seems less immediately evident. However in some of the following areas the data provides valuable references that can be examined and drawn upon.

HUMAN RIGHTS AND GOVERNANCE

When considering the data in terms of human rights and governance, it seems as if, once again, the EU has very little visibility. Yet in terms of news coverage the few relevant reported stories can offer insights as to whether certain countries view the EU contribution positively or negatively. The same trends can be identified from the public opinion data and the elite interviews. These trends might not in themselves provide sufficient leverage for serious policy debate but can serve to supplement existing information for policy-makers.

PUBLIC HEALTH AND PANDEMICS

ASEF's newest area of work, public health and pandemics presents a challenging area in which to build mutual understanding across and between Asia and Europe. First and foremost it is an area of work that has been thrust onto the global agenda in a profound way with the recent H1N1 outbreak raising fear levels and causing a global panic. The media and public attention given to the H1N1 outbreak offers the upcoming "EU through the Eyes of Asia" research teams in India, Malaysia and Macau potentially divergent data than that of the previous nine research locations. It seems that Asian countries, given their experience with SARs in 2003, are taking the lead globally in preparation for a future outbreak. This may leave EU policy-makers with an opportunity to communicate their strategies and policies on the H1N1 issue due to the dominance of the issue in Asian societies. Given the relatively sudden emergence of the H1N1 outbreak as a major global issue, the findings from the next phase offer to provide interesting data in terms of the awareness of the EU's global standing in pandemic management and public health.

CONCLUSION

At a minimum, the rich information gathered under the "The EU through the Eyes of Asia" research project enables us to build some understanding on how Asians view the EU and on the way in which relations vary across the Asian region.

While the overriding finding is the low visibility of the EU generally, clearly this is not a true reflection of the sophisticated and complex strategic partnerships that the EU has built with Asian countries whether this is through trade links, development aid or political negotiations. The then Minister of Foreign Affairs of Ireland, Dermot Ahern TD, referred to this reality in the context of Ireland's Asia Strategy which he stressed "is also embedded in the context of the wider relationship between the European Union and Asia. The relationship has been dramatically transformed from one of

European political and economic dominance to a partnership of equals".[11]

The dominance of the EU as an economic and political actor is something that can be easily identified but the discrepancies of the EU as an environmental actor, and in addition a development actor, is not reflective of the global weight of the EU in terms of these issues. Nor does it take adequate understanding of the areas where the EU has competence.

In terms of influencing policy-makers, the data provided by the project in the nine research locations to date offers a wealth of resources to not only policy-makers but to local and international stakeholders including media, academe, and civil society at large. The main benefits that can be drawn from the data is the ease of access to clear and concise scientifically valid feedback on the EU's external image in Asia. In terms of policy recommendations, the findings mirror the existing policy and provide identifiable missteps on behalf of policy-makers both from the EU and in the research locations themselves. These missteps can be quantified in concrete terms through the lack of EU visibility across the board and in particular the invisibility of EU actions in key areas.

ASEF and NCRE welcome and encourage the further use of the collected data and are ready to provide access to people interested in looking at a particular aspect for comparative or study analysis. In fact, we have initiated the ESiA's Young Academics' Workshop with the aim of providing a platform for next generation European studies academics in Asia and Europe to exchange ideas, acquire new skills and present their work to the larger European studies community.[12]

---

[11] Dermot Ahern, Irish Minister of Foreign Affairs, Extract from a speech delivered at the Royal Irish Academy in Dublin, Ireland reprinted in the *Asia Europe Journal*, June 2007.

[12] ASEF, NCRE and the College of Europe co-organised the 1st Young Academics' Workshop 'How is the EU Perceived in Asia: Media, Public and Elite Perceptions', in Bruges, Belgium, on 1–4 September 2008. The intensive workshop brought together 20 junior researchers and Masters/PhD level students from across Asia and Europe. The participants came from a broad variety of institutes and educational backgrounds.

In addition, recognising the importance of balance and the dearth of information on the subject, ASEF is working with a number of partners to measure the perceptions of Asia in the European Union, in a counterpart project to the ESiA work. We are hoping that the "Asia in the Eyes of Europe" research project will help to improve the understanding between the two regions and to create a permanent platform to enable civil society, business, researchers, students, policy-makers, media gatekeepers and a broad range of cross-sectoral stakeholders to understand one another better.[13]

The "Europe through the Eyes of Asia" project is a flagship for ASEF and we thoroughly value the partnerships we have developed as a result of this work — while at the same time we recognise that Martin Holland, Natalia Chaban and their team at the NCRE have been fundamental to the smooth implementation of the project. We look forward to the extension of the project to include India, Macau and Malaysia over the coming year, which will bring even greater geographical coverage to our study of Asian perceptions of Europe.[14]

---

[13] ASEF organised a panel dialogue at the 6th International Convention of Asian Scholars (ICAS) in Daejeon, Republic of Korea on 6 August 2009.

[14] In June 2009, ASEF, NCRE and the Asia-Europe Institute of the University of Malaya in Kuala Lumpur, Malaysia co-organised the first of a series of three methodology workshops for the upcoming phase.

About the Contributors

EDITORS

Dr. Natalia Chaban
Deputy Director
National Centre for Research on Europe
University of Canterbury

Natalia Chaban is a Senior Lecturer and Deputy Director of the National Centre for Research on Europe (NCRE), University of Canterbury. Since 2002, she has been a research leader and co-supervisor of the comparative cross-national research project "Public, Elite and Media Perceptions of the EU in Asia Pacific Region" currently involving 19 locations in the region. Dr Chaban has an extensive publication record actively pursuing her research interests in cognitive and semiotic aspects of political and mass media discourses, cross-cultural adjustment, image studies, and EU identity studies outside the EU.

Prof. Martin Holland
Director
National Centre for Research on Europe
University of Canterbury

Martin Holland holds a Jean Monnet Chair ad personam and is the Director of the National Centre for Research on Europe (NCRE) at the University of Canterbury. Since writing his PhD at the University of Exeter, United Kingdom, on the 1979 direct elections to the European Parliament, he has specialised in the analysis of the European Union (EU)'s external relations, initially in terms of European Political Co-operation and latterly through the Common Foreign and Security Policy (CFSP).

His research on EU-South African relations during the apartheid and post-apartheid eras is particularly well-known and saw Holland involved as a practitioner in one of the EU's first election observer missions to monitor the first democratic non-racial South African election in 1994. More recently, he has focused his research interests most broadly on the EU's global development policy and on the perceptions of the EU in third countries.

Mr. Peter Ryan
Director for Intellectual Exchange
Asia-Europe Foundation

Peter Ryan, a career diplomat from Ireland, joined ASEF as the Director of the Intellectual Exchange Department in September 2006. He received his undergraduate and postgraduate degrees from the National University of Ireland in Dublin and worked in Ireland and Australia in the banking sector before joining the Department of Foreign Affairs of Ireland in 1994.

His strong interest in Asian-European relations stems from his appointments to the Irish Embassies in Japan, Korea and Singapore. In addition, he served as Deputy Director, Asia-Pacific in the Bilateral Economic Relations Division of the Department of Foreign Affairs.

Prior to joining ASEF he was based in Singapore covering eBusiness and New Technologies in the Asia-Pacific Region for the Department of Communications, Marine and Natural Resources of Ireland.

Peter Ryan is married with two children.

AUTHORS

Vietnam National University

Dr. PHAM Quang Minh
Dean
Department of International Relations
Vietnam National University — Hanoi

Having received a PhD in Southeast Asian Studies from Humboldt University in Germany, Pham Quang Minh became Vice Dean and then Dean of the Faculty of International Studies, Vietnam National University-Hanoi, a well-known university in the country. He is the co-ordinator of several international projects such as "Vietnam's access into WTO" supported by the German Konrad Adenauer Foundation, and "Renovating the Undergraduate Teaching of International Relations/Studies in Vietnam" supported by the Ford Foundation. His dissertation was on land reform in Vietnam from 1950s to the 1980s, which is still a topic of debate in the modern history of Vietnam, and was published in Germany in 2002. Among his current interests and concerns are international relations and politics. He is the author and co-author of several books and many articles published in Vietnam and abroad.

Mr. Bui Hai Dang
Vice Dean
Faculty of International Relations
Vietnam National University — Ho Chi Minh City

Bui Hai Dang is Vice Dean of the Faculty of International Relations in the University of Social Sciences & Humanities, Vietnam National University Ho Chi Minh City, in charge of research and international co-operations affairs. He graduated with a Masters degree in European studies from Jagiellonian University, Krakow, Poland. Bui Hai Dang is currently a PhD candidate in Cultural studies, University of Social Sciences & Humanities, with the dissertation about European identity in the process of EU development.

His teaching and research interests include the political and legal system of the EU; European cultures, introduction to Area studies, European identity, European integration, European Union.

Universitas Indonesia

Dr. Cornelis Pieter Frederik Luhulima
Senior Researcher
Graduate School of European Studies Programme
Universitas Indonesia

Cornelis Luhulima was a Member of the Eminent Persons Group on the Association of Southeast Asian Nations (ASEAN) Vision 2020 (1999–2000) and has been a Researcher at the Indonesian Institute of Sciences, Jakarta, since 1964. He has been heavily involved in policy studies and proposals on Indonesia's foreign policy since 1986, particularly Indonesia's ASEAN policies. He was Project Manager of the International Area Studies Program of the National Institute for Cultural Studies, Indonesian Institute of Sciences (1973–1980), and lectured at the Indonesian Army and Naval Staff Colleges, the National Institute of Defence, and the Foreign Office Training Institute for career diplomats since 1974, while serving as the Executive Secretary of the National Institute of Cultural Studies, Indonesian Institute of Sciences from 1971 to 1980. Since 1984, Luhulima has been a member of the Board of Advisors for the Indonesian Ministry of Foreign Affairs. At the same time, he is a Senior Fellow at the Centre for Strategic and International Studies and a Research Professor of International Relations at the Indonesian Institute of Sciences

Mr. Edward M.L. Panjaitan
ESiA Researcher
European Studies Program
Universitas Indonesia

Edward M.L. Panjaitan is a lecturer and the Secretary of the Graduate School of European Studies Programme, Universitas Indonesia and

Chief Editor of *Jurnal Kajian Wilayah Eropa* (Journal of European Studies). He has an LL.M in International Law and the Law of International Organisations from the University of Groningen, the Netherlands. His main research interests are related to International Law, EU Integration and ASEAN.

Ms. Anika Widiana
ESiA Researcher
European Studies Program
Universitas Indonesia

Anika graduated from Universitas Indonesia European Studies Program having majored in the Economy of Europe. She is currently working for the European Studies Department as a researcher for the ESiA "EU through the Eyes of Asia" project. Her research interests include EU–Asian Trade Relations.

Ateneo de Manila

Assistant Prof. Alma Maria O. Salvador, Ph.D.
Chair, Department of Political Science
Ateneo de Manila University
The Philippines

Alma Maria O. Salvador is an Assistant Professor at the Department of Political Science at Ateneo de Manila, the Philippines. She teaches international relations, politics and governance and decentralisation. Her research includes state and society relations and institutionalism as frameworks for analysing environmental management and resource management. She has been involved in work in globalisation as well the European Union.

A full time faculty of her department, Alma is currently the Chair of her department. She obtained her PhD in Development Studies at the De la Salle University, Manila, the Philippines.

Ms. Leslie Lopez
ESiA Researcher
European Studies Program
Ateneo de Manila University
The Philippines

Leslie Lopez is currently pursuing her PhD in Sociology at the University of the Philippines Diliman.

She graduated with a Bachelor of Sciences degree in Human Ecology from the University of the Philippines Los Banos in 1997 and a Masters in Social Development from Ateneo de Manila University in the Philippines in 2005.

Mr. Manuel Enverga III
ESiA Researcher
European Studies Program
Ateneo de Manila University

Manuel Enverga III is a part-time graduate student, doing his Doctorate in Sociology at the Ateneo de Manila University. It is in the same that he finished a Master's Degree in Global Politics and a Bachelor's degree in European Studies. At present, he is a full time faculty member of the university's European Studies Program.

National Centre for Research on Europe

Ms. Suet Yi (Cher) Lai
Researcher
National Centre for Research on Europe
University of Canterbury

Suet Yi Lai graduated from European studies (French stream), Hong Kong Baptist University in 2006. She focused on French politics as well as France's role in the EU during her undergraduate studies. In the academic year of 2004–2005, she studied at the Institute of Political Science in Lille, France, as an exchange student. Starting from 2006, she became a researcher in the "EU through the

Eyes of Asia", the inaugural project of the European Studies in Asia (ESiA) network.

Shortly after graduation, she did a three-month internship at Hong Kong SAR's Legislative Council. Upon completion of the ESiA project, she left for New Zealand to start her PhD at the National Centre for Research on Europe (NCRE), University of Canterbury. Her current research focus is on Inter-regionalism as well regional integration in Europe and Asia, with specific attention on the Asia-Europe Meeting (ASEM) process.

About the Partners

CO-ORDINATORS

The Asia-Europe Foundation (ASEF) seeks to promote better mutual understanding and closer co-operation between the people of Asia and Europe through greater intellectual, cultural, and people-to-people exchanges. These exchanges include conferences, lecture tours, workshops, seminars and the use of web-based platforms. The major achievement of ASEF is the establishment of permanent bi-regional networks focused on areas and issues that help to strengthen Asia-Europe relations. Established in February 1997 by the partners of the Asia-Europe Meeting (ASEM), ASEF reports to a board of governors representing the ASEM partners. ASEF is the only permanent physical institution of the ASEM process.

In 2000, the forerunner to the **National Centre for Research on Europe (NCRE)** — the Centre for Research on Europe — was founded at Canterbury. In 2002 a grant from the European Commission was awarded and at this time the Centre became the NCRE. It remains the only EU-dedicated tertiary level centre in New Zealand. Since then, the NCRE has developed significantly in both academic and outreach activities, involving a variety of roles and mechanisms. In 2006 the NCRE was awarded a further EU grant to establish the EU Centres Network of New Zealand, a grouping involving seven of the country's eight universities. In 2009 the NCRE was also designated a Jean Monnet Centre of Excellence for the Asia-Pacific in partnership with Keio University, Fudan

University and the University of Melbourne. Above all, the NCRE has begun the essential process of encouraging and promoting a new generation of New Zealand graduates who have a high level of expertise and interest in the European Union (EU).

RESEARCH PARTNERS

The Ateneo de Manila University's European Studies Program equips students to understand the cultural, economic and political relations between the Philippines and Europe, specifically the European Union (EU). The program seeks to develop future professionals who will enhance the Philippines' role in the global community, particularly in that region of the world. The program thus educates professionals who will help the country respond to the challenges and opportunities presented by the European integration.

Universitas Indonesia (UI) was founded in 1849. UI is a modern, comprehensive, open-minded, multi-culture, and humanism campus that covers wide arrays of scientific disciplines. UI simultaneously strives to be one of the leading research universities and the most outstanding academic institution in the world. As a world class research university, UI seeks to achieve the highest level of distinction in the discovery, developing and diffusion of advance knowledge regionally and globally. In the meanwhile, UI is distinctive among research universities in its commitment to the academic invention and research activities through various scientific programs.

Since September 2003, UI has been offering a Graduate School of European Studies Programme which is based on a multi-disciplinary approach. UI is the country's first and only university currently offering this particular Programme. The main objective of the Programme is to produce highly qualified Indonesian experts on European affairs. It is expected that through this Programme, a better mutual understanding between Europe and Indonesia can also be achieved. The Programme offers a two-year master's programme with four areas of specialisation, namely European Economics, European International Relations, European Law, and European Culture.

Vietnam National University, Hanoi (VNU) is the first modern university established in Vietnam. VNU has undergone various development stages: the University of Indochina established on 16 May 1906; Vietnam National University (November 1945); the University of Hanoi (June 1956). In December 1993, VNU was reorganised on the basis of amalgamating the University of Hanoi, Foreign Language Teachers' Training College (established in 1967) and other leading universities in Hanoi.

VNU is the largest multidisciplinary higher educational and research centre in Vietnam. VNU is entrusted with the task of producing qualified human resources for the industrialisation and modernisation of the country. VNU holds a special position in the system of tertiary education in Vietnam, operating according to a special regulation promulgated by the Prime Minister. VNU reports directly to the Prime Minister and has the high autonomy in organization-personnel, training programs, scientific research and technological development, planning — finance, international relations and other fields. VNU is entitled to work directly with ministries, ministerial level organizations, governmental bodies, people's committees of central cities and provinces concerning affairs related to VNU. VNU's colleges and institutes maintain their juridical person status of a higher education and scientific research institution as regulated by the Law on Education and the Law on Science-Technology.

About the ESiA Network

The European Studies in Asia (ESiA) network was initiated to stimulate European studies in the Asian region by providing a reliable platform for exchange and co-operation between European studies academics both in Asia and Europe. As an all-inclusive network, ESiA embraces all academics, institutions and networks in the field of European studies in Asia-Europe Meeting (ASEM) countries. It endeavours to strengthen existing academic links in Asia as well as facilitate the creation of new synergies within Asia as well as between Asia and Europe, through networking meetings, academic collaborations and the use of online tools.

ESiA is the flagship initiative of the Asia-Europe Foundation under the framework of the ASEM Education Hub.

For more information please contact:

Ms. Sol Iglesias
Acting Director for Intellectual Exchange
Asia-Europe Foundation
31 Heng Mui Keng Terrace
Singapore 119595
Tel. +65-6874-9744
Fax +65-6872-1207
E-mail esia@asef.org
Website http://esia.asef.org